ANCIENT LAVA CLIFFS ON THE NA PALI COAST

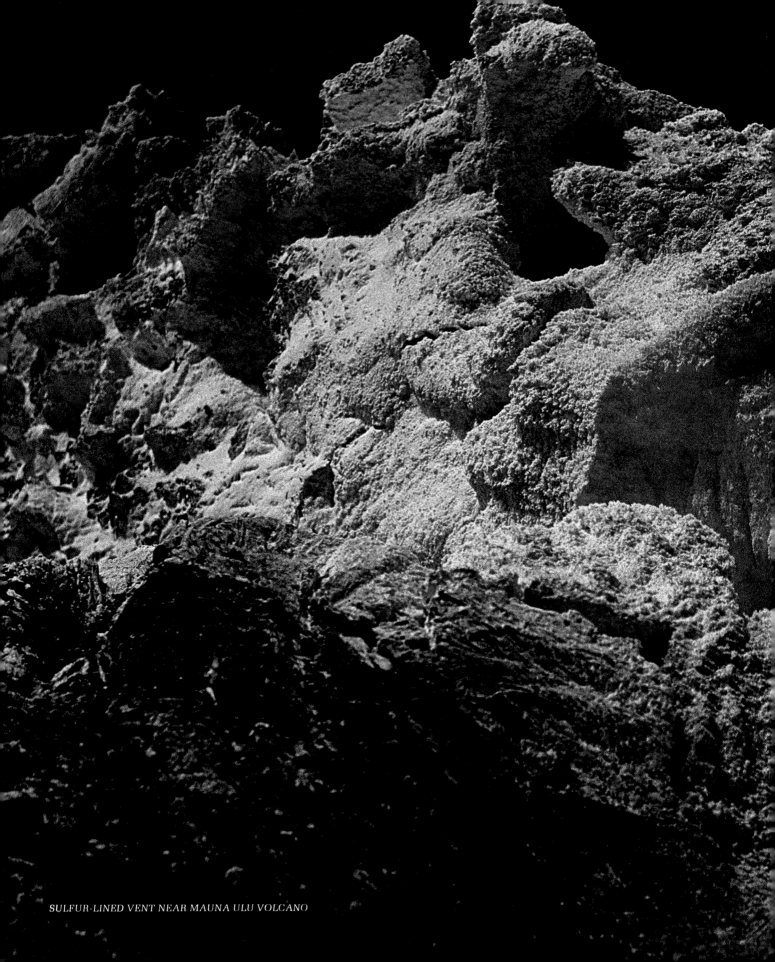

SULFUR-LINED VENT NEAR MAUNA ULU VOLCANO

BLACK-FOOTED ALBATROSSES ON PEARL AND HERMES REEF

OHIA TREES AND CIBOTIUM FERNS IN KIPUKA PUAULU

SNOW-CLAD CONES OF MAUNA KEA VOLCANO

STARBURSTS OF THE ILIAU PLANT RIMMING WAIMEA CANYON

HAWAII

THE AMERICAN WILDERNESS/TIME-LIFE BOOKS/NEW YORK

BY ROBERT WALLACE
AND THE EDITORS OF TIME-LIFE BOOKS

The Author: Robert Wallace is the author of six previous TIME-LIFE books: *The Rise of Russia* in the Great Ages of Man series; in the Library of Art, *The World of Van Gogh, The World of Rembrandt, The World of Leonardo* and *The World of Bernini;* and *The Grand Canyon* in The American Wilderness series. He gathered the material for the present volume on visits to wild areas on the islands of Hawaii, Maui, Lanai, Molokai, Oahu and Kauai, and during a stay on uninhabited Pearl and Hermes Reef, a remote atoll in the Hawaiian archipelago.

The Cover: A branch of the Kalalau Stream courses through the valley of the same name, on the island of Kauai. The eerie spires through which it winds were once part of the lava cliffs behind them, and have been separated and sculptured into their present shapes by millions of years of water erosion.

Contents

An Ancient Archipelago

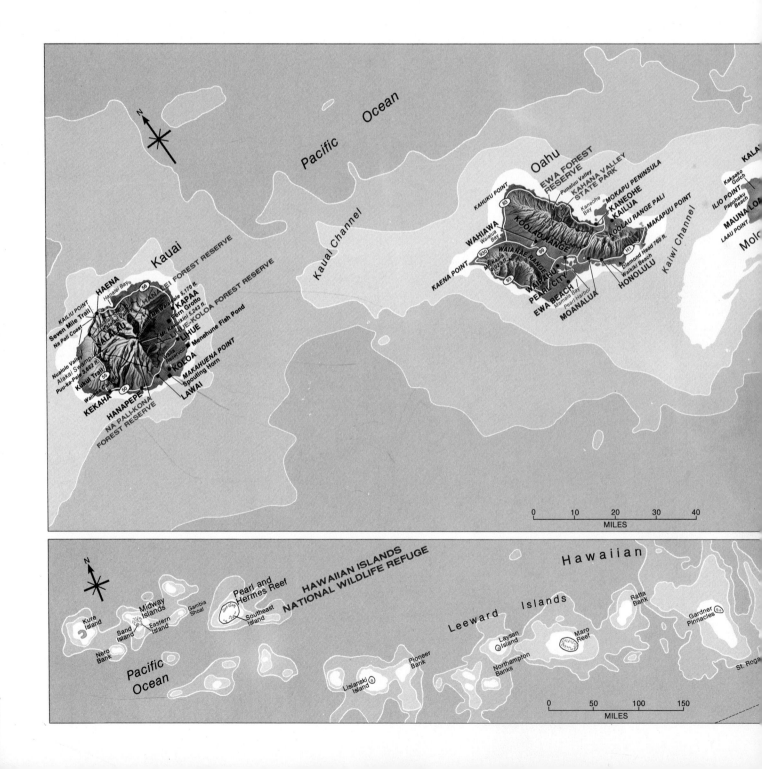

The long reach of the Hawaiian archipelago, a chain of volcanic islands ranging in age from 700,000 years to 16 million years and stretching 1,600 miles across the mid-Pacific Ocean, is indicated by the green rectangle at right and by the more detailed map at bottom. Washed on all sides by the sea—its increasing depths shown by deepening shades of gray—the islands have a total land area of 6,500 square miles. The oldest geological formations, such as Pearl and Hermes Reef (also shown on the map on page 108), stand above sea level only because of coral built up on eroded volcanoes. The major islands at the eastern end of the chain (large relief map) emerged last. On one, Hawaii, there are active volcanoes. Green lines indicate rivers and streams. Red lines (on both maps) define the boundaries of parks and forest reserves. White lines represent major roads; black lines are trails. Black squares mark points of special interest.

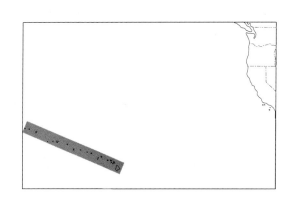

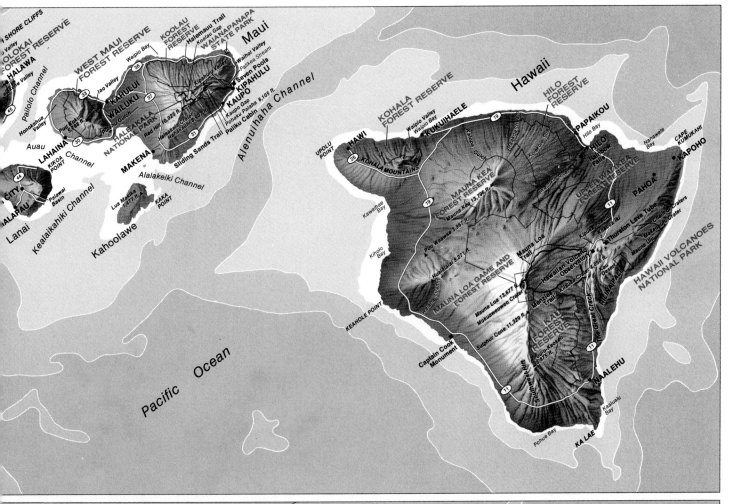

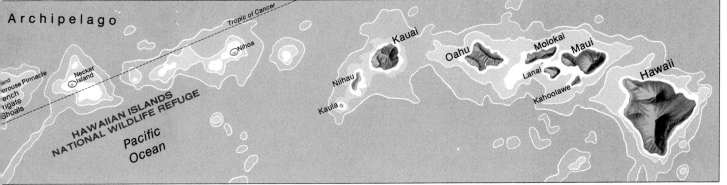

1/ A Handful of Jewels

*Midway across the North Pacific, space, time, and life
uniquely interlace a chain of islands named "Hawaiian"....
These small fragments of land appear offered to sky
by water and pressed to earth by stars.* CHARLES A. LINDBERGH

A good many people find it difficult to believe that there is any wilderness left in Hawaii. Waikiki has become Miami Beach West. Belief is hard even for those who have taken a standard tour of several of the islands. They wake each morning in what seems to be the same plastic hotel room and at breakfast find the same small, mass-cultivated purple orchid decorating their scrambled eggs. Yet the wilderness does exist; and in fact some of the world's most naturally wild places exist in the Hawaiian Islands. There are hidden valleys in Hawaii so remote, so overgrown with jungle and walled off by towering green-black cliffs that few men have ever entered them. Year after year the valleys are silent except for the spatter of rain on the canopy of leaves, the splash of waterfalls and the call of birds. Faraway and mysterious, called by such Polynesian names as Waihoi and Kipahulu, the valleys are in a sense among the experimental greenhouses of the world. Many of the plants growing there, from the lowliest moss to the loftiest trees, belong to unique species found nowhere else on earth. Very likely a few of them have never even been glimpsed, let alone named and classified by botanists.

There is almost impenetrable wilderness in the wet mountains, where the rainfall may exceed 50 feet a year; and on the slopes of the volcanoes, where floods of orange lava, cooling into metallic gray, constantly change the face of the earth. And wilderness exists, too, in the Leewards, the far outlying islands where the rarest of birds and seals are making a last stand against extinction.

The wilderness areas are small by continental standards, to be sure. No one expects the High Sierra in the middle of the Pacific. But the wild places of Hawaii are extremely valuable, a handful of jewels on the green velvet sea, and what they contain is to the mainlander wondrously strange: silverswords and quivering *lapalapa* trees, six-foot violets and birds with curved bills that draw nectar from curved flowers. These things are not only rare but delicate—otherworldly and fragile as dreams. They are the plants and birds one imagines in the background of Shakespeare's *Tempest*. Touch them and they vanish. It is brutish to go blundering among them without knowing their nature, without knowing at least something of the singular, almost enchanted life of sea islands.

Many islands are created by erosion along the edges of continents. The gnawing of waves, currents and even of wind may cut a channel through a peninsula, isolating a bit of land that may be less than an acre in size or as large as Trinidad, nearly 2,000 square miles. A continental island of this sort is somewhat like Noah's Ark, launched with a living cargo that can reproduce itself. The flora and fauna of Trinidad are much the same as those in nearby regions of the parent continent, South America. But the case of Hawaii is far different.

There are eight major, or "high," Hawaiian islands—Niihau, Kauai, Oahu, Molokai, Lanai, Kahoolawe, Maui and Hawaii. The latter is much the largest and geologically the newest, and lends its name to the entire group. The eight are clustered fairly close together and contain 99.9 per cent of the land area of the state. However, there are more than 100 other visible islets, atolls, pinnacles and shoals in the Hawaiian archipelago, which is 1,600 miles long and stretches far out into the north central Pacific to include Midway and Kure, which are mere atolls. Most of these remote dots of land—among them French Frigate Shoals, St. Rogatien Bank, Laysan Island, Lisianski Island and Pearl and Hermes Reef—are administered as part of the city and county of Honolulu, which, as a result, is 540,000 square miles in area and includes a good many more whales in its population than other cities.

Despite the length of the archipelago, it occupies only a tiny fraction of the vast Pacific and its situation is isolated and lonely indeed. From the eastern end of the Hawaiian chain it is 2,000 miles to San Francisco; from the center, 2,400 miles north to the Aleutians; from the western end, 2,400 miles to Japan. To the south the first really major landfall is Antarctica, 7,000 miles away. Thus it is apparent that the Hawaiian Islands are not continental in origin. They were never attached to any mainland. How then did they get out there?

The islands are all volcanic. They arose from the bottom of the sea. To a layman the idea is stunning. Consider it. The Pacific is very deep in the neighborhood of the archipelago, about 18,000 feet; and although it has been shallower in earlier times, the volcanic eruptions must still have occurred at great depth. They are among the most eerie events that have ever taken place in the natural world. Three miles deep in the ocean it is totally dark, extremely cold, and the pressure of the water is about three and a half tons to the square inch. In this crushing blackness a fissure opens and incandescent molten rock gushes out of it. The clash of light and dark, heat and cold, pressure and counterpressure is almost too much for the mind to grasp. No man has seen such a thing and only deduction can tell him what it is like. Although it might seem certain that there would be a prodigious explosion, there is none at all. The weight of the water contains it. Instead the lava, rapidly cooling, spills out quietly on the ocean floor. Not even a bubble of gas arises. On the face of the sea there is no sign of the fantastic event below.

As eruptions continue, layer upon layer of lava spreads across the sea bottom. During a few million years a mountain takes shape and slowly the pressure on its summit diminishes as it nears the surface. At last clouds of steam burst out of the ocean; fragments of rock are thrown up and fall back into the boiling water; and the volcano thrusts clear of the surface and keeps on growing. In this manner the Hawaiian chain has been formed. On the island of Hawaii two volcanoes, Kilauea and Mauna Loa, are still erupting. The latter has reached a height of 13,680 feet above sea level while nearby Mauna Kea, which is probably though not certainly extinct, stands at 13,796.

When the islands emerged from the Pacific they were quite the opposite of Noah's Ark. They were sterile, as antiseptic as it is possible for anything in nature to be. The temperature of molten lava can be as high as 2,200°F., intolerable to any form of life. Even the marine organisms in the ocean nearby must have been killed when the water boiled. Yet in time the steaming lava cooled and became populated with a great variety of living things. The population had some broad gaps—the only mammals that reached the islands unaided by man were bats and seals. Many plant species made the journey but, oddly, no conifers. Land snails arrived in large numbers; amphibians and reptiles never did, except for the green sea turtle. Still, it is impressive that the islands should have been reached and colonized by so many species, all of which were obliged to cross many hundreds of miles of open sea.

There are three ways—setting aside the agency of man—in which the plants and creatures may have traveled: by drifting in the water, sailing on the wind, or by attaching themselves to other organisms. The spores of ferns, lichens and fungi are so small and light that they can be carried enormous distances in the air. The seeds of a few flowering plants, particularly orchids, are so tiny that they too can be airborne for hundreds of miles. Heavier seeds may drift in ocean currents. Others, indigestible but contained in edible fruits, may be eaten by shore birds and waterfowl and transported overseas. Experiments by biologists in recent years have shown that certain birds may retain seeds in their bodies for hundreds of hours. Still other seeds, either burrlike or covered with sticky coatings, may cling to birds' feet and feathers. Among sea birds the wide-ranging albatrosses, petrels, shearwaters, terns and boobies would have had little difficulty in reaching Hawaii. Several species of shore birds, among them the Pacific golden plover and the ruddy turnstone, migrate to Hawaii from the mainland each year; some of them remain for the winter and others pass on to more tropical islands. Small land birds, however, probably made the journey while caught in storms, and bats doubtless arrived in the same way.

Dr. Elwood C. Zimmerman, author of the classic *Insects of Hawaii*, wrote of a means of travel known as rafting. "Large rafts or masses of debris making up 'floating islands' are commonly washed out to sea. . . . A survey of these rafts probably would reveal that numerous plants and animals were riding them. . . . It is possible that some of them, on rare occasions, could travel more or less intact for many hundreds of miles and deposit at least part of their living cargoes on foreign shores. I have seen large trees washed from stream sides during a storm in Tahiti and have seen them floating out to sea with their large branches riding high out of the water. . . . Some of the branches may be held 20 or more feet above the waves. . . . It is conceivable that over a period of several millions of years a few such floating trees have been beached in Hawaii and that from them there escaped ancestors of some of our insects, terrestrial mollusks and plants."

The odds against any particular species reaching Hawaii and becoming established were immense. But so is geological time. The botanist F. Raymond Fosberg estimates that more than 1,700 species of flowering plants now found in Hawaii had only about 275 ancestors, and

Towering above a stand of withered
ohia trees and coco palms, fiery
lava and billowing steam rise from the
main vent of the Kapoho cinder cone,
which is situated in a rift zone
of Kilauea Volcano. The picture was
taken during the volcano's longest
eruption of this century: it began
in early October 1959 and continued in
three stages until mid-February 1960.

that in the 25 million years since the first of the islands emerged from the sea there need only have been one successful colonization of seed plants every 20,000 years. Thus it is not surprising that Hawaii has a substantial, varied plant and animal population and that its progenitors have journeyed there from North, Central and South America, Australia, Asia, other Pacific islands and perhaps even Africa.

Upon reaching the islands the ancestral plants, insects and birds encountered circumstances quite different from those in which they had earlier evolved. In general these circumstances were easier, more free, less competitive. A good many plants, for example, have developed strong defenses against being eaten by sheep, goats, cattle and wild herbivores. The plants have sharp thorns, a rank smell, a bad taste. They may also be poisonous. But in ancient times there were no herbivores in Hawaii and the plants' defenses were unnecessary. Therefore in the inexorable logic of nature the defenses were bred out; they vanished. Now there are very few native plants with thorns, only one or two that are poisonous and none that are particularly foul-smelling. Another characteristic of Hawaiian plants, even those that are not consumed by cattle and goats, is their lack of aggressiveness. Their mainland ancestors were obliged to fight for moisture and places in the sun, and no doubt the Hawaiian immigrants still possessed the same toughness when they arrived in the islands. But there they found ample space, moisture and sun and their competitiveness slowly diminished.

While the plants (and insects and birds) were becoming, in an anthropomorphic sense, meek, they were also changing into new species. As they spread out into the many small environments or microclimates of the islands, wet and dry, high and low, they underwent a process called adaptive radiation. Different foods, temperatures, humidities and other factors caused them to change in habit and appearance, often so drastically that they no longer bore much resemblance to their common ancestors. The range of local environments in Hawaii is remarkable. Consider rainfall. The summit of Mount Waialeale on the island of Kauai is the rainiest place in the world. The constant trade winds blowing from the northeast are heavily burdened with moisture. When they reach the mountain they are forced upward. This rising causes the air to cool, condensing the moisture, which then falls as incredible torrents of rain. As much as 50 feet of rain a year drops on Waialeale and into the nearby Alakai Swamp, a depression on a slope of the ancient volcano. The plants that live there are, to say the least, unusual. Yet within a very few miles, in the "rain shadow" of the mountain where almost all the moisture has been removed from the air, other plants have evolved in near-desert conditions. While the islands' temperature range in the valleys is mild, there are extremes (at least for subtropical islands) of heat and cold. On any night of the year the temperature may fall below freezing on the nearly 14,000-foot peaks of Mauna Loa and Mauna Kea on Hawaii; a dust of snow often covers their tops in winter. Not far away the climate is always balmy. Throughout the islands, because of local differences in soil, moisture, exposure, altitude, temperature and wind, there are isolated colonies of plants whose range may be only a couple of hundred yards.

Hand in hand with adaptive radiation went two other factors that have made the Hawaiian plant and animal population unique on earth. Most of the plants and birds are the descendants of a few individuals —in the case of plants, perhaps only one—and show the results of prolonged inbreeding. In continental areas many members of the same species from broad geographical regions are constantly crossbreeding and thus the species as a whole tends to remain the same. Variants and eccentrics do appear, but crossbreeding suppresses or absorbs them. However, in a small island community where little or no fresh genetic material can be added in the breeding process, individual eccentricities may be emphasized and new species are created fairly quickly.

The second factor that has led to rapid speciation—the biologists' word for the process by which new species are formed—lies in the volcanic origin of Hawaii. Lava is not uniform in hardness; some of it is easily eroded, some very durable. However, a glance at the awesome cliffs pictured on pages 165 and 168, for example, makes plain that the forces of rain, wind and waves have deeply carved the face of the islands. In some areas sharp ridges and pinnacles, separated by sheer-walled valleys, have become in effect islands upon islands. It is difficult or impossible for certain plants and creatures—land snails, for example —to move from one ridge to another and thus they have become doubly marooned and even more likely to develop into new species.

Today there are about 1,660 species of flowering plants in Hawaii that are classified as endemic—that is, they are found nowhere else on earth. Another 100 species are indigenous, growing naturally in Hawaii but also found elsewhere. Beyond these there are scores of exotic plants, introduced purposely or accidentally by man, that come from all parts of the globe. Among birds there are perhaps 45 endemic species still surviving; the exact number is unknown because a few rare individuals may—or may not—still be found in remote valleys and mountain jungles. One might suppose that the discovery in Hawaii of 1,660 plants and 45 birds new to science would be a source of joy unconfined, certainly among botanists and ornithologists. And to be sure, it has been. But the sense of joy has long since been replaced by anxiety and gloom because of the destruction of these unique species by man and by the alien plants, animals and diseases that man has imported. Within the past 200 years at least 25 endemic birds have become extinct in Hawaii. The number of plants that have been exterminated by men, sheep and goats cannot be determined with great accuracy (some plants may well have disappeared before botanists ever saw them), but it is surely large. As the botanist Sherwin Carlquist puts it, "there have been more animal and plant species extinguished in the Hawaiian Islands than in the entirety of North America."

One major reason for the mass extinction has already been suggest-

When Captain James Cook explored the Hawaiian Islands in early 1779, the people believed him to be one of their gods and feted him royally. But a fracas that ensued from the theft of a dory from his flagship cost the celebrated Englishman his life. In this 19th Century engraving of the incident, Cook is the figure with outstretched arm, about to be stabbed in the back.

ed: the peculiar passivity, the Eden innocence of island species. Its complement is the peculiar virulence of introduced species. The idea may be extended without too great distortion into the world of men. In 1778, when Captain James Cook of the British Navy discovered the islands, he was well aware of certain dangers. ("Discovered" is an unpopular word among Hawaiians. Cook was indeed the first European to find the islands, but Polynesian navigators of great skill and daring discovered them about 1,000 years before he did.) Cook's fear was that his crew would spread venereal disease among the natives. In contrast to the stereotype of callous skippers roistering across the Pacific leaving syphilis on every atoll and not caring a damn, Cook was an intelligent, decent soul. Unfortunately his efforts at quarantine were foredoomed—after glancing at his lusty sailors and the half-naked maidens swarming around them, he gloomily confided to his journal that "No women I ever met with were less reserved. Indeed, it appeared to me that they visited us with no other view than to make a surrender of their persons." Still, Cook tried. He ordered the crews of his small boats not to go ashore and "all female visitors to be excluded from the ships. Many of them had come off in the canoes. . . . They would as readily have favored us with their company on board as the men; but I wished to prevent all connection which might, too probably, convey an irreparable injury to themselves, and through their means to the whole nation. . . . Whether these regulations, dictated by humanity, had the desired effect or not, only time can discover."

Within two weeks of Cook's arrival the infection had been spread. A party of men who had been sent ashore to trade was held on the beach by heavy surf for two days and nights and somehow neglected to remember the captain's orders. Although Cook was chiefly concerned with one disease there were others to which the natives were disastrously susceptible. Epidemics of smallpox, measles and influenza brought in by subsequent colonists reduced the population from about 300,000 at the time of the discovery to 50,000 a century later. Today there may be fewer than 8,000 pure-blooded Hawaiians left, largely because of the ravages of disease and in part because of interbreeding with the many foreign races that have come to live in the islands.

The introduction of exotic species among plants has had an effect comparable to the introduction of germs and viruses among men. The lantana, which on the American mainland is a modest, maidenly flower sometimes used in borders of home gardens, becomes tigerish in the nourishing climate of Hawaii. It grows 8 or 10 feet tall, develops thorns

The pandanus or hala tree, a form of screw pine, carpets the Puhaluu Valley on Oahu. The plant, introduced to the Hawaiian Islands by the colonizing Polynesians about 1,000 years ago, now thrives along the islands' shorelines.

and goes rampaging across the countryside. Fireweeds, guavas and blackberries have spread explosively in many areas, overwhelming native species that could not compete with them. On the island of Oahu, by far the most developed of the group, about 85 per cent of all the native vegetation has been wiped out and replaced by plants brought in by man. Today the importation of foreign species is subject to strict legal control but the laws are largely too late.

Cattle, pigs and goats have been ruinously destructive in Hawaii almost from the days of their introduction. Polynesian colonizers brought the pigs, and apparently also brought rats as stowaways in their great seagoing canoes. Captain Cook fetched goats to the islands in 1778; his fellow British explorer, George Vancouver, introduced cattle and sheep in 1793. Each of the animals is a menace in its own fashion. Wild pigs are particularly troublesome because of their habit of rooting up large areas of the forest floor. The freshly turned earth affords a lodgment for foreign plants that might not otherwise be able to take hold and multiply. Goats, which both graze and browse, eat the native grasses down to the roots and destroy small trees and shrubs by devouring their twigs and tearing off their bark. Cattle, pastured in the uplands that once were forest, eat and trample rare plants well-nigh at will. Botanist Carlquist in *Hawaii: A Natural History* writes of *Delissea undulata*, a fantastic relative of the common lobelias of many flower gardens. The plant has white-and-green flowers and purple-black fruit, clustered at the top of a bare, 20-foot fish-pole stem that enables it to reach up toward the light in dense forests. "*Delissea undulata* was very nearly extinct when I saw it in 1966, when 23 plants were counted in the one cinder cone where it was known to have survived," Carlquist reported. "At that time one could see plants only recently demolished by cattle or pigs. Most of the remaining plants were fenced off in 1967 and this curious plant may have been saved."

Goats and pigs run wild in the islands; cattle once did, but now are confined to ranches, some of which are surprisingly large; the Parker Ranch on the island of Hawaii has 250,000 acres. In the 19th Century cowboys on the Parker Ranch, to preserve the purity of their breed of cattle, killed all the wild bulls and cows they could find. Many were captured in pitfalls on the slopes of Mauna Kea, and in one of these pitfalls —probably not by accident—an eminent botanist met his death. The man was David Douglas, who had botanized along the west coast of North America and given his name to a number of plants, including the Douglas fir. When Douglas climbed Mauna Kea in search of new specimens he was accompanied by an ex-convict who, it seems likely, shoved him into a pit where a bull gored and trampled him to death.

The destructiveness of domestic animals gone wild, particularly goats and pigs, seems unlikely to be curbed until they are wiped out. Hawaiians hunt and eat them but do not kill enough to make much of a dent in the population—the breeding potential of wild goats is such that 100 of them in 15 years can increase to about 20,000. Recently on the island of Hawaii alone as many as 18,000 of the animals have been wandering ravenously across the land. Although extermination is preferable, another means of dealing with goats is to fence them out of certain areas. In 1972 in Hawaii Volcanoes National Park the rangers, after great labor, completed a 2,500-acre goat exclosure at a cost of $4,000 for each mile of its three-and-a-half-mile-long fence. It is not easy to drill postholes in lava. The close-cropped vegetation in this large exclosure may revive and flourish, as it already has in an experimental one-acre exclosure fenced a couple of years ago. Indeed, a very startling and heartening event took place in this exclosure not long after it was completed. The grass returned, its leaves providing shade and its roots holding moisture, and then among the tufts of grass there appeared a plant the rangers had never seen before. It proved to be a pea-like vine, hitherto unclassified and unknown, a new species. Apparently its seed had lain dormant in the ground for half a century or more awaiting the right opportunity to sprout.

There are other encouraging gleams and glimmers in the dark Hawaiian scene. Birds thought to be extinct have been found in Kipahulu Valley on Maui and in the Alakai Swamp on Kauai. A new tree belonging to a rare genus has been found deep in Kauai's Waimea Canyon. The creatures that inhabit the remote outlying islands are holding their own. As to the choice of wilderness areas that are described and pictured in this book, it may be well to repeat what was earlier said of them: there are many such areas, small and jewel-like. To include the Na Pali coast of Kauai is not intentionally to slight the north coast of Molokai; a discussion of Kipahulu on Maui is not meant to denigrate Moanalua on Oahu or any of a score of other wild places beloved by Hawaiians. It is only a question of choosing among riches.

An Island Chain Forged by Fire

The ancient Hawaiians drew comfort from a legend that the same great lava flows that occasionally devastated their fields also built up their islands. About a century ago scientific fact began to catch up with the myth. The Hawaiian archipelago, geologists realized, was an island chain stretching some 2,100 miles roughly northwest and encompassing the Leeward Islands. It was also noted that the island of Hawaii, the southernmost point in the archipelago, was geologically young—relatively unaltered by erosion and very active volcanically—while the other end of the chain consisted of extinct remnants of much older volcanoes.

These observations led scientists to conclude that all the islands in the chain were peaks in a colossal submarine ridge built up by lava flows from an enormous crack in the ocean floor. To account for the differences in the islands' ages, they suggested that the land-building eruptions had begun at the northwestern end of the crack and proceeded slowly southeastward over millions of years. Confirmation that the Hawaiian Islands were formed more recently than the Leeward Islands came in the 1960s, with the development of radioactive dating methods.

But a radical new theory has been advanced to explain the formation of the island chain. According to this concept, the part of the earth's crust that underlies the chain consists of a continent-sized plate that for ages has been slipping northwestward at a rate of about four inches a year. Beneath this vast plate, and centered at a point slightly to the north of the island of Hawaii, is a stationary "hot spot" of magma, about 175 miles in diameter, that spews up tremendous volumes of lava—perhaps through weak points in the plate—as the plate slides across the hot spot. The lava forms new islands, but as the plate carries them beyond the hot spot, they are no longer subject to lava flows, and ultimately succumb to the forces of erosion.

Graphic evidence of this theory appears in the photographs on the following pages. Most of the Hawaiian Islands have already slid northwestward past the hot spot; their volcanoes are extinct and in time they will be worn down to fragments resembling the Leeward Islands of today. Yet even now, under 15,000 feet of water south of the island of Hawaii, earth tremors and incipient volcanoes suggest that new islands will eventually be formed.

Shooting as high as 1,900 feet, a fiery fountain of lava and gases erupts from a crater on Kilauea Volcano on the island of Hawaii. In time, when the lava flow solidifies and cools, it will create new areas of land; meanwhile the temperatures within this lava fountain range from approximately 2,000°F. at the yellowish-red core to 1,200°F. at the darker red fringes.

Kilauea: the Youngest, Liveliest Land-Builder

On the southeastern shore of Hawaii —youngest and southernmost island in the archipelago—is its youngest and most active volcano: Kilauea. Local seismographs have registered literally millions of earth tremors signaling lava movements within the mountain. The focal point of these churnings is the Halemaumau fire pit, a lake of molten lava in the four-square-mile caldera atop the mountain. When the lake is full, the lava in it circulates constantly; the surface cools and forms a rocky crust that convectional currents in the lake continually pull under to melt again. Occasionally, prodigious up-wellings cause the lake to overflow. In a series of eruptions between 1967 and 1968 Halemaumau gushed incandescent lava *(right)* at the rate of 1.5 million cubic yards per hour.

For all these pyrotechnics at the top, the lava eruptions chiefly responsible for the recent building up of Kilauea and the land around it come from two long rift zones on the volcano's broad flanks. The numerous vents along these rifts sometimes eject great boulders and tons of cinders, but for the most part the lava that pours forth is so thin and fluid that great molten rivers have flowed downslope at 35 miles per hour and traveled 12 miles before they congealed. When such streams hit the sea below Kilauea to extend the land-building process, the result is often an inferno of smoke, steam and fire *(overleaf)*.

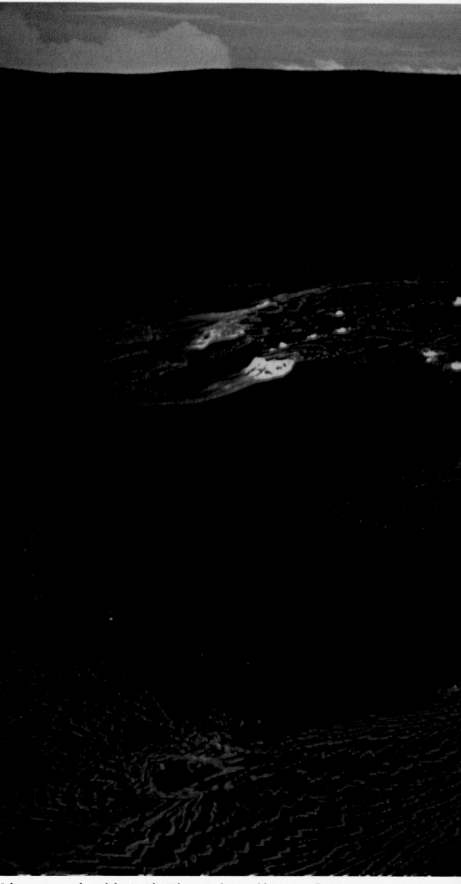

Halemaumau, a lava lake inside Kilauea's deep caldera, overflows in 1968, engulfing

about 1.6 square miles of the caldera floor. The rising lake built its own retaining walls as molten lava cooled and hardened around it.

Roaring down from Kilauea, steaming streams of pahoehoe lava, a thin, ropy variety, pour over a sea cliff in 1971. This eruption lasted three months and created 100 acres of new land.

Flowing from Kilauea's east rift zone in 1955, aa lava, chunky and slower-moving than pahoehoe lava, explodes on contact with the sea, forming black sand particles for Hawaiian beaches.

The gently sloping profile of western Maui's volcano typifies the classic shield shape of all Hawaiian volcanoes before erosion transforms

them. *Lava that is unusually free-flowing, hence far-ranging, accounts for the shape.*

A Tranquil, Aging Volcano

The island of Maui, 30 miles north-west of Hawaii, is perhaps a million years older, and two volcanoes on its eastern and western ends have reached later stages in their geological life cycle. Land-building lava flows on western Maui's volcano (*left*) ceased entirely about 10,000 years ago, leaving the forces of erosion unopposed. Though they have not yet altered the exterior shield profile of the volcano, they have reduced its interior to a gutted shell. The caldera at the summit, a great cavity left when the mountain's empty magma chambers collapsed under the weight of ejected lava, has been worn down some 1,200 feet; at the same time the height of the summit rimming the crater has been lowered —almost a half mile—from its former 7,000 feet to 5,700 feet.

Erosion on an even grander scale has eaten away at eastern Maui's huge volcano, 10,000-foot-high Haleakala. Its main crater, in fact, was created not by volcanic activity, as is usually the case, but by the erosive power of water. Sometime in the remote past, protracted torrential rainfall wore away as much as 3,000 feet of the volcano's summit and gouged canyons thousands of feet deeper into the heart of the mountain. When volcanic activity later resumed, and before it eventually stopped around the end of the 18th Century, new lava flows slowly filled the canyons and built up the plateau-like floor of today's crater (*overleaf*).

Eastern Maui's Haleakala Crater, hollowed out by long erosion and later overlaid with lava flows, is now an immense oval bowl seven miles long, two miles wide and half a mile deep. The photograph at left, taken from the crater's rim, reveals rain-carved inner walls with a much gentler slope than the steep sides of a crater formed by volcanic action. The jagged pinnacle in the foreground, contrasting vividly with the smooth cinder cone beyond, is a so-called dike—a finger of lava that filled a crack in the crater wall, hardened, and was exposed when the softer material around it eroded. A view of the crater from the air (above) reveals a line of cinder cones that crosses the crater along a rift zone. From the vents below these cones came the lava flows that raised the crater floor to the level seen here. The reddish tint of the entire rockscape results from iron oxides in the lava.

Dense plant life and silvery waterfalls on Mount Waialeale, seen from a plane, give evidence of rain water's impact on an extinct volcano.

The Changes Wrought by Rainfall

The moaning of the trade winds is a kind of dirge for Kauai, the oldest major island in the Hawaiian archipelago. Buffeting Kauai from the northeast, the moisture-laden winds dump more and more rain as they blow inland, up the long broad slope of Mount Waialeale, the extinct volcano that long ago built up the island. The mountain's upper slope, a nearly vertical wall *(left),* is the wettest place on earth, with an average annual rainfall of 450 inches.

This incredible deluge nurtures such lush vegetation that Hawaiians call Kauai the "Garden Island." But as the rain drains downslope in streams laden with abrasive debris, it hastens the island's destruction. Waialeale's vast crater—the largest in the islands, 10 to 12 miles across —has already become a broken-down, overgrown Eden. On Kauai's north coast, erosion has carved out a colossal valley amphitheater and slashed its walls with many secondary valleys *(right).* Succumbing to this relentless attack, the Kauai of the future will much resemble the present-day remnants of islands farther to the north *(overleaf).*

Water-carved buttresses form a somber line along the west ridge of Kalalau Valley.

A fragment of volcanic rock, 910 feet high at its peak, is all that remains of Nihoa Island.

The Final Ravages of Time and Water

Once-active volcanoes, the 12 Leeward Islands, which extend the Hawaiian archipelago more than 1,200 miles to the northwest of the main islands, are the oldest links in the island chain and the most battered by time and erosion. Each successive Leeward island is older than the one to its southeast and hence displays greater ravages by wind, rain and sea. On Nihoa, the second youngest of the Leewards and some 2.3 million years older than the island of Hawaii, land-building lava flows that countered the forces of erosion ceased so long ago that the island, once 20 miles across, has shrunk to a rock one quarter of a square mile in area *(left)*. Ages of rainfall and wave action have even more thoroughly worn down Kure *(right)*, the oldest and outermost of the Leewards, at one point lowering it to sea level. But the shell of its volcano provided a foundation on which tiny sea creatures slowly built up a spacious, gleaming white coral atoll.

The low-lying atoll of Kure, oldest point in the island chain, outlines the site where a great volcano once towered above the sea.

2/ The Fire Goddess

The fire-rivers, already rushing to the sea, were narrowed and driven downward so rapidly that they leaped out from the land, becoming immediately the prey of the remorseless ocean. WILLIAM D. WESTERVELT/ HAWAIIAN LEGENDS OF VOLCANOES

Kaha-wali was a chief who enjoyed sledding. Lacking snow, except on the relatively inaccessible summits of Mauna Loa and Mauna Kea, the Hawaiians slid down steep slopes covered with dry grass. Their one-man sleds were long and very narrow, with polished hardwood runners only a few inches apart, and they went so fast they scorched the grass. One day when Kaha-wali was sporting on Kilauea he was approached by an ugly old woman who asked to borrow his sled. Foolishly, he refused. Kaha-wali should have known who the woman was: the goddess of volcanoes, Pele—in Hawaiian pronunciation, *pay-lay.* Sometimes Pele goes among mortals as a crone, asking for help or a loan of some sort. Sometimes she appears as a beautiful young woman, demanding that a man sleep with her. When she is turned down she gets angry.

As soon as Kaha-wali spurned her request Pele's eyes turned to glowing coals and her hair to a banner of flame. She stamped on the ground, opening a fissure from which lava burst forth. Kaha-wali flopped on his sled and rode for his life downhill while floods of molten rock pursued him, Pele riding on the foremost billow. When his sled ran out of momentum he scrambled to his feet and raced toward the ocean. On the way he passed his mother and yelled, "Aloha ino oe eia ihonei paha oe e make ai, ke ai manei Pele!" (May you receive mercy, because your death is probably close at hand. Pele comes devouring.) Then he passed his wife, who suggested that he remain with her so that they might die together. Kaha-wali thanked her but kept on running. Then he passed his pet pig, whose name was Aloi-puaa. Kaha-wali paused to greet the pig by rubbing noses but he did not linger. Finally he came to the beach, one jump ahead of the lava, leaped into a canoe and saved himself while Pele threw hot rocks at him.

Hawaiians were afraid that ignorant and inexperienced visitors might not believe this story without corroborative evidence, so they immediately began to collect a mass of it, which they can produce when asked. One of the first men who asked was the Reverend William Ellis, an English missionary, who toured the site in 1823. The Hawaiians showed him the very hill where the incident took place. Ellis described it as "a black frowning crater about one hundred feet high, with a deep gap in the rim on the eastern side (toward the sea) from which the course of a current of lava could be distinctly traced." What is more, Kaha-wali's mother, his wife and his pig can all be seen turned to stone in the lava flow, and if a man goes snorkeling off the beach he can see strewn on the bottom the volcanic rocks Pele threw.

There are many stories of Pele in the written and unwritten literature of Hawaii and most of them have curious inverted nubs of truth in them, hyacinths planted upside down. The Hawaiians were keen and articulate observers of the natural world and their myths are like those of ancient Greece, full of apt explanations of events that scientists do not fully understand even now. Lava *does* suddenly burst out of the ground and rush downhill at surprising speed; it does harden around the shapes of living things; volcanic projectiles do splash into the sea. Hawaiians have on occasion been obliged to flee to safety in canoes.

The story of Kaha-wali accounts for some particular bits of local scenery; the tales of Pele herself explain the past and present volcanic activity in all the islands. Why is it that the volcanoes in the northwest are cold and dead, those in the central islands seemingly still warm, and those in the southeast vigorously erupting? The answer is Pele. At some ancient time she came to Hawaii to build a home, or rather to dig one. She likes to live in deep pits lined with fire. At first she dug on the island of Kauai, where she threw up a great mound of cinders called Puu-o-Pele, the hill of Pele, but sea water seeped into the pit and put out her flames. Then she moved southeast to Oahu and made several more pits and mounds with the same result. The last of these was Diamond Head, which is so close to the sea that it must have become uninhabitable for her very quickly. Pele moved on to Molokai, Lanai and then to Maui, where she was able to live until fairly recently in the immense crater of Haleakala. When her fire was extinguished there she went at last to the southeasternmost island, Hawaii, where she dug *two* homes that she still inhabits. The higher of the two, on the summit of 13,680-foot Mauna Loa, she has temporarily abandoned for the more salubrious climate of lower altitudes. She has not been seen there in 20 years, although she will surely be back. Her lower, favorite residence is in the fire pit of 4,090-foot Kilauea, from which smoke and fumes rise night and day. The volcano, one of the most active on earth, has been in almost continuous eruption in recent years, mainly from vents on its flanks where Pele can be seen swimming in the orange-hot lava.

Hawaiians still have a proverb that says "Watch out for old ladies; one of them may be Pele," and the goddess remains a real and terrifying presence to more than a few people who live within sight of Mauna Loa and Kilauea. In recent years offerings of roast meat and papayas have been tossed into lava flows to placate her. To the majority of Hawaiians, however, Pele has become only an outworn memory. The decline of her influence was hastened by an act of magnificent courage on the part of a lady named Kapiolani. A high chieftainess (women as well as men inherited rank in old Hawaii), Kapiolani became a Christian convert in the 1820s soon after the first boatload of missionaries arrived. To assist them in making other converts Kapiolani undertook to defy and humiliate Pele, and thus indirectly all of the local deities. Carrying a book given to her by the missionaries, she made a long journey on foot to the brink of the fire pit, announcing her iconoclastic intentions all the while. On Kilauea she flagrantly violated various taboos, going so far as to eat some *ohelo* berries without offering any to Pele. The *ohelo,* a relative of the huckleberry, grows in profusion near the volcano and was thought to be Pele's private property. Before eating any of the berries Hawaiians threw some into or toward the fire pit, saying, "Pele, here are your *ohelo.* I offer some to you; some I also eat." Failure to carry out this ritual would result in quick incineration.

Kapiolani was approached by a priestess from one of Pele's temples who showed her a letter of warning said to have been written by the goddess herself. "I too have a letter," said Kapiolani, taking the missionaries' book from under her arm and bravely reading aloud from it. Then she advanced to the edge of the lake of blazing lava, contemptuously tossed a few stones into it and made a speech, for which she may have received a little coaching. "Jehovah is my God. He kindled these fires. I fear not Pele. If I perish by the anger of Pele, then you may fear the power of Pele. But if I trust in Jehovah, and He shall keep me from the wrath of Pele when I break through her taboo, then you must fear and serve the Lord Jehovah. All the gods of Hawaii are in vain."

Nothing happened; there was no explosion, no fire fountain, nothing. Wrapped in her pride and her courage, Kapiolani walked home with her book. It was not a Bible, for she had not yet mastered the reading of complicated English. It was her spelling book.

Today any visitor may follow Kapiolani's path on Kilauea, more or less, and a great many do, particularly when Pele is having one of her frequent outbursts of temperament. Hawaiians attend volcanic eruptions with the enthusiasm of crowds descending on a major football game. They arrive by bus and by car, by public and private plane, often fetching drinks and sandwiches. When they reach Hawaii Volcanoes National Park they follow freshly set-out signs that say "To Eruption Site" just as motorists far to the east follow signs to the Yale Bowl.

The people of Hawaii flock to eruptions instead of fleeing from them because the local active volcanoes put on spectacular performances but never kill anyone; or hardly ever. The lava released from them, like all other lava, contains gas—chiefly water vapor, with small percentages of carbon dioxide, nitrogen, sulfur dioxide and several others. In volcanoes famous for deadly violence, such as Vesuvius or Krakatoa, the lava is sticky, viscous and likely to form solid plugs in the vents, trapping the gas and holding it under increasing pressure until it bursts forth in a terrific explosion. In Hawaiian volcanoes, however, the lava is much more fluid, of about the consistency and color of thick tomato soup. Gas escapes from it easily, often whooshing upward in great fire fountains, but without major explosions. Rarely, a sudden draining of ground water into a hot volcanic vent may produce a series of steam blasts, but there has been only one such event in this century, at Kilauea in 1924. It killed one man, who ignored advice to stay away from the area and was hit by a flying rock. Ordinarily Hawaiian eruptions produce boiling lakes of lava, rivers, gushers and geysers of incandescent liquid stone spurting as high as 1,900 feet into the air. As the lava spreads away from the vents it gradually cools and solidifies, often destroying roads, crops and houses.

Highly fluid lava may flow as far as 30 miles before cooling into immobility or running into the ocean, and for short distances on steep slopes it may move as fast as 35 mph. Often, however, the lava partially hardens, acquiring a clinkery, rubbly surface and a dense semisolid core that may take all day to travel half a mile. Both the slow and fast flows are fascinating to watch but the fast ones create by far the more interesting forms. The top and sides of a rapidly running stream may congeal into a hard black crust, making a tube within which the lava continues to flow like water in a pipe. When the supply is shut off the liquid drains out of the tube, which may later be buried beneath succeeding flows to become a tunnel within a growing mountain. Some of the lava tubes in Kilauea and Mauna Loa are as large as subway tunnels; the best known of them, the Thurston lava tube in the National Park, has been fitted with electric lights and accommodates hundreds of strollers every day.

At times fluid lava may pour through a forest, hardening around the cool, moist trunks of trees as it passes. The heat sets the trees afire and the wood is burned out. The ashes disappear, leaving hollow pillars with molds of the long-dead trees inside them. If the flow does not drain away but remains to cover the forest, the tree molds appear as holes in the ground.

Hawaiian lava tends to cover broad areas with thin flows, many of them only a few feet thick. Mauna Loa, at nearly 14,000 feet above sea level and 30,000 feet above the ocean floor, has thus been built up of thousands of layers. It has no sharply defined peak, but is shaped like an inverted circular shield. Both Mauna Loa and Kilauea, which is several thousand feet lower and built against the side of its larger brother, are in fact called shield volcanoes. Their long, flattened profiles contrast with the steep truncated cones that come to mind when one thinks of volcanoes such as Shasta or Fuji. However, the gentle curves of the Hawaiian volcanoes disguise astonishing bulk. Mauna Loa, with a volume of 10,000 cubic miles, is by far the largest volcanic mountain on earth, a hundred times larger than either Shasta or Fuji.

The principal vents of Kilauea and Mauna Loa are at their summits, where signs of forthcoming eruptions often first appear. Sometimes the eruptions are confined there, but frequently the lava issues from a zone of rifts (or fissures) on the flank of the mountain 5, 10 or even 25 miles away. Both volcanoes have two major rift zones, lines of weakness trending generally southwest and east, that are marked by craters, fractures, cinder cones and recent lava flows. In the southwest rift zone of Kilauea there is an enormous fissure called the Great Crack, which extends without interruption for 14 miles. In places it is as much as 50 feet wide, and a man can climb down into it for 60 or 70 feet before it becomes too narrow for further descent. From the air the rift zones appear like battlefields where armies have been fighting with flame throwers: black, melted slopes strewn with scorched pillboxes, smoldering forts, charred forests, trenches oozing steam and fumes. Yet, wherever the lava has not flowed in recent times, plants and trees have returned.

To the old Hawaiians the legends of Pele were all the more real because eruptions of lava might, and did, suddenly occur at any time anywhere, near a village, in a taro patch or on a hill that was good for sledding. When such things happened it was easy enough for witnesses to recall that there had been an ugly old woman or a beautiful young one prowling somewhere in the neighborhood; there usually is. But today the unpredictability of eruptions has been largely eliminated. Scientists at the Hawaiian Volcano Observatory, perched almost on the rim of the main vent of Kilauea, have learned to forecast—within reasonable limits—when another outbreak is likely to occur. Kilauea is a fine volcano to study. Indeed there is no other on earth that lends itself quite so well, in accessibility, docility and frequency of action, to the purpose. There has been a volcano observatory at Kilauea since 1912, established through the efforts of the late, brilliant geologist Thomas A. Jaggar. It was originally supported by M.I.T. and by scientifically inclined Hawaiian businessmen; today it is maintained by the U.S. Geological Survey.

The general mechanics of Kilauea and Mauna Loa, although not all the important details, are fairly well understood by now. A complex mixture of melted rock and gases, called magma when it is below the surface and lava when it emerges, originates about 40 miles underground. Because it is lighter than the solid rock pressing down around it, it is squeezed upward through vertical channels and accumulates in chambers or reservoirs only two or three miles below the summits of the volcanoes. When the pressure within the reservoirs becomes great enough—whoosh! Before an eruption the summit of a volcano inflates or swells, often by as much as four or five feet, sometimes in a few days and sometimes over a period of months. The swelling is imperceptible to the eye because it takes place all across the top of a huge, flattened dome; but instruments at the volcano observatory can measure it with great precision. Surveyors' levels determine how much the ground rises or falls. Geodimeters, using laser beams, measure changes in distance between various points. Tiltmeters, anchored firmly in the mountain, can translate the smallest motion into a variable electric current that is then translated back into the motion of a stylus on a graph in the laboratory. The accuracy of the tiltmeters has given rise to a local figure of speech that, however extreme it sounds, is true enough: if you have a steel girder one mile long, and you raise one end of it high enough to slip a nickel under it, the instruments can measure the tilt.

A network of seismographs, which record earth tremors not only beneath the volcanoes but throughout the island and under the surrounding sea, provides a good deal more information for the scientists. As a rule several dozen quakes are recorded each day, although occasionally there are "swarms" of a few hundred or even 2,000 to 3,000 in 24 hours. Only rarely, however, is a quake strong enough to be felt throughout the island. Still, the depth and duration of the seismic patterns are revealing, and there is a particular sort of record that can raise the hair on the back of any geologist's neck no matter how many seismograms he has looked at in his lifetime. That is harmonic tremor, a steady, heavy pulsing or pounding that indicates that magma is coursing through underground conduits on the way to the surface. The signature of harmonic tremor on a seismogram is unmistakably distinct from the blips made by ordinary quakes; it goes on and on, for hours or months, a rhythmic, wide swinging of the stylus not unlike an exercise in the old Palmer Method of penmanship.

Although the volcanologists in Hawaii have learned much about the prediction of eruptions, they can do little but offer suggestions as to how to cope with the whopper that seems likely to come—not necessarily tomorrow but, as geological time goes, pretty soon. The third largest city and seaport in the state, Hilo, with a population in the mid-1970s of about 30,000, is located some 40 miles from the summit of Mauna Loa in line with the course of many past lava flows. And when the volcano erupts it discharges almost unbelievable quantities of lava—the flow of 1950, luckily on the southwest rather than the northeast rift that faces Hilo, was on the order of one billion tons. On several occasions lava from Mauna Loa has menaced Hilo—the flow of 1881 came within a mile of the center of the town and there were serious threats in 1855, 1899, 1935 and 1942. The eruption of 1942 received no notice in the press—the Japanese had attacked Pearl Harbor only four months before, the islands were under a nightly blackout, and there seemed no reason to inform enemy submarine captains that they could find Hawaii the way Moses found the promised land, by following a pillar of smoke by day and of fire by night.

The eruption of 1942 began in late April and by May 1 the lava was only 12 miles from Hilo, advancing at 300 to 500 feet an hour on a front

Vapors released by lava rise from the Halemaumau fire pit, a 3,200-foot-wide crater contained within the sunken top of Kilauea Volcano.

half a mile wide. It seemed about to inundate an aqueduct and a main highway, vital for military purposes, and its approach to the city was particularly alarming to residents because of the noise that accompanied it. The flow was advancing through swampy jungle, where in the clouds of smoke and brown steam could be heard what sounded like a rolling artillery barrage: pockets of methane gas, generated in the decomposing vegetation, exploding.

Volcanologists and local authorities made up their minds to meet violence with violence, or at any rate with the comprehensible, almost quaint sort of violence that was available in those days. Once before, in 1935, the U.S. Army Air Corps had used old Keystone bombers to try to alter (without much success) the course of a lava flow headed toward Hilo, and now the scientists called on the Army again. Several 500-pound bombs were dropped high on the rift zone at points where the flow might have been turned aside and there was, briefly, a minor diversion. However, by good fortune the eruption soon ceased of its own accord. There was no evidence that the bombs had done any good. The question remains open. If Hilo is threatened again it is quite possible that the Navy or the Air Force may be asked to use the remarkably accurate "smart bombs" developed during the war in Vietnam. An alternative defense for Hilo, seriously proposed by one of the most respected geologists in Hawaii, is to build a wall 17 miles long and 25 feet high across the rift zone to deflect the lava away from the city.

Unlike Mauna Loa, Kilauea menaces no cities because there are none within its reach, although in 1960, without loss of life, it wiped out the small town of Kapoho along with some papaya groves, sugar cane and fields of cultivated orchids. The eruption took place more than 20 miles from Kilauea's summit, but it is at the summit that any close look at the volcano should begin.

In the top of Kilauea's flattened dome there is a roughly oval, sunken area, typical of shield volcanoes, called a caldera. Created by the collapse of the interior of the mountain, the caldera is about two miles across and has clifflike walls that plunge as much as 400 feet down to a flat floor 2,600 acres in area. When he first saw this sunken plain Mark Twain remarked that all the armies of Russia could camp there and have room to spare. The shape of the caldera raises an odd image in the mind of a visitor. It appears that the volcano contains a gigantic cylinder and piston: at the moment the piston is on the downstroke, creating the caldera, but on the upstroke it will rise flush with the surrounding area and all will be level again. The caldera floor is covered with fairly recent flows of lava, poured out at intervals in the last 150 years, dark gray or black, dull or shiny, smooth or wrinkled as the light chances to strike it. In the southwestern quadrant of the caldera there is a circular crater more than half a mile across and (as of early 1973) 300 feet deep. This is the great fire pit, the home of Pele and for countless years the center of action on Kilauea.

The fire pit is called Halemaumau, the House of the Ferns, probably in reference to the tall *amaumau* ferns that grow nearby. The ferns were once used by Hawaiians to make temporary shelters when they came to pay their respects to Pele. The name persists, although since the 19th Century more substantial material has been used to construct guesthouses on the rim of the caldera. In 1866 a wooden hotel, Volcano House, was erected for the tourist trade and was visited by Twain, who was then a 31-year-old correspondent for the *Sacramento Union*. After various remodelings and rebuildings Volcano House still stands above the dark volcanic depression; visitors today stare out its windows at Halemaumau smoldering below.

Not far away, in another building even closer to the fire pit, volcanologists stare out of *their* windows at the rising smoke and steam, or read the seismograms and tiltmeter reports that are constantly wired into their quarters. Halemaumau, despite its ominous appearance, no longer contains the lake of molten lava that made it world-famous for a century prior to 1924. Tourists used to peer down into it, seeing—as did Mark Twain—a great cauldron "ringed and streaked and striped with a thousand branching streams of liquid and gorgeously brilliant fire! It looked like a colossal railroad map of the state of Massachusetts done in chain-lighting on a midnight sky. Imagine it—imagine a coal-black sky shivered into a tangled network of angry fire!" Other visitors saw other visions, perhaps depending on the states they came from or what preachers they had lately been listening to, but everyone saw something astonishing. At times the lake rose and overflowed onto the caldera floor; at times black rafts of hardened lava drifted on its crimson surface, or dozens of fountains leaped and splashed there. But suddenly in 1924, at the time of the steam explosion mentioned earlier, the lake disappeared and one of the great sights of the earth vanished. Since then it has returned only at brief, infrequent intervals.

Visitors are politely discouraged from entering the observatory, although they may look through a window at a row of working seismographs that the volcanologists have placed close behind the glass.

Dead ohia trees, victims of hot cinders, ash and sparks from the 1959-1960 eruption of Kilauea Volcano, loom over a slope of Kilauea Iki Crater, where all vegetation was destroyed—an area now aptly called Devastation Trail.

Visitors may also wander across the slopes of Kilauea, following paths marked by stakes, cairns and bits of bright plastic tape set out by rangers of the National Park Service. Although the rangers' prime consideration is safety, they will often, when conditions are right, allow sightseers to walk to the brink of a crater where newly erupted lava is boiling below. However, it is the scientists who go out almost daily into the unmarked, steaming, boot-scorching wilderness, and the scientists who occasionally get blistered.

Men who choose to study volcanoes at close range are not ribbon clerks. They are an unusual breed. Dr. Donald Peterson, the scientist in charge of the observatory, has been scorched more than once, and perhaps a glance at a typical scorching will serve somewhat to describe him. A while ago he was asked, as a favor to a fellow scientist, to provide a sample of fresh lava that had been contaminated as little as possible by contact with organic matter—that is, a bit of lava that had never flowed along the mortal earth or even remained long exposed to the spore- and germ-rich air. It seemed to Peterson, who is a trim, athletic man in his late forties, that the way to obtain such a sample was to pick it up with tongs immediately after it popped out of a volcanic vent. Lava often emerges in half-melted blobs that sail 10 to 20 feet into the air, fall, and build up formations called spatter cones. One variety of blob, because of its striking resemblance to the genuine article, is called a cow-dung bomb. While Dr. Peterson was searching with his tongs for a suitably fresh blob, venturing courageously close to the active cone, a large number of them suddenly flew out of it all at once. As he turned and ran, a ball of lava hit him on the back of the neck and fell down inside his shirt, causing what he calls "a little discomfort." However, he persisted in his attempts with the tongs, finally snatched up a likely specimen, clapped it into a container and sent the sample off.

On a midsummer morning Dr. Peterson invited me to take a walk with him out into the east rift zone of Kilauea where an eruption was in progress. It was a lovely day for a stroll, as Beelzebub might have said, with just the tiniest seasoning of sulfur in the air and a nice showing of harmonic tremor on the seismograph. Because the eruption site was several miles from the observatory, we covered much of the distance in a jeep, accompanied by a young geologist from the National Aeronautics and Space Administration, Grant Heiken. NASA is interested in hot places and may establish its own volcano laboratory in Central America. Heiken, lending a hand with Peterson's equipment, was carrying a newly designed 10-foot-long thermocouple, a device for measuring temperatures. When we came to a convenient pool of molten lava Peterson was going to stick the thermocouple into it.

On the way to the eruption site Peterson talked briefly about the function of the observatory, which does a good deal more than study volcanoes. It cooperates with physicists investigating magnetism and isotopes, with botanists who are interested in the return of vegetation to devastated areas, and with astronomers studying gases by spectroscope. At the moment there is some interest in the nonpollutive production of electric power by using the volcanoes as sources of heat, but many problems must be solved before this source is successfully tapped. A power plant requires a good deal of fresh water for the generation of steam, but not much is available locally. The volcanic rock is so porous that water sinks into it quickly. Although there are many streams, there are few fresh-water lakes in the entire state of Hawaii. Even if ample water were available for geothermal power, Peterson says, the location of a plant in an active volcanic area is no casual matter. The source of heat beneath the plant might migrate to some other spot, making the plant useless, or perhaps a new eruption might bury the plant in lava or reduce it to a heap of cinders.

After driving for about 10 miles along the east rift we reached a place where the jeep could go no farther; the road was blocked by hardened billows of recent lava. Behind us there was a fairly luxuriant growth of trees, bushes and grass; ahead there was only a dead, solidified ocean, gunmetal in color but streaked here and there with ocher and dry lizard gray. On the surface of the lava there was a sheen created by innumerable flat threads of volcanic glass—it resembles fiberglass in appearance and materializes on the crust as it cools. About half a mile distant against the sky faint puffs of smoke marked the vent from which the lava had poured.

A foot trail, indicated by white metal rods jammed into crevices, led across the stone ocean to the summit of the shield, which was about 300 feet high and a couple of square miles in area. A good many people had walked along the trail before us and their feet had worn away the threads of glass, making the trail dull black in contrast to the shiny lava nearby, and quieter to step on. Whenever a man happened to wander off the worn path the glass threads made a faint, crisp, grinding noise beneath his boots. (Mark Twain, walking across the floor of the Kilauea caldera at night, lost his way and got back on the trail only after a companion relocated it by sound.) As we walked, Peterson remarked that the shield, called Mauna Ulu (Growing Mountain), was the largest new volcanic land form to arise in the United States in many centuries, and that it had been created by the longest flank eruption in the recorded history of Kilauea. It began in May 1969, continued for two and a half years, paused briefly and resumed in February 1972.

It was an easy walk to the low summit of Mauna Ulu. Little gusts of heated air and steam emerged from cracks in the lava, tinged with faint whiffs of gas. City people walking over subway gratings in the winter encounter much the same warmth and smell, although what is running underground in Mauna Ulu is hotter than the A train to Harlem. At the top of the shield behind a rope barrier a score of visitors were peering down into the crater. Nearby, seated on a lump of lava that suggested a throne, sat a guardian park ranger. He was not wearing a Smokey-the-Bear hat but a helmet and seemed a figure from Milton or Dante, staring hard at the visitors and occasionally cautioning them with his voice or merely with a flick of his eyes. Several of the visitors had cameras and were pressing against the rope, within three or four feet of the brink, to take pictures. The crater at this point was not very wide, perhaps only 70 yards, and about 25 yards deep. Heavy smoke drifted inside it, parting at times to reveal a pond of glowing orange lava below. The lava appeared to be welling up at one side of the pond and disappearing at the other, in steady circulation although the level of the pond remained constant. In the past several months the pond level had fluctuated greatly, the lava sometimes sinking to a depth of 60 yards below the crater rim and sometimes rising to overflow the spot on which we were standing.

Peterson exchanged greetings with the ranger and then, passing a sign that said, "Danger. Do not pass," set out in an easterly direction along the rim of the crater. He moved briskly and easily although he was wearing a 40-pound backpack full of instruments, cameras, heavy gloves, first-aid equipment, rock hammers and other geologist's gear. The crater, or trench, was about a third of a mile in length and maintained its 70-yard width throughout that distance. Peterson occasionally glanced down into it but noted little that had changed since his last visit. Fumes were rising from the depths but we rarely caught a whiff of them; the trade-wind breeze, coming steadily from the northeast, pushed them away. In any case they would not have been troublesome because we were out in the open where the fresh air could dilute them. "A while ago," Peterson said, "I saw a bat fly in there and die."

Hawaiian bats sometimes sleep in crannies in the walls of craters, and when they emerge they may be engulfed by rising gases. "This one came out of a hole," Peterson went on, "fluttered for a few seconds, fell into the lava and winked out like a match." The same fate sometimes overtakes the white-tailed tropic birds that nest in the walls of the Kilauea caldera. During an eruption in 1969 several of these large birds, which have wingspreads of three feet or more, flew into fume clouds, lost consciousness and fell like meteors.

Leaving Mauna Ulu, Peterson continued east toward the site of Alae, which until the current eruption had been one of several deep pit craters that mark the upper part of Kilauea's east rift zone. During the Mauna Ulu eruption, however, Alae had been filled with new lava, drained, refilled, drained and refilled still again. And even now it was filled to the brim and overflowing with lava that was creating a new shield where the crater once had been. As we climbed its gentle slope I could see above us small clots of soupy liquid flying into the air.

At the summit of Alae's shield stood a spatter cone perhaps 30 feet high and 50 feet in diameter at its base. From a vent near the top of the cone came a deep sloshing, woofing noise, the sound of an enormous, infernal piece of plumbing, and out of the base of the cone, not its top, gushed the lava. It was bright yellow-orange and moving with great speed, a torrential river compressed within close banks. In a short distance the banks flared out and the lava poured into a large lake that was contained within a recently hardened levee all around the summit. Peterson walked toward the sideways-gushing fountain, studying it with a pleased eye. I asked him what he estimated the volume of flow to be and he began to work out the problem in his head, staring at the gusher to gauge its diameter and speed.

The gunmetal lava underfoot was hot. The heat penetrated the thick soles of my boots but it was not strong enough to make them smoke. A good deal of heat was radiating from the wide-open hydrant of lava, too, but it was not unpleasant at a distance of 30 or 40 feet. The surface of the lake, which was several hundred yards long, was covered with a thin, fragile black crust. Choppy waves constantly broke the crust, revealing the brilliant liquid beneath, and in several places low fountains, 5 or 10 feet in height, spurted and splashed. The level of the lake was only a few feet below its levee and visibly rising. It appeared that it would overflow, somewhere, within the next few minutes.

Peterson completed his calculation. The flow from the gusher was about 40 cubic meters or 1,000 gallons per second, only a trickle in comparison with the major outpourings, sometimes a hundred times greater, that Kilauea occasionally releases. Still, 1,000 gallons of hot lava per second is a considerable amount. I did a quick calculation of my own and concluded that it would completely fill a large church—say, the Presbyterian church where as a lad I learned about infant damnation —in one minute. The lake was also being fed from underground sources, probably being connected by tubes with the crater of Mauna Ulu. Peterson glanced hopefully in various directions, looking for a spot where a breakthrough and overflow might occur. Our own elevation was about three feet above lake level but there were other places where the lava was lapping only a few inches from the top of the levee. Peninsulas and bays made it impossible for us to see the entire shore, however; we were thus unprepared for the breakthrough when it came. The level of the lake simply began to drop; somewhere close by but out of sight a stream of lava had begun to pour down the side of the shield.

Instead of walking around the summit to find the break Peterson went downhill toward the base. It was possible that the break might suddenly widen, causing problems for pedestrians in the neighborhood, and Peterson wanted to be well removed from it. He would approach the stream of lava from a lower level and from the side. The surface of the shield, like that of Mauna Ulu, was covered with glossy black billows. But here no one had staked out a trail around the treacherous spots. Many of the billows were hollow, their interiors having drained away, and though they appeared solid they were only brittle crusts a few inches thick. As we walked on them the billows cracked and sagged. Sometimes they broke completely, dropping a man up to his knees in sharp-edged shards that clattered and tinkled. A continual breaking-crockery noise accompanied us down the slope of the shield.

At the bottom Peterson headed east again, his backpack joggling as he hopped along the lava. He has a doctorate in geology from Stanford, has worked for the U.S. Geological Survey for 20 years, and is of course a public employee. As I hurried to keep up with him it struck me that the taxpayers were certainly getting their money's worth from him. Soon he stopped short and pointed out into the sloping field of lava in front of us. "There."

At first I saw only the black, frozen sea, but as I stared it suddenly became apparent that a long strip of the sea was moving. In the middle distance, bounded in the foreground and background by fixed, seemingly firm banks, a stream of lava was flowing downhill from right to left. There were small streaks of orange in it but in the main it was crusted

Lava from a volcano can take many different forms, depending on its temperature and composition when it emerges into the air. The common variety the Hawaiians call aa, consisting of large amounts of gas in a relatively cool (1,000°F. to 1,500°F.) mixture of rough, clinkery chunks of basalt, moves quite slowly but can cover extensive areas. At higher temperatures (1,600°F. to 2,000°F.) lava pours out in a liquid form called pahoehoe, which contains fewer and smaller gas bubbles, and travels farther and faster than aa. Lava also occurs in rarer forms such as obsidian and Pele's hair—varieties of volcanic glass that cool and harden in shimmering strands on the lava surface.

GLOWING AA

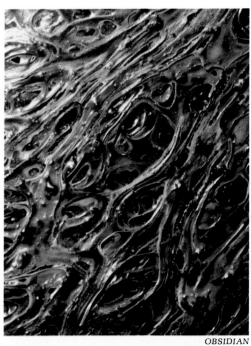

OBSIDIAN

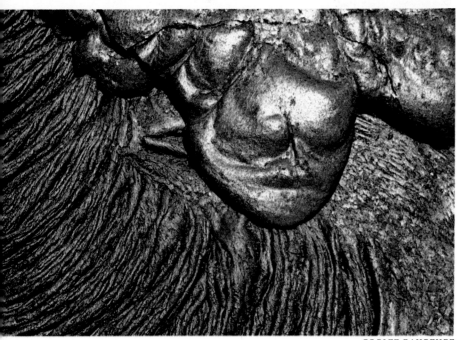

COOLED PAHOEHOE

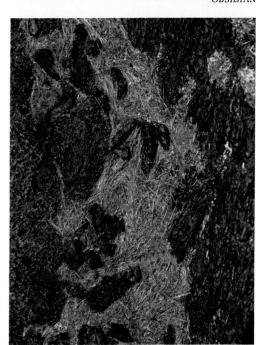

PELE'S HAIR (CENTER)

over, distinguishable from the hard lava on both sides of it only by the fact that it was in motion. The motion was steady and sedate, only a mile or two an hour on the gentle slope. Strange shapes swept silently along like black ice floes on a black river, or like figures and floats in a truly Godforsaken parade.

Peterson, full of enthusiasm, headed for the river with all deliberate speed. As we approached it, circling the lower part of the shield, we could look up and see the break in the levee of the lake perched above us. In truth it was not a break but merely the lowest spot in the levee over which the lava was pouring. That was the manner in which the shield grew: the lake rose and fell, constantly building its levee higher and higher, and at intervals it poured over the low spots. Sometimes several flows would come over the levee at once, radiating like spokes from a wheel hub. Peterson knew about that, and as we approached the river he mentioned the possibility. In the next few minutes, he said, he would be busy testing the thermocouple and would not have time to keep his eye on the levee, which was perhaps 20 yards above us and 200 yards away. Would someone please glance up occasionally, and let him know if a new flow of lava started to come down behind us? His words were, "It is not a good idea to be caught between two flows of lava." I volunteered to look up at the levee once in a while.

The lava at the edge of the river was sluggish, cooling and building banks. Its crust, however, was very thin and flexible. Peterson found a convenient place to test the thermocouple and, helped by Heiken, the geologist from NASA, prepared to do so. The principle of the device, long known, is this: when two dissimilar metals such as copper and iron are joined and simultaneously heated, a tiny electric current is generated. The current can be run through an ammeter and expressed on a gauge as temperature. The particular instrument that Peterson was testing resembled a long curtain rod with a meter connected by wires to one end; the other end was to be thrust into the lava.

Peterson put on a pair of gloves and, shielding his face from the heat with his forearm, advanced to the riverbank. The thermocouple rod was 10 feet long but its effective length was somewhat shorter because he had to stick it well into the lava to get a fair temperature reading. I moved up close to him for a few moments to feel the heat but then retreated, dropping a plastic ball-point pen I had been using to take notes. As it lay on the hard lava where Peterson was standing the pen turned into a piece of macaroni.

As Peterson held the rod tip in the molten lava, Heiken, some distance behind him, read the gauge and called out the temperature in degrees Fahrenheit. "1,600 . . . 1,650 . . . 1,675 . . . 1,700."

Peterson withdrew the rod and stepped back. Because the rod was relatively cool a blob of lava had hardened around the end of it, making the temperature reading inaccurate. With the blunt end of his geologist's hammer he carefully knocked off the blob, and then decided that he would stick the rod into a lava toe. Soft, liquid lava, of the sort we were dealing with, advances by thrusting forward rounded pillow-like protuberances called toes, not human in appearance but such as might be seen on an enormous black gingerbread man oozing across a cookie sheet. Peterson bent over a toe, which appeared to have an inch-thick crust on it, and struck it with the pointed end of his hammer. He poked a hole in it from which several spurts of orange lava flew up. A pea-sized drop hit him on the back of the wrist and fell down inside his glove. He quickly shook it out, muttering, and thrust the end of the thermocouple into the hole. In a few moments Heiken reported that the needle on the temperature gauge had touched 2,000°F.

Peterson had only one more task: he wanted to collect a sample of fresh lava, and so he stuck the pointed end of his hammer into the hole in the toe and hooked out a red-hot lump. He allowed it to cool briefly on the hammer, then popped it into a little cloth bag and put the bag into his backpack. As we walked and floundered across the hollow billows on the way back to the jeep he said, "A while ago I failed to let a sample cool long enough and it set fire to my pack. Embarrassing."

After we returned to the volcano laboratory I took leave of Dr. Peterson and drove down to Hilo, wondering where I would place a 17-mile-long 25-foot wall if someone asked me to build one. I was traveling alone, on my way to Hilo airport to catch a plane to another island. On the road I passed an old lady who had a flower stand, really only a table with some local orchids and anthuriums in tin cans. I had no use for flowers, not then, but she was staring at me with an odd expression. Although she was not ugly she was scarcely beautiful and she was in a sense asking me a favor. It dawned on me that a few flowers might not be a bad investment, so I bought some, and my car got all the way to Hilo without catching fire.

NATURE WALK **/ In Kipuka Puaulu**

PHOTOGRAPHS BY DAVID CAVAGNARO

On the slopes of Mauna Loa the overlapping and intertwining flows of lava have created islands called *kipuka*—the Hawaiian word for an opening. Sometimes *kipuka* form small hills, but more often they are pockets in the mountainside surrounded by more recent lava flows. Within the *kipuka,* plants have escaped the devastation that has swept past them on all sides; birds and butterflies find refuge there; and in the green shadows are echoes and fragrances of a time long vanished.

One of the most luxuriant of the *kipuka* on Mauna Loa lies at an altitude of 4,000 feet. It is called Puaulu, a combination of the words *pua,* which means both flower and a collection of things bound together, and *ulu,* to grow. Puaulu is so lush because it lies in the path of warm moist air that sweeps up the mountain from Hilo, at the base of Mauna Loa's fellow volcano, Kilauea.

Puaulu comprises 100 acres, which is large as *kipuka* go; many are only a few dozen square yards in size. It is roughly oval, with a trail that makes a loop of about a mile around its edge. Its age cannot be accurately determined but its huge *koa* and *ohia lehua* trees, some of them standing in small glades and others in patch-es of dense climax forest, are part of a community that has been undisturbed for hundreds of years—perhaps since the birth of Christ.

It takes about an hour to walk around Puaulu, allowing time for pauses to look and smell and listen, but even a dozen circuits of it reveal only a fraction of the *kipuka's* varied attractions. The rangers of Hawaii Volcanoes National Park have explored it many times and still consider themselves to be merely acquainted with the place, and not thoroughly knowledgeable about it. In fact, several basic studies of Puaulu remain to be made, to discover more about the evolution and interrelationships that distinguish this isolated community.

However, it is not a scientific interest that moves a man on first approaching Puaulu, but a sense of wonder and even of mystery. To me the trees and plants, though not at first glance dramatically different from those of the American mainland, were still unfamiliar enough on a recent visit to make me stop and stare. My thoughts then turned to the Hawaiians themselves, who enjoyed a greenwood instead of a metallic culture, who intimately knew these plants and put them to shrewd or cu-

KOA (LEFT) AND OHIA TREES

rious uses that have now slipped almost beyond memory.

The way to the *kipuka* passes over lava flows of recent centuries where the topsoil is still shallow and the vegetation stunted. Here and there on the rocks patches of gray beard-like lichen grow, slowly and invisibly breaking down the stone into

PIONEER LICHEN ON LAVA ROCK

earth by means of minute amounts of organic acids that the lichen secretes both when it photosynthesizes and when it decomposes. Entering the *kipuka* I passed quickly into the cool shade of a mixed forest. For the rest of the walk, save in a few small, grassy, sunlit areas, I was enclosed in the woods and saw no large vistas. I could fix my attention on the greenery around me.

The ground cover alongside the

OAK FERN IN THE OPEN FOREST

trail was thick with delicate oak ferns—their fronds characteristically thinner at the base than in the middle—and also with crane's-bills, otherwise known as wild geraniums. Overhead were the intermingling branches of soapberry trees and Hawaiian olives, whose fruit is inedible but whose hardwood was once used for spears and adz handles. I had the good luck to glimpse a Kamehameha butterfly perched on a knee-high bracken fern. Highly colored, with a wingspan of about four inches, the Kamehameha is found in the forests of all the major Hawaiian Islands —but nowhere else in the world.

A few of the plants visible from the trail are familiar to mainland gardeners. The broad-leaved *ti* is widely known for its decorative qualities; its flowers, appearing in spring, grow in branched clusters at least a foot

A KAMEHAMEHA BUTTERFLY

long, bearing half-inch-long white buds tinged pale purple. In times past, the Hawaiians found the *ti* useful as well as decorative. The leaves were used as thatch, stitched together to make skirts, or wrapped around food that was to be cooked or stored. In those innocent days the Hawaiians brewed a weak alcoholic drink

from the *ti*'s thick roots, which are rich in sugar. But around 1800, white men showed them how to make stills from blubber kettles and musket barrels, and the *ti* became the source of a skull-popping rumlike concoction called *okolehao.* A civilized version of the liquor is sold in Honolulu liquor stores today.

A Nut for Burning

Near the *ti* plants along the trail was a *kukui,* or candlenut, tree. It too looked familiar—in this case deceptively so. With the sun shining down through them, the leaves were shaped much like the leaves of mainland maples. Totally unlike the maple, however, the tree bears a nut that used to be burned for illumination—hence the name. The nut was also put to other purposes, including ritualistic retribution against criminals. Scattered in a fire kindled for

A DECORATIVE, POTENT TI PLANT

LEAVES OF THE CANDLENUT TREE

POMPON BLOOMS OF THE OHIA TREE

the occasion by priests, the kernels of the nut furnished magic that was guaranteed—provided the ceremony was accompanied by the proper incantation—to make a thief give himself up, on pain of certain death.

Some of the towering *ohia lehua* trees beside the trail were tilted at fantastic angles by the wind but still thriving, in full bloom with brilliant clustered scarlet flowers. The *ohia* has shallow roots, a disadvantage at times of hurricane, but in other ways a source of strength: since the seeds of the tree are light and easily airborne, the *ohia* is a pioneer among plants in revegetating newly lava-covered areas. Sailing out of the *kipuka,* the seeds lodge in lava crevices where only shallow-rooted plants may take hold; in time these

crack the stone and make room for other plants that delve more deeply.

Common throughout all Polynesia, the *ohia* as it appears in Hawaii is remarkably varied in form. There are so many subspecies that it is impossible to classify them all. In the Kau region, a stone desert on the southeast side of Mauna Loa, the *ohia* may be a tiny shrub only a foot tall but fully mature, producing seeds and beautiful crimson pompon blooms.

In such inhospitable places the young *ohia* may hitch a ride on an even earlier arrival—the sadleria fern. Airborne *ohia* seeds may take root in the branches of the sadleria, extend their roots earthward and eventually strangle the fern. This ability of the *ohia* to grow as an epiphyte, or air plant, led the early

BRACKET FUNGUS ON OHIA BARK

Hawaiians to think of the fern as the parent of the tree. In Kipuka Puaulu the oldest *ohia,* with their bark encrusted at intervals on the trunk by bracket fungus resembling outsized clams, reach heights of about 100 feet. *Ohia* wood is dark red, handsomely grained and tough. From it the Hawaiians made planks that were pegged as gunwales on their big dugout canoes. Rubbing against these hard boards, the relatively easily made paddles wore out, while the softer sides of the laboriously hollowed boats went unscathed.

A Medicinal Relic

Beside the trail, both on the ground and in clefts in the trees, grew a strange primitive plant called *moa* by the Hawaiians and *Psilotum nudum* by botanists. Its stems are triangular, its scales grow no more than one eighth of an inch long; in its general appearance—somewhat like seaweed—it resembles certain other plant species so long extinct that they are known today only as fossils. By boiling the *moa* the Hawaiians produced a medicinal tea that they found useful in curing thrush, a

AN OHIA TREE TILTED BY THE WIND

A PRIMITIVE, MEDICINAL MOA PLANT

fungus infection of the mouth common in infants. They also employed the tea as a laxative, while to combat diarrhea they swallowed the *moa*'s powdery spores.

About halfway around the loop I came upon a rare *holei* tree, a native plant with boldly decorative leathery leaves. Nearby were a few dwarfed but hardy *hapuu* tree ferns, which ordinarily thrive better at lower altitudes, where they reach heights of 35 feet or more.

At several points the edge of the trail was adorned with the fleshy white fruit of the *mamaki*, a large shrub about 15 feet high that was once among the Hawaiians' most prized plants. Its inner bark furnished a durable cloth, resembling cotton, that was made into skirts for women and loincloths for men.

LEAVES OF THE RARE HOLEI TREE

Also thriving in the *kipuka* was the *koali,* a common morning-glory whose pale violet blooms form a startlingly delicate contrast to the coarse leaves of the vine on which they grow. Known in Hawaiian legend as a source of rope, the vine is celebrated in even older Polynesian folklore as the source of the human race; its juice once produced worms that the Creator, Tangaloa, transformed into people and endowed with intelligence.

In experimenting with the properties of the plants and trees in their islands the Hawaiians always had an eye for any amusement they could derive. Such was the case with the *papala,* which I recognized beside the trail by the tiny flowers that stippled the tips of its branches. The *papala* supplied the Hawaiians with fireworks. The wood of the tree is very light and flammable; coated with oil, it burns briskly. Discovering this, the Hawaiians fashioned long *papala* spears, set them alight and hurled them at night from high cliffs above the water. To the delight of watchers floating in their canoes below, the spears would sail great distances on the trade winds—like a swarm of comets in the dark sky —before sputtering into the sea.

A White Strawberry

As I reached the open forest at the halfway mark on the trail, the spacing of the trees enabled me to get a better look at the ground cover, and I was struck by its great variety. Among the most widespread of the ground huggers was a strawberry bearing a white fruit. Though not a

STEMS AND FLOWERS OF THE FLAMMABLE PAPALA

THE MAMAKI: SOURCE OF NATIVE CLOTH

A HARDY HAPUU TREE FERN

DELICATE KOALI MORNING-GLORIES

native of Hawaii—it originated in Europe and North America—the plant is strange, with its pale berry that never reddens even when ripe. Interspersed among the strawberry plants was the luxuriant foliage of the *kopiko*, a member of the coffee family that accounts, along with its 10 or so Hawaiian relatives, for a large percentage of the native forest vegetation. Another somewhat larger ground cover, formerly considered sacred to the goddess Pele, was the shrubby *ohelo*, which bears berries the Hawaiians also considered good to eat; they could not eat the fruit, however, until they had propitiated the fire goddess by throwing *ohelo* branches, berries attached, into the lava pit of Kilauea.

A Majestic Giant

Past its midpoint the loop trail on Puaulu has a short spur that leads out almost to the edge of the *kipuka*, within sight of the newer lava that surrounds it. There in lone majesty stands a giant *koa* tree, 10 feet in diameter at its base. It is doubtless hundreds of years old, but there is no way of knowing its precise age. In tropical and subtropical latitudes trees do not produce well-defined growth rings that can be counted. In attempting to determine their age from samples withdrawn from their trunks by core bits, botanists can only make estimates. The huge *koa* tree I saw had a many-branched trunk, but the species also produces trees with one trunk of great girth. It was from these that Hawaiian craftsmen fashioned their canoes.

The making of canoes, particularly

WHITE HAWAIIAN STRAWBERRIES

the large vessels designed for war or long ocean voyages, was accompanied by a good deal of ceremony and prayer. When a Hawaiian located a suitable *koa* tree in the forest he told a *kahuna* (priest) about it, and the *kahuna* went into a temple to sleep in the hope of having an auspicious dream. If in his dream he saw a naked man or woman the tree was considered rotten and unfit; but if the person was well clothed the tree was deemed suitable. Other signs being propitious, the priest then went into the woods and cut down the *koa* with a stone ax. Finished canoes were very narrow, between one and three feet in width, but as much as 100 feet long and 10 feet deep.

The *koa* tree also furnished wood for Hawaiians' surfboards, which

THE UBIQUITOUS KOPIKO

were a good deal larger than those
in use today—in the collection of
boards in the Bishop Museum in
Honolulu there is one 16 feet long.

From the giant *koa* tree the Puaulu trail curves gently rightward toward where it began, at the entrance
to the *kipuka*. Beside the trail at this
point, mingled with the endemic Hawaiian plants, are several interesting
foreigners, such as an avocado tree
whose weighty seed can only have
been left there by some picnicker
years ago. At the *kipuka*'s 4,000-foot
elevation the avocado is far above
its optimum range, yet it thrives. Indeed, all plants thrive in the *kipuka*,
whose soil is made not of decomposed lava but of many layers of
volcanic ash, rich in nitrates and other nutrients. In one place this hos-

THE SACRED OHELO

A MAJESTIC KOA

THE IMMIGRANT PUKAMOLE

PUKIAWE: A RITUAL FUMIGANT

pitable soil nourishes a bed of enormous nasturtiums, two or three times the size of garden nasturtiums. Nearby flourishes a colorful *pukamole,* which has somehow found its way there from Peru.

Near the exit from the *kipuka* I noticed a low shrub with small stiff leaves, some of them with red or white berries: this is a native plant called the *pukiawe.* The Hawaiians found the berries unappetizing but sometimes threaded them into *lei.* The notion that *lei* are always made of flowers is relatively recent; in earlier times they were often made of berries, feathers or nuts.

Another use of the *pukiawe* was an odd ritualistic one. The Hawaiian world was hedged about with taboos; if, for example, a commoner allowed his shadow to fall on a chief, the penalty was death. The chiefs found this a trifle inconvenient when they wished to attend a feast without killing their people. A temporary dispensation, however, was possible: a chief smoked himself in the fumes of burning *pukiawe* branches to remove his lethal taboo long enough for a public frolic.

Emerging from the cool *kipuka,* I glanced to the west at the quiet peak volcano of Mauna Loa. Its low gentle curve stretched for miles along the horizon. No trace of smoke or steam was visible at its summit. It seemed sunk in slumber from which it would never awaken. Yet common sense and the record of the past insist that it will indeed awaken, and that this green island on its flank will someday sink in a sea of fire.

THE EDGE OF THE KIPUKA—MAUNA LOA IN BACKGROUND

3/ The Magic of Maui

---

*We lived and breathed in cloudland....Forests laced with
frost; silvery, silent seas; shores of agate and of
pearl; blue shadowy caverns; mountains of light, dissolving
and rising again.* CHARLES WARREN STODDARD/ *SOUTH-SEA IDYLS*

The names of most of the major Hawaiian islands are so ancient that
no interpretation of them is possible. To be sure, the names once had
specific meanings, in times lost beyond all memory. However, one island—the nearest to the main island of Hawaii—has a name that is readily understood: it is called Maui after a famous demigod. Now, Maui
was not born on the island that bears his name. He has been well known
for countless years throughout Polynesia, the vast ocean expanse extending northward from New Zealand through the Society Islands and
the Marquesas, and no one can say where he came from. But it is only
to this island in the Hawaiian chain that Maui's name is attached.

To the ancient Hawaiians, Maui was not one of the great gods in the
Polynesian pantheon: Lono, god of harvest and peace; Kane, father of
living creatures; Ku, god of war; or Kaneloa, ruler of the world of ghosts.
Maui was a youthful player of tricks, innocent ones as a rule. He was
quick-witted, a benefactor of humanity, and he was mortal himself—he
was killed while trying to steal the secret of eternal life from a goddess
called The Guardian of the Night, so that he could give it to mankind.

Maui had several brothers, less smart than he, whom he could often
bamboozle into doing his bidding. Once he went fishing with a magical
line and hook, and while his brothers dutifully paddled the canoe Maui
sat in the stern and caught something enormous far below the surface.
As the brothers struggled to move the canoe forward to pull up the

heavy catch, Maui warned them not to look backward. He had hooked a small continent lying on the bottom of the sea and he feared that it might break in pieces if his brothers paused to stare at it before he had it safely moored. Unfortunately they did not heed him; they turned around to look and the continent did indeed come apart, separating into the eight Hawaiian Islands.

Maui could not only pull islands from the depths. When the sky fell down, pressing so close to the earth that the trees were bent over and men had to crawl about on their knees, Maui summoned the strength to push it back up. Today clouds occasionally come close to the earth again but they do not stay long for fear that Maui will return and shove them so far into the heavens that they will never find their way back. People who doubt the story need only glance at the trees for proof. The trunks, branches and twigs, being resilient, have regained their normal shape but the leaves are still pressed flat.

Many of the tales of Maui are ancient but a few are even more recent than the arrival of the Polynesians in Hawaii, perhaps only a thousand years ago. On the island that bears Maui's name there is a great mountain called Haleakala—The House of the Sun. It could as well be called The Prison of the Sun because of Maui. When he lived on the island with his mother and brothers, the length of the days was only three or four hours. The sun was fond of sleeping, so it raced across the sky in order to get back into bed as quickly as possible. Because of the short days Maui's mother did not have time to make her *tapa* cloth from the bark of the mulberry or the *mamaki* tree. By nightfall the *tapa* was still soggy and not sun-dried as it ought to have been.

Studying the situation, Maui observed that the sun rose in the morning by thrusting first one long leg—or beam—above the rim of Haleakala, and then another and another. The sun had 16 such legs spaced evenly around its circumference, on which it strode through heaven. Maui therefore secured 16 long ropes that he made into lassos, and in the darkness before dawn he hid in a crevice high up near the top of the mountain. When the first of the sun's legs appeared Maui threw a rope around it and tied it to a *wiliwili* tree; and so he did with the second, third and all the others until the sun was hopelessly caught.

At first Maui announced that he was going to kill the sun with an ax he had brought with him for the purpose, but when the sun craftily pointed out that *tapa* cloth would *never* dry in total darkness, a bargain was struck. The sun agreed to walk slowly across the sky, while Maui agreed to cut the ropes and release his prisoner.

It was probably not Maui's benefactions to man that caused the Hawaiians to name the island after him. More likely it was because there was a magical charm about the demigod that the Hawaiians found somehow reflected in the beautiful, haunting land. Visitors, and even permanent residents on others of the islands who are able to set aside their local pride, tend to agree that there is a special air about Maui —or at any rate about east Maui—a bewitching place where a man can see strange things and believe he sees things even stranger. A good many years ago, in 1909, as staid an organization as the U.S. Bureau of American Ethnology published a book called *Unwritten Literature of Hawaii.* In it is this passage: "Of what nature were the gods of the old times, and how did the ancient Hawaiians conceive of them? As of beings having the form, the powers, and the passions of humanity, yet standing above and somewhat apart from men. One sees, as through a mist, darkly, a figure, standing, moving; in shape a plant, a tree or vine-clad stump, a bird, a taloned monster, a rock carved by the fire-queen, a human form, a puff of vapor—and now it has given·place to vacancy. . . . Or again, a traveler meets a creature of divine beauty, all smiles and loveliness. The infatuated mortal, smitten with hopeless passion, offers blandishments; he finds himself by the roadside, embracing a rock." The vision and the roadside would be, surely, in east Maui.

Haleakala is a national park. A well-engineered road, full of switchbacks, leads to the summit of the 10,000-foot mountain where Maui caught the sun. From the summit one can look down to the southwest and see, across a narrow channel, the low-lying island of Kahoolawe. It is one of the two islands in the archipelago that are almost never visited. The other is Niihau, which is owned in its entirety (72 square miles) by a family named Robinson whose members operate a cattle ranch there. The Robinsons have long been fanatical in their refusal to admit visitors, on the ground that they wish to preserve the bloodlines, language and customs of the 250 or so Hawaiians who live on the island and work for them.

Kahoolawe is a different case and deserves mention in a book about wilderness for a gloomy reason: it is a *man-made* wilderness. The island is on the lee side of Maui and thus is screened from rainfall, receiving only about 20 inches a year. Nonetheless Kahoolawe, within the memory of living Hawaiians, was green with drought-resistant grass and trees. But in the 1920s and 1930s it was overgrazed by herds of sheep and cattle, and after it could no longer support these animals it was turned into a bomb target for the military. Today it is a barren expanse of red dusty clay littered with shell casings, shrapnel and the black pellet droppings of seemingly immortal goats.

The sad little island of Kahoolawe is worth only a glance from the summit of Haleakala. The real spectacle lies down past a man's boots, where he can see spread out below him a huge crater 3,000 feet deep, eight miles long and three wide. The whole inner top of the mountain is missing. The great depression is commonly called Haleakala Crater, to the annoyance of geologists who keep pointing out that it was only partially caused by volcanism. Most of it was excavated by stream erosion in ancient times when the pattern of wind and rainfall must have been quite different from today's. The streams cut two large gaps through the wall of the then-dormant volcano—Koolau at the head of Keanae Valley to the northwest, and Kaupo to the southeast. After this occurred Haleakala became active again and erupted several more times, sending flows of lava pouring out through the gaps and covering almost all the signs of erosion.

From the mountaintop a trail leads into the crater, across its long floor, out through Kaupo Gap and down to the sea, a hike of about 20 miles through one of the most strangely beautiful landscapes on earth. The trail, its upper reaches called Sliding Sands for a reason that soon becomes clear to anyone walking on it, descends a slope of reddish-brown ash and cinders. For the first 1,000 feet of descent no plants are visible among the scorched stones. In the clear still air at that high altitude the crunch of cinders underfoot seems uncommonly loud. Tiny puffs of dust arise and hang motionless. The division between areas of sunlight and shadow is very sharp. Below, scattered on the level crater floor, there are several symmetrical volcanic mounds and cones in shades of ocher and orange, black and gray. In the distance they seem small but as a man approaches them they turn out to be several hundred feet high. He half expects to see two globe-helmeted figures in suits of metallic cloth, wearing little American flags as shoulder patches, come hopping out from behind one of the cones and start setting up a package of instruments.

Growing on the sides of the cones are round moon-colored plants, some of them as large as bushel baskets: Haleakala silverswords. The Hawaiians, who had no word for metal in their language before the coming of white men, called the plant ahinahina, or "gray-gray," a repetition that served to make the point for people who had never seen polished silver or burnished steel. The leaves of the silversword are long and narrow, incurving to the shape of a globe, and they derive their color from a dense feltlike covering of fine hair.

All plants of course are adaptations or designs that are successful in their particular environments, but on close inspection the silversword seems to go beyond mere success to something close to a miracle. It is found only at elevations of 7,000 to 10,000 feet on Haleakala—although a few specimens may still be surviving at similar heights on the volcanic island of Hawaii—and only in conditions that would be quickly fatal to other plants. It is desert-dry within the crater; at night the temperature often falls below freezing while by day the sun is merciless. Yet the silversword survives to an age of as much as 20 years and then, having reached a diameter of about two feet, it suddenly produces a magnificent flower stalk perhaps six feet high on which nod hundreds of purplish blossoms. After this effort it dies.

As a protection from cold the growing point of the silversword is buried deep in its globe of incurved leaves. Against the drying sun and wind the plant presents the narrow leaves characteristic of most desert vegetation. But within the leaves, where other plants have countless microscopic air spaces, the silversword has a jelly-like substance that stores water. Outside, the tiny gray hairs both deflect wind and turn sunlight aside. In cross section, instead of being round or convex like most hairs, they are seen to be flat or concave. Thus they do not focus light on the leaves, like lenses, but reflect it.

It would seem that so well designed a plant would have little difficulty surviving, but a careful count in 1927 turned up barely 100 specimens remaining in Haleakala, where once there had been so many that the cinder cones seemed bathed in perpetual silvery moonlight. Mountain climbers destroyed some of them; as Europeans fasten sprigs of edelweiss on their hats to signify that they have climbed one alp or another, people who ascended Haleakala used to carry down small silverswords. Or they would uproot the largest ones and roll them like huge snowballs down the cones. At one time thousands of the plants were picked, dried and shipped to the Orient as ornaments. Goats, however, did even more damage than men, devouring the seedlings as fast as they sprouted. The species was saved at almost its final moment by the National Park Service, which planted some specimens and fenced them off; they then began a program to wipe out the goats, deputizing hunters as rangers so they could shoot the animals on park land. (Many Hawaiians are fond of the meat. A prime goat is worth as much as $25

The silversword, named for the silvery hairs on its leaves, is one of the world's rarest plants, growing only in Haleakala Crater on the island of Maui. The plant takes as much as 15 years to produce its soaring six-foot bloom, after which it withers and dies.

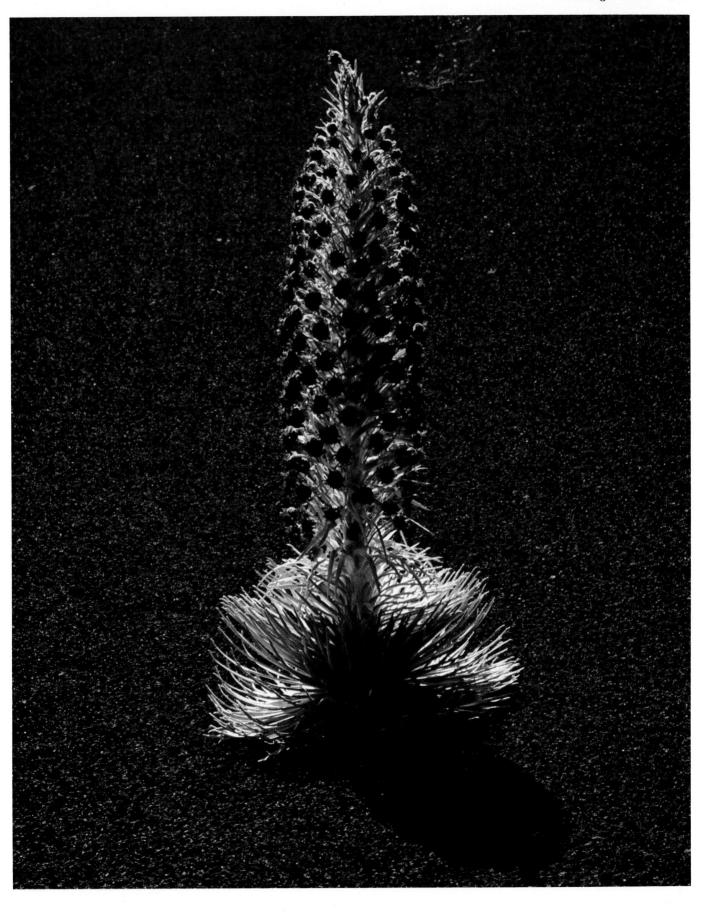

on the market.) By 1973 the silversword, though still endangered and in need of every bit of protection it could get, had increased in number to about 2,000, and the goats, though still in the neighborhood, had become skittish about venturing across the open floor of the crater to reach the plants on the cones.

Archeologists have uncovered a good many stone platforms and terraces in and around Haleakala Crater, together with several ancient graves—it was the custom of Hawaiians to bury their dead, particularly people of prominence, in remote and inaccessible places. Near the midpoint of the crater there is a black hole about 10 feet in diameter, rimmed with a jagged rampart of lava spatter, that was apparently thought by the Hawaiians to be a bottomless pit. (Today it is choked with rubble about 70 feet underground and appears to have been a vent for escaping gas in some long-ago eruption.) The Hawaiians used the pit to dispose of the umbilical cords of babies, which were wrapped in *tapa* cloth or, more recently, placed in bottles. It was believed that this would make the children strong and prevent them from becoming thieves, as might happen if the cords were casually discarded, then found and eaten by rats.

At the eastern end of the crater near Paliku Cabin, a park service rest hut, the trail turns south to descend the Kaupo Gap. At this point there is a notch like a rear gun sight high in the crater wall. On the other side of the wall, on the outer slope of Haleakala, lies the cloud-filled valley of Kipahulu. Trade winds constantly push clouds up the valley toward the notch in the high wall and often they spill through into the crater in a swirl of rain and mist. Thus for a few hundred yards around Paliku there is an area of vegetation unmatched anywhere else in Haleakala; the clouds, drifting deeper into the dry crater, quickly lose all their moisture and vanish in the brilliantly clear air.

The trail approaches Paliku across a field of broken, spiny blocks of lava crazily jumbled together. If clouds are coming down through the notch, the lava field is wrapped in thick mist with low, twisted bushes and trees materializing and disappearing in it. Their crooked, beckoning branches seem to be clutching at shreds and streamers of fog slowly gliding past. The idea inevitably strikes a man that Macbeth must have encountered the three witches in a place very much like this —an idea that loses nothing when a wild, forlorn, nonhuman cry comes curling through the mist from somewhere close at hand.

There may be, on a good day, several wild, forlorn, nonhuman cries,

Elusive and rarely photographed, the Hawaiian honeycreepers are the most colorful and diversified family of native songbirds in the islands. Of the 20-odd species of honeycreepers, four are shown at right in Kipahulu Valley on Maui. Each of the four has a bill suited to the bird's preferred diet. The iiwi's bill is long and curved, enabling it to dip deep inside tubular flowers to get at their nectar. The bills of the apapane, the amakihi and the akohekohe are shorter and only slightly curved; these species favor the nectar of more open flowers, as well as insects, for food—in the case of the akohekohe, caterpillars.

THE IIWI, ADULT (LEFT) AND JUVENILE

THE APAPANE

THE AMAKIHI

THE AKOHEKOHE

and after an instant's hesitation a listener is glad to hear them. They are the calls of the Hawaiian goose, the *nene* (pronounced *nay-nay*), which is being bred in captivity and set free to establish itself in the wild at Paliku. *Nene,* which are believed to have evolved from Canada goose stock, are the state birds of Hawaii, and had been so cut down by hunters, predators and disease that in the late 1940s there were probably fewer than 50 of them left in the world. Since then federal and state propagation projects have increased their number to more than 1,000, some of them reared by the Severn Wildfowl Trust in England and air-freighted halfway around the globe for release on Maui. They often remain near the release site for some time, feeding on the cloud-watered grass and shiny black *kukaenene* berries there.

Nene bear a superficial resemblance to Canada geese, though their necks appear silvery instead of black. Their natural habitat is brushy upland between 5,000 and 7,000 feet, both on Maui and the island of Hawaii, and they are a great curiosity among waterfowl in that they forsook the water thousands of years ago. They rarely swim, except in a clumsy way in captivity, and in the process of evolution they have lost half the webbing on their feet.

When clouds lift away from the cliff above Paliku, a prominent rock called Pohaku Palaha becomes visible up there. It is the central reference point of bygone times, the surveyor's mark from which royal land grants were measured. Hawaiian kings had a remarkably equitable, sensible method of distributing real estate, at least among the chiefs, or *alii,* as they were called. Land grants were made in great triangles, with their apexes on mountaintops and their broad bases extending out into the ocean far below. The logic was that the necessities of life are to be found at various altitudes: each man needs hardwood for weapons and tools, *koa* trees for canoes, land for dry farming, land for wet farming, birds for eating and birds for ornament, a share of the sea for fishing and for recreation, and so on, all of which can be found only in triangular plots radiating down from pinnacles.

The trail leading out through Kaupo Gap goes down about 6,000 feet in eight miles to the sea, a pleasant slope easily descended. The vegetation grows thicker along the way; in its midst there are a good many large shrubs or small trees with leathery, dark green leaves and, in summer, clusters of brick-red flowers. These are sandalwoods, of which about eight species are found in Hawaii, where the tree has had a melancholy history. Sandalwood was—and still is—highly prized in the Orient, where its close-grained heartwood is used in ornamental carving and cabinetwork. It is richly scented, and is burned both for incense and as an insect repellent. When white men discovered that sandalwood was abundant in Hawaii a hectic and almost maniacal trade sprang up in it. In exchange for money or goods, mostly the latter, local chiefs traded great quantities of sandalwood at prices that ranged upward from $125 a ton, an important sum in the period (1815-1830) when the traffic was at its height. The actual collection was done, of course, by the common people, who were forced to go up into the mountains to cut trees and carry down the logs. If a chief wished to buy a shipyard-built schooner or other small ship, his subjects were ordered to dig a large pit that had the dimensions and shape of the proposed vessel and to fill the pit with closely packed sandalwood. This was considered a fair swap by white traders, who then transported the wood to China and received silks, porcelain and other goods worth 10 times as much as the ship. Hawaiian chiefs drove their subjects so hard to collect wood that there was little time for anything else, even farming, with the result that the islands were seriously threatened by famine. However, by about 1830 all the marketable sandalwoods had been cut down and the trade ended. Hawaiian workers, who were not only strong-backed but smart, also surreptitiously destroyed as many sandalwood seedlings as they could find so that they would not have to return in later years to harvest the trees. Today the sandalwoods have made a fair comeback, but it will be another century or two before truly large ones are again common.

As the trail from Kaupo Gap approaches the sea, the white waves breaking along the coast come increasingly into focus. With binoculars a man can look out into the Alenuihaha Channel, which separates east Maui from the island of Hawaii, and see—particularly in the months from November to May—humpback whales frolicking there with their calves. Considerable numbers of these creatures, which weigh as much as 60 tons, congregate in Hawaiian waters to breed. Humpbacks are black with white undersides, although occasionally a pure white one appears. Moby Dick was a sperm whale, not a humpback, but the sight is enough to bemuse any reader of Herman Melville.

The green coast and the constantly changing blue of the sea, the coconut palms nodding by the shore in the steady, gentle breeze of the trades, can hold a man transfixed for hours. He can, with Mark Twain, "sun himself all day long under the palm trees, and be no more troubled by his conscience than a butterfly would." But the long downhill

trail ends at a coastal road and sooner or later the road must be followed. Several miles to the east lie the entrances—or, at any rate, the access points—of two wild valleys, beyond the utmost capability of jeeps, requiring an uphill scramble on foot. The valleys are Kipahulu, from whose upper end the clouds glide down through the notch into Haleakala Crater, and Waihoi.

In the summer of 1972 photographer Dan Budnik climbed into Waihoi and emerged with the pictures on pages 98 to 105. Kipahulu was explored in 1967 by a group of scientists sponsored by The Nature Conservancy. Theirs was the first study of the whole ecology of the valley and to this day it remains unsurpassed, although nonscientists will find parts of it a good deal more fascinating than others. Botanically, Kipahulu proved to be the greatest stronghold of endemic plants in all of Hawaii. Only 10 per cent of those found there have been introduced to the islands by man; all the rest, some 200 species including at least 15 previously unknown, are endemic, or indigenous. One of the expedition's botanists, Dr. Charles Lamoureux of the University of Hawaii, was so impressed that he concluded—in language a good deal more exuberant than scientists generally use—that "Kipahulu . . . offers an opportunity [for study] not available elsewhere on this planet."

The birds of Kipahulu, some of which are pictured on page 87, are perhaps of more interest to laymen. Indeed, one species that had been thought to be extinct since the 19th Century was found to be living in the valley. However, the names of Hawaiian birds have so odd an appearance in print, and their extinction or near-extinction has been so puzzling, that some preliminary explanation seems worthwhile.

A written language for Hawaiians was devised in the 19th Century by missionaries, who tried to express the rich, spoken language with an alphabet of only 12 letters—the five vowels plus the consonants h, k, l, m, n, p and w. Because there are so few letters it is necessary to make the most of them; a man cannot go far wrong if he pronounces every letter he possibly can. Thus the bird called the *ou* is pronounced *oh-oo;* the *o-o* is *oh-oh,* and so on. To some non-Hawaiians the names may *look* silly, but in fact they are musical and in some cases onomatopoeic —to some, *elepaio* suggests the call of the bird itself. As one Hawaiian ornithologist has observed, not without annoyance, "People on the mainland would be a lot more concerned with our endangered species if only they were named the Red, White and Blue Warbler or the American Golden Owl. As it is, our only endemic owl is the *pueo.*"

Waterfalls wide and narrow, powered by 200 inches of rain a year, feed the Palikea Stream and its tributaries in Maui's Kipahulu Valley.

Now to the loss of Hawaii's birds. When the islands were discovered by white men there were 69 species found nowhere else in the world. Twenty-five of them are now known or believed to be extinct and another 27 are considered rare or endangered. How this depletion should have come about was for many years a mystery.

Explanations that at first seemed obvious and conclusive turned out on thoughtful examination to be only partially true or not true at all. Only two things were certain: first, that for a century after the arrival of Captain Cook competent observers on all the islands had seen Hawaii's endemic birds ranging in goodly numbers from the beaches to the high mountain forests; and second, that by the end of the 19th Century the birds were fast disappearing or had already vanished. It seemed likely that one cause was the destruction of part of their habitat, taken over by huge plantations and ranches; another was that their food plants had been devoured by cattle and goats or crowded out by rampaging imported vegetation. Still another probable factor was the introduction of continental predators such as house cats, which ran wild, and the small Indian mongoose, *Herpestes auropunctatus,* which was brought to Hawaii in 1883 to prey on rats in the sugar-cane fields. (Although mongooses do destroy rodents, they also destroy ground-nesting birds and have been known to kill animals many times larger than themselves. Full-grown mongooses weigh only a couple of pounds but can fell fawns and even donkeys by attacking them around the mouth and throat.) But these factors did not provide the whole answer. Something strange and unaccountable was also taking place.

In 1902 the ornithologist H. W. Henshaw wrote in bafflement: "The author has lived in Hawaii only six years, but within this time large areas of forest, which are yet scarcely touched by the axe save on the edges and except for a few trails, have become almost absolute solitude. One may spend hours in them and not hear the note of a single native bird. Yet a few years ago these areas were abundantly supplied with native birds. . . . The ohia blossoms as freely as it used to and secretes abundant nectar for the Iiwi, Apapane and Amakihi. The ieie still fruits, and offers its crimson spike of seeds, as of old, to the Ou. So far as the human eye can see, their old home offers to the birds practically all that it used to, but the birds themselves are no longer there. . . . The abandonment of forest tracts under such circumstances seems inexplicable, and the writer can recall no similar phenomenon among American birds."

The native birds did not vanish on all the islands simultaneously

—on Lanai, for example, they flourished until 1923, when a sudden decline began. And on one of the remote Leeward Islands the Laysan finch is probably as numerous today as it ever was. Further, extinction and survival are related to altitude—in lowland areas the endemic honeycreepers have disappeared, yet remnant populations still exist in upland forest areas like the Kipahulu Valley, above 3,000 feet, and in the Alakai Swamp on the island of Kauai, at 4,200 feet.

The elements of the mystery were pieced together and published in 1968 in a brilliant scientific paper by Dr. Richard E. Warner, who had spent several years studying Hawaiian birds. It was plain enough that the major factor in their disappearance was disease; encroachment on their habitat, reduction of food supply and increase of predators were important but secondary. But what were the diseases and how had they been spread?

Just as the Hawaiian people had never developed resistance to influenza or measles, Hawaiian birds had no resistance to avian malaria, which is common among mainland birds and is caused by a microscopic parasite in their blood. Hawaiian birds were also highly vulnerable to bird pox, or bumblefoot, a tumor-producing disease of domestic poultry. In Warner's view, the potential for avian malaria had probably existed in Hawaii for thousands of years. Migratory shore birds and ducks, coming to the islands from the mainland, undoubtedly carried the blood parasite—but for some reason it was not transmitted to the native birds. Caged pet birds and foreign birds introduced by the early colonists might also have caused the disaster. Bird pox was a different matter; it had come to Hawaii with the barnyard fowl of white men. Still, how it had been passed from chickens to wild forest birds remained a puzzle.

The answer, Warner found, lay in an incident that had occurred in the port of Lahaina on Maui in 1826. In that year the ship *Wellington,* having last filled her water casks at San Blas on the west coast of Mexico, put in at Lahaina to fill them again. The sailors assigned to this duty dumped the dregs from the casks into a pure stream, not noticing or more likely not caring that the dregs were alive with small wriggling larvae. In that manner the mosquito, which had failed to reach Hawaii in 20 million years, arrived at last. The particular mosquito was *Culex pipiens fatigans,* which inhabits tropical and subtropical regions. It is now found on the main Hawaiian islands from sea level to elevations of about 3,000 feet.

Culex was the carrier that transmitted blood parasites and viruses from migratory birds and domestic poultry to Hawaii's endemic birds. As *Culex* made its way from island to island the forests one after another fell silent. Even at altitudes above 3,000 feet, where the mosquitoes are not found in significant numbers, the silence spread. The insects did not go up to the birds; the birds came down to the insects. It had been the long-established habit of Hawaiian birds to migrate, during the season of winter storms, from the high country to the lowlands—and when they descended into territory occupied by *Culex* they were bitten and mortally infected.

In some conclusive experiments Dr. Warner captured small numbers of Laysan finches on their tiny home island, 900 miles from Honolulu, where the mosquito had never become established. The birds were taken to Honolulu in a cage shrouded in several layers of cheesecloth, and for two months they thrived in it. But when the cheesecloth was removed and mosquitoes were allowed to enter the cage, all of the finches developed bird pox and perished. In a similar test on the island of Kauai, other Laysan finches prospered in cages but died of avian malaria soon after the screening was removed. Later Dr. Warner captured a few individuals of other endemic species—*apapane, amakihi* and lesser *amakihi*—at an elevation of about 4,000 feet on Kauai and took them down to the lowlands, where they too developed malaria and died.

Today it is only in the highlands that Hawaii's rare endemic birds are found. Warner thinks they may be developing disease-resistant forms and hopes they may someday be able to return to the pestilent lowlands. However, this is at best only a hope, and some powerful factors are arrayed against it. In recent years, introduced game birds such as pheasants and wild turkeys have been found to carry, among other diseases, avian encephalomyelitis and botulism. It is impossible to say what resistance to these diseases the endemic birds may have, although very likely they have none. And in California there exists a mosquito called *Culex pipiens pipiens*, a cousin of the insect already established in Hawaii, that can thrive in higher altitudes. If *pipiens* establishes itself in the islands, having reached them not in a water cask but in the cabin of a jet plane, the last of the rare birds may be doomed.

It was Dr. Warner who led The Nature Conservancy's expedition of scientists into Maui's Kipahulu Valley, which slopes gradually upward until at 7,300 feet it ends at the wall that separates it from the crater of Haleakala. As they ascended from the lower elevations to 2,500 feet

Ohia trees thrust their limbs through the Kipahulu Valley cloud forest, where constant moisture helps them grow 50 to 100 feet tall.

they found exactly what Warner had expected—dense populations of *Culex* and not a single bird belonging to Hawaii's remarkable honey-creeper family. But by about 3,000 feet the mosquitoes disappeared and the honeycreepers began to be seen in increasing numbers, among them *apapane, iiwi, amakihi* and Maui creepers. Only the latter is considered a rare and endangered species but the relative abundance of the other birds seemed an encouraging sign, suggesting that in the upper reaches of Kipahulu—where in all the years since Cook's arrival in 1778 only a handful of white men have ever ventured—there might be something very surprising.

Among the scientists there were four who had special competence in ornithology: Warner; Dr. Andrew Berger of the University of Hawaii; Winston Banko, a research biologist in the Bureau of Sport Fisheries and Wildlife of the U.S. Department of the Interior; and Gerald Swedberg of the Hawaii State Division of Fish and Game. It is worth stressing the competence of the men—when amateurs report the sighting of unusual birds doubts can be raised, but in this case there are none. All four men saw the *akohekohe,* or crested honeycreeper, described by the Hawaiian Audubon Society as "possibly the rarest of the living native Hawaiian mountain birds," not once but several times each. Some of the birds were feeding on the crimson blossoms of an *ohia* tree almost directly above a campsite at 6,000 feet.

It fell to Winston Banko to make the two most startling discoveries of the expedition. Binoculars in hand, Banko was walking alone on a trail at about 5,800 feet when he saw "a small, dull, yellowish bird with a dark eye stripe and a moderately long, distinctly sickle-shaped bill." He held his binoculars on it for nearly half a minute at fairly close range but was unable to recognize it. However, he did have time to make note of every field mark that might be useful in identification, noting in particular the downcurving bill with an upper segment more than twice the length of the lower.

Half an hour later Banko saw a second such bird at a slightly lower elevation, and still later he spotted a third. He made a leisurely examination of it with his glasses at a distance of only 25 feet, so close that he could pick out every feather, but still he could not identify it. "The problem," he says with a wry smile, "is that I had studied all the *living* birds of Hawaii, but not having studied the extinct ones, I wasn't prepared for what I was looking at. As soon as I got back to camp I grabbed a reference book and there, among the old photographs, it was." The birds he had rediscovered were Maui *nukupuu,* believed by almost all ornithologists to have vanished many years ago. The last sighting had been in 1896.

Banko was also fortunate enough to have a long close-up view of another exceptionally rare honeycreeper, the Maui parrotbill, that had been seen only once before in the 20th Century, in 1950. "I had been looking particularly for the parrotbill," he says, "and suspected it might be found—if at all—high up in the valley. I saw it at nearly 6,500 feet —and of course, there's no mistaking a bird like that." In its particular adaptation the parrotbill has developed by far the most formidable beak of all the honeycreepers, enabling it to tear the bark from trees or crush twigs to get at insect larvae inside.

The discovery of the rare birds has been, not only for Banko and Warner but also for every naturalist in Hawaii, a source of delight and fear. Without exception they feel that Kipahulu Valley, which through the efforts of The Nature Conservancy was added to Haleakala National Park in 1969, must be kept closed indefinitely to everyone but qualified researchers who can demonstrate a genuine need for going there. "The preservation of this area intact," Banko says, "is of paramount—absolute—importance." But it is no easy proposition, politically, to exclude the taxpayers from land the taxpayers own. "Prayer may help."

It may indeed. It may also be helpful if men develop the sort of love for Maui, the unwillingness to inflict even the slightest injury, that filled Mark Twain when he saw Hawaii and that remained with him for the rest of his life:

"No alien land in all the world has any deep strong charm for me but that one, no other land could so longingly and so beseechingly haunt me, sleeping and waking, through half a lifetime, as that one has done. Other things leave me, but it abides; other things change, but it remains the same. For me its balmy airs are always blowing, its summer seas flashing in the sun; the pulsing of its surfbeat is in my ear; I can see its garlanded crags, its leaping cascades, its plumy palms drowsing by the shore, its remote summits floating like islands above the cloud rack; I can feel the spirit of its woodland solitudes, I can hear the splash of its brooks; in my nostrils still lives the breath of flowers that perished twenty years ago."

The Remaking of a Valley

PHOTOGRAPHS BY DAN BUDNIK

Lying just inland from the east coast of the island of Maui the secluded three-and-a-half-square-mile Waihoi Valley imparts an almost palpable air of mystery. Its very look is strange. Carved out of the lower flank of the Haleakala Crater and bounded by near-vertical cliffs, the valley rises from a floor rather like a broad, tilted plate, gently sloping up to about 3,600 feet, then sharply climbing in ridges to the rim of the crater at almost 7,000 feet.

The main mystery of Waihoi, however, is not geological but botanical. Unlike other valleys on Maui, particularly Kipahulu to the southwest, Waihoi has no stands of giant trees and little diversity of plant life. The birds that abound in the forests of Kipahulu find no haven in Waihoi and seldom appear there.

Trying to explain the reasons for this lack of luxuriance, botanists theorize that at some point in the past something interfered with the valley's primeval growth. The nature of the disturbance is unknown. It may have been a volcanic eruption, even though no recent lava flows are visible. The cause may have been landslides, animals rooting for food, ancient Hawaiians planting taro, or a combination of these factors.

Whatever the agent, it interrupted the growth of the plants that, left undisturbed, might have made Waihoi as lush a place as Kipahulu, where some trees reach 100 feet in height.

But now there are signs that Waihoi is staging a comeback, spontaneously reforesting itself (opposite). A thick matting of three-foot-high false staghorn fern covers the valley's floor and lower slopes and lines its shallow streams. This pioneer plant grows not only in the Hawaiian Islands but in several other tropical and subtropical areas as well. In Waihoi, however, a number of plants endemic to the islands—growing nowhere else—have begun to reestablish themselves. Ohia and olapa trees, naupaka, broussaisias and others poke uncertainly through the ferns here and there on the lower slopes, increasing in number, fullness and stature on the ridges.

The growth is slow; the soil on which the staghorn ferns and endemic plants have gained a hold is thin and nutrient-poor. Men now living cannot expect to see the ultimate outcome, but it may be that, given no further disturbance, the increasingly sturdy endemic plants will eventually crowd out the ferns and give a new luxuriance to Waihoi.

False staghorn ferns fringe a rocky stream in a southern corner of the Waihoi Valley. This species of fern is a pioneer plant—one of the first to recolonize a disrupted area; currently the most abundant plant in the lower valley, it may in time be crowded by the scrubby ohia trees seen growing sparsely among the ferns. The cloud-shrouded ridge in the background separates the Waihoi from its much lusher neighbor, the Kipahulu Valley.

Inundating the area, false staghorn fern covers the Waihoi Valley, unchallenged by other plants until it reaches the base of the ridge.

An Aggressive Pioneer

The first plant to reclaim the floor of Waihoi Valley, and its principal cover up to an altitude of about 3,600 feet, is the false staghorn fern. It is called staghorn probably because of its forking leaves, which look much like the antlers of a stag, and it is called false to distinguish it from the true staghorn, another Pacific fern to which it bears a little resemblance but no kinship whatever. The Hawaiians call it *uluhe*. In the old days they used its sturdy tangled branches for thatching their houses, and the juices of the plant for a laxative.

In the meager soil of the lower part of the valley the false staghorn is the only plant that grows in any abundance. Below ground it advances by putting out rootstocks; above ground it forms a dense tangle of wiry fronds that range from a few inches to a few feet in length. No matter how matted false staghorns become as they grow, they are recognizable from a distance by their yellowish-green color.

Nevertheless, this seemingly indomitable fern should eventually be driven out. For in flourishing it fortifies and enriches the soil with its roots and nutrients, thus preparing the way for other plant life to follow. *Ohia* and *olapa,* the most common trees throughout the Hawaiian Islands, will take root after them; in time the *ohia* and *olapa* will put up a forest cover, displace the false staghorn and encourage the colonization of a diversity of other plants.

A clump of fern fronds shows the tangled growth that chokes out most other vegetation.

Flanked by ferns and yellow broussaisia flowers, a Cyanea aculeatiflora spreads its leaves over the delicate white bloom at its base.

A Flourishing Forest on the Heights

One of the enigmas of the Waihoi Valley is evidence that whatever upheaval disturbed the valley floor apparently did not reach its ridges. Here a number of endemic plants compete with the staghorn fern for living space. In the lower altitudes they are sparse in number and small in stature; but above 4,000 feet they multiply and thicken. They finally surpass the fern along the tops of the ridges, flowering into a full-fledged forest that spills over into the canyons of adjoining Kipahulu Valley.

None of the plants in this forest grow anywhere but in the Hawaiian Islands; some, like the *Cyanea aculeatiflora (left)*, are endemic to the east coast of Maui. The graceful, broad-leaved cyanea belongs to the lobelia family, species of which occur elsewhere in the islands and other parts of the world. But through long isolation on Maui the *Cyanea aculeatiflora* has evolved prickly flowers lacking in other lobelias.

The antiquity of the cyanea and of the other flowers of the Waihoi forest *(right and overleaf)* has given many of them a place in Hawaiian folklore. One legend about the *naupaka* attributes its peculiar form—as if it were minus one petal *(overleaf, lower left)*—to a lovers' quarrel. The piqued maiden is said to have torn apart a *naupaka* flower and told her lover that if he wanted her back he must find her a perfect bloom. He could find only the odd-shaped *naupaka* and died of a broken heart.

Seen in detail, the blossom of the Cyanea aculeatiflora reveals the prickles that distinguish the plant from lobelias elsewhere in the world.

A labordia, a member of the poisonous strychnine family, flaunts its vivid yellow-orange flower against a backdrop of glossy green leaves.

Small yellow blossoms mark the Broussaisia arguta, a relative of the hydrangea.

The Nothocestrum longifolium, called the aiea by the Hawaiians, is related to the tomato, the potato and tobacco. Its seeds are dispersed by birds that dote on its orange-red fruit.

A naupaka (below), looking as though it were missing one of its petals, grows on a Waihoi Valley ridge. It is one of the relatively few Hawaiian plants that are in flower all year round.

A Trematolobelia macrostachys, a species of lobelia, leans over the south ridge, extending its nectar-filled blossoms out over the valley.

4/ Refuge on a Reef

Against the illimitable blue of the sky, over the unfathomable blue of the ocean the sea birds of the Pacific wing the cycle of their lives. For them the ocean is a larder: the islands and atolls their mating ground and nurseries. GEORGE C. MUNRO/ *BIRDS OF HAWAII*

Before dawn the sky over the Pacific was like a sheet of dark blue glass. From below the eastern horizon, light and heat began to play on it. The stars squeezed shut and the sky expanded, growing pale and taut. Suddenly the sky shattered, falling in countless tinkling fragments, while overhead, replacing the stars, white birds soared.

The island is small, a sand-covered coral platform only about half a mile long and a few hundred yards wide. There are no trees on it, only broad patches of tough narrow-leaved grass and mats of yellow-flowered puncture vine. Along one side of the island runs a beach of coral sand; on the other there are limestone reefs and shelves. During the night a half-dozen green sea turtles, big as overturned wheelbarrows, have hauled themselves up on the beach to sleep. Not far away two brown-gray seals, each with her single black-velvet pup, are dozing on the sand. In the shallow water near them the silhouette of a little wave, less than a foot high, suddenly turns solid and moves against the grain of the other waves—a shark's fin.

The island is very low. The highest point on it is only 12 feet above the level of the sea. From there one can see about seven miles to the horizon where in all directions there is no smoke, no sail, no ship, nothing. The island is far from any traveled sea lanes; almost no one ever goes there intentionally. The discoverers of it surely went there by mistake.

In 1822 two English whaleships, the *Pearl* and the *Hermes,* cruising in consort, ran into the coral reef and broke up. The survivors built a 30-ton craft out of the wreckage, the *Deliverance,* and navigated it 1,100 miles southeast to Honolulu. Today the charts show this coral bank as Pearl and Hermes Reef.

Pearl and Hermes is in fact an atoll, a half-submerged coral ring about 15 miles wide enclosing a very pale green lagoon in the dark blue sea. There are a few tiny islands along the rim of the lagoon but this one, Southeast Island, is the largest and of greatest consequence. The rest are big sand bars. The atoll marks the place where once there existed a high volcanic island, perhaps as large as Oahu. Now it is worn down by rain, wind and waves so that no trace of it is visible, although if a drill bit were sunk through the sand and coral it would strike black lava roots a few hundred feet down.

In the early-morning light two structures appear on the island. One is a flimsy tower of metal posts and angle irons with something white lashed to its top: a five-gallon metal water can completely covered with sea-bird droppings. It might serve to alert a navigator approaching the low island. The other is a redwood sign. Carved on it in large half-inch-deep letters is "Hawaiian Islands National Wildlife Refuge/Pearl and Hermes Reef/Southeast Island." Below that there is "No Trespassing" in English and Japanese. Aside from the tower and the sign there are not many evidences of human life except for a temporary camp in which a few men are living.

The birds that had replaced the stars were white albatrosses and red-tailed tropic birds. At lower levels shearwaters, petrels, boobies and frigate birds dipped and soared. On the sand, in the grass and on the bare limestone rock there were white eggs and speckled eggs, oval eggs and conical eggs, eggs that weighed less than an ounce and others that weighed three quarters of a pound. Chicks were everywhere. The newly hatched sooty terns were little gray fluffballs spotted with brown. The infant frigate birds were ugly enough to rouse religious thoughts in the mind of a heathen. Surely nothing could be *that* homely without being part of some grand design: stark naked, without even a visible hair or pinfeather; bright gray skin, the color of a bookmaker's felt hat; covered with permanent large goose-pimples; potbellied, scrawny; mad-eyed and squirming with lust for food.

The young albatrosses, although they were already about six months old, two feet tall and had six-foot wingspreads, were still only chicks and not nearly as ferocious as they tried to appear. Some were just learning to fly and would make 20- or 30-foot hops that often ended in ridiculous crashes that seemed to embarrass them a good deal. When a man approached them they would snap their beaks rapidly with a sound like castanets but then they would trip over their own feet and fall down. Sometimes they made little peeping sounds. There were about 6,000 of them on the island, so that it was impossible to walk very far without running into one. Perhaps 80 per cent of them were Laysan albatrosses, with white heads, breasts and underparts; the upper surfaces of their wings and their tails are brownish black. The remaining birds were black-footed albatrosses, first cousins of the Laysans, with black bills and sooty brown heads and bodies. When they are standing on the ground both birds, at least at first glance, suggest enormous sea gulls. In the air, with their long, narrow wings outstretched in gliding flight, they look like sailplanes. Their common name is gooney, or gooney bird, a sailor's term that may derive from the old word "gawney," meaning a clownish fool. Still, although they have comical habits and often get into ludicrous scrapes, they are—as birds go—fairly intelligent.

The air over the island was not, as might be expected in a rookery, full of uproar and stench. The trade winds blew steadily from the northeast at about 10 miles an hour and the birds were fairly quiet except when a man intruded directly among their eggs and chicks. At such times they set up an incessant screaming, as they were doing now. Walking in a blizzard of sooty terns so thick he could reach out and catch them in midair in one hand was the man who has charge of the refuge, looking after the interests of the birds and the people of the United States. Although he had arrived on the previous afternoon, a good deal of time had been consumed in setting up camp; and now he was taking his first careful look around. "Please," he said to the terns in a reasonable tone, "stop dropping guano on the administrator."

The name of the administrator is Eugene Kridler, pronounced with a long "i," as in rider. He is a rugged man in his early fifties who works for the Fish and Wildlife Service of the U.S. Department of the Interior. Two or three times a year he leaves his office on Oahu and journeys out to the refuge to see what has been going on there. The refuge extends for more than 800 miles northwestward from the main Hawaiian islands and comprises a chain of reefs, islets and atolls—Nihoa Island, Necker Island, French Frigate Shoals, Gardner Pinnacles, Maro Reef, Laysan Island, Lisianski Island and Pearl and Hermes Reef—that are collectively one of the world's most important sea-bird nesting areas.

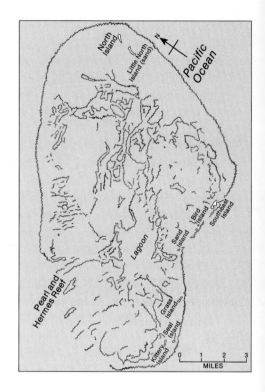

The classic semicircular shape of a coral atoll appears on this map of Pearl and Hermes Reef. Only 15 miles wide, Pearl and Hermes covers more than 100,000 acres of reefs, islands and lagoon within the barrier reef (outermost line) separating it from the ocean. The shorter lines mark coral formations that are usually below water; only the islands, which are labeled, stand above the tide level.

The refuge also contains most of the Hawaiian monk seals still surviving on the planet, and is the last remaining nesting ground in the United States of the green sea turtle.

To reach the island, Kridler relies on the cooperation of the Coast Guard and the Navy, which sometimes have ships or helicopters operating in the neighborhood and will take him along. In this instance a big Navy helicopter flying out of Midway Island had set him down on Pearl and Hermes with all his equipment, including aluminum bands for the birds, metal tags for the seal pups and turtles and an enormous slide caliper of the sort used by foresters to determine the diameter of trees. Kridler measures turtles with it.

The Navy had also provided him with a couple of burly assistants to help wrestle the turtles and the seals, which weigh as much as 300 and 700 pounds respectively. One of the assistants, a Chief Hospitalman named Marvin Cunningham, was an amateur naturalist who had accompanied Kridler on previous visits to the island. This time Cunningham hoped to find a seal, dead of natural causes, intact and not too fragrant, so that a skeleton could be secured for a museum. Museums are glad to have the skeletons of rare creatures so long as they are collected by people who know what they are about. Cunningham, whose main medical interest is in bacteriology, spent considerable time in Vietnam and sent back scores of carefully prepared rodent skins and skeletons to the Smithsonian Institution.

On this trip Cunningham was looking for Hawaiian monk seals, so called because the silhouette of their head and neck is thought to resemble that of a monk in a cowl; monk seals belong to an interesting branch of the pinnipeds, or fin-footed mammals. There are (or perhaps were) only three species, unusual among their kind in that they live in warm or subtropical waters. Several hundred of them still inhabit the Mediterranean, principally along the North African coast. At one time monk seals were numerous in the Caribbean, in the Bahamas and off the Florida coast, but they have probably all been slaughtered. The last sure sightings of them were made in 1949. Hawaiian monk seals were nearly wiped out as well, for their oil and skins, but have made a comeback since Theodore Roosevelt established the refuge in 1909. Kridler estimates their number today at about 1,000.

As Kridler made his morning reconnaissance he looked for signs that anyone had landed on the island since his last visit. "Do you know what could happen if there were a shipwreck out here?" he said.

It struck me that this would be a poor place for a man to be stranded.

"I wasn't thinking about *people*," he said. "What I worry about is rats. If a ship plows into one of these islands and the rats get ashore, they can wipe out a whole species before you know it. Ground-nesting birds are very vulnerable to rats." A few years ago a scientist from the Smithsonian, working in the outer islands, watched a rat attack an albatross on its nest. The albatross was so intent on brooding its egg that it defended itself only feebly and was killed.

Although it would be grim news if rats got ashore anywhere in the refuge, it would be disastrous on a couple of the islands because of the extreme rarity of the species living there. On Nihoa, and nowhere else on earth, live some grayish-brown millerbirds, so called because of their fondness for eating miller moths. When Kridler last estimated their number he put it at about 600. The island also is the only home of the Nihoa finch, a member of the Hawaiian honeycreeper family. In size and color the birds resemble large canaries, with yellow heads and bodies, but they have powerful crushing beaks like those of miniature parrots. About 4,000 of them still survive. On Laysan in the highly saline interior lagoon there are some handsome little ducks, unique to that island, that have been fighting nip-and-tuck with extinction since 1923. In that year only seven of them existed; today there are probably about 175. The ducks, the finches and the millerbirds would vanish quickly if rats became established on their islands. In 1969 a Japanese fishing trawler ran aground at a speed of eight knots on Laysan. After the men were rescued they swore a great nine-jointed oath that rats had never set foot on *their* vessel, but when he inspected the wreck Kridler found several boxes of rat poison. "I had nightmares about it for some time," he said, "but either there really weren't any rats aboard or they failed to get ashore. That time, anyway."

There were no signs that strangers had been prowling on Pearl and Hermes in the immediate past, so Kridler turned his eye to legitimate visitors, the turtles on the beach. A full-grown green sea turtle is surprisingly powerful and when it is alarmed it moves like a bulldozer across the sand, heading straight for the water. To capture the turtles, which were asleep, Kridler and Cunningham sneaked up on them from the side and turned them over with sudden strong charges reminiscent of interior line play in football. They were careful to avoid the turtles' flippers, which are hard and bony on the front edges and can break a man's wrist with a solid blow. They also took heed of the turtles' mouths —green sea turtles do not snap aggressively, but may bite off a hand if it is carelessly offered to them. The two men turned over four big tur-

Scrawny and bare, a newborn frigate bird (above) hugs its nest in a clump of solanum shrub on Pearl and Hermes Reef, waiting to be fed small pieces of fish and squid that its parents steal from boobies. The adult male at right, gliding to the nest on its seven-foot wingspan, prepares to disgorge tidbits to its young as its mate looks on. Adults also eat tern chicks and turtle hatchlings when such delicacies are in season—mostly in summer.

tles with little trouble. A fifth one awakened, however, and began making for the water. Cunningham jumped in front of it and put his foot on its head, shoving it down hard into the sand. The turtle halted and in a moment Kridler hurried over and flipped it.

When green sea turtles are overturned they cannot right themselves again as can various other members of their kind, including snapping turtles. Upside down they can survive for weeks or months and were often carried in that manner for fresh food on long sailing voyages, to be butchered when needed. Kridler's turtles, as though they had some dim racial recollection of this, lay on their backs without struggling, occasionally uttering long, loud sighs. Two of them already had numbered metal tags attached to the trailing edges of their right front flippers, close to the body, where Kridler or his fellow workers had placed them in previous years. He took note of the numbers and then tagged the others, using pronged tags that are pinched shut with pliers. The turtles seemed not to notice, apparently being fairly insensitive to pain. One of them had been attacked by a shark that had bitten a semicircular piece out of the side of its shell about the size of half a dinner plate. The wound had healed in the manner of bark covering a gash on a tree.

Kridler took the dimensions of the turtle shells with his caliper, measuring length, width and thickness of body, which in a fair-sized creature came to 38.1, 29.2 and 13.7 inches. In weighing the turtles he and Cunningham slid them one at a time onto a piece of heavy canvas that had a slack loop of rope threaded through metal grommets around its edge. When the rope was pulled taut the canvas enclosed the turtle as in a hammock. The rope was then hooked onto a spring scale fastened to the middle of a stout eight-foot pole. They strained to lift the pole on their shoulders and when the hammock was clear of the ground I read the scale. The fair-sized creature weighed 295 pounds. Released, right side up, it rapidly heaved itself over the sand into the water and swam off at what seemed great speed, although it was probably only about 10 miles an hour.

"We're building up a file of information on the migration and growth rates of these turtles," Kridler said. "They're not an endangered species yet, but they soon may be. They're a great delicacy and bring high prices on the market. Right now we're cooperating with a scientist at the University of Hawaii who's trying to figure out if they can be raised commercially." Thus far Kridler has recaptured a number of turtles that have traveled from island to island within the refuge, and to some of the main inhabited Hawaiian islands—as much as 600 miles at times.

It was midsummer noon. Pearl and Hermes is not far from the intersection of the international date line and the Tropic of Cancer, and the sun there is like a sledge hammer. The water and the white, coarse coral sand reflected light and heat. The young albatrosses, facing into the wind, stood with wings outstretched, occasionally waving them to exercise and strengthen them. To cool off, the birds rocked back on their heels, lifting the soles of their triangular webbed feet so that the air could circulate under them. Networks of fine blood vessels enable their feet to serve as radiators, dissipating body heat. It is an effective mechanism except in one regard: unlike land birds, sea birds have no strong rear toes to support them when they rock back, and albatross chicks take some humiliating pratfalls before they get the hang of it.

Not all of the albatross eggs on the island had hatched. Some had been infertile and now, several months old, they were baking in the sun, full of green slime and gas. *Pow!* If a man picked up one of them, joggling it, there was a fair chance that it might explode in his hand. Sometimes an egg would burst spontaneously when no one was near. The sound was like a small light bulb breaking but the smell was thunderous, fortunately soon swept away by the breeze.

Scattered along the beach were scores of corked or capped glass bottles, seemingly a strange litter to be found in the far wilderness of the sea. Almost all of them were liquor or Japanese sake bottles tossed overboard from trawlers, merchantmen and passenger ships in many latitudes and carried to Pearl and Hermes by the wind and the ocean currents—the Kuroshio, the California and the Equatorial—that create a slow-moving clockwise flow of water in the North Pacific. A well-stoppered bottle will float for years or decades in the currents, and since there are literally millions of them adrift, even the most remote islands become strewn with them. In fact the remote islands, rarely reached by beachcombers and souvenir hunters, have many more bottles than the accessible ones. Among perhaps 200 bottles on Pearl and Hermes, two had messages or, at any rate, communications in them. One contained a tract from a West Coast Bible society announcing good news for sinners: the word of the Lord will reach them even at the ends of the earth. The other contained somewhat more earthly comfort: a photograph of a pretty Japanese girl, some Japanese cigarettes and matches.

Among the beached bottles were Japanese fishing floats, beautiful hand-blown glass globes of pale green, light blue and lavender that are used to hold nets upright in the water or to support lines of baited hooks. Many of them were the size of small grapefruit, others as large as basketballs and one, measured with Kridler's caliper, was nearly 16 inches in diameter. In use the floats are secured by light rope netting that sometimes breaks and sets them adrift. Occasionally in a storm a fishing boat may lose part or all of a tuna line, perhaps a mile long, with dozens of the big glass balls attached. They are eagerly sought by beach-combers in Hawaii, British Columbia, Washington and Oregon, who sell them to collectors and curio shops for as much as $50 apiece. There were at least 100 of various sizes on Pearl and Hermes, waiting for someone to pick them up.

In the heat of the afternoon Kridler took a census of some small birds commonly called Laysan finches. Canary-like, with heavy bills, they very much resemble Nihoa finches, and they too belong to the honeycreeper family. They are the only land birds on Pearl and Hermes and arrived as recently as 1967, when 50 pairs of them were transferred from their ancestral home on Laysan Island. They were in no immediate danger on Laysan, but it seemed a good idea to establish a colony of them on another island as insurance. To make an approximate count of the little birds, Kridler followed the wildlife biologist's standard procedure of sampling by transects, or swaths. At random in all parts of the island he selected 100 pieces of ground, each 100 feet long and 16½ feet wide, and walked down the center of each one, counting finches as he went. The population could be calculated by a ratio: the number of birds counted is to the total number of birds as the area of the 100 transects is to the total area of the island.

I set out to walk a few transects with Kridler. He began in the middle of the island, which was covered with wiry bunch grass in which the finches had built nests. On the ground between the bunches, terns were nesting too. Below the ground, in burrows they had dug in the soft earth, wedge-tailed shearwaters were nesting. Shearwaters are about 18 inches from bill to tail tip, gray brown above and whitish below, and can dig at a remarkable rate. It is very unsettling to walk across their nesting ground. Inevitably one steps on a concealed burrow, sinks to his knees in the earth and stands there horrified, not knowing if he has crushed an adult bird, a chick or an egg. Twice when I caved in their tunnels, adult shearwaters, hopping mad, dug their way out and scuttled and bounced away unhurt.

After 25 transects I left Kridler, found a patch of shade in the lee of a tent and sat watching him. Back and forth he went under the hammering sun, changing direction, counting his steps, counting birds, sinking into the earth and getting up, plodding across the hot sand and coral rock. Kridler believes in the old-fashioned virtues and regards himself as employed not by the bureaucracy in Washington but by his fellow citizens. On that small island, although it was 6,000 miles beyond eyeshot of civil-service headquarters on the Potomac, he seemed to have no thought of dogging the job by walking only 72 transects or even 99. He walked 100. He was dripping with sweat and limping when he came over to the tent and sat down to work out his ratio. The 50 pairs of finches had multiplied in five years and now, he figured, there were about 350 birds.

In the afternoon, isolated clouds drifted over the green lagoon, and the reflection of the sunlight from the water tinted the bottoms of the clouds. It was a good strong tint that must have been visible for many miles, if anyone beyond the horizon had been looking for it. Polynesian sailors, who were among the best the world has known, used to find atolls by searching the sky for green-tinted clouds. At sea they also studied the flight of birds heading from their fishing grounds to their colonies to feed their young, and the men turned the prows of their seagoing canoes to follow. Now the birds were beginning to straggle back to Pearl and Hermes, carrying in their gullets and stomachs small fish and squid that they would regurgitate for their chicks.

Albatrosses feed largely on squid, and their digestive systems contain reservoirs of oily squid chowder. When a chick inserts its beak crosswise into its parent's beak the adult expels a jet of liquid that the chick catches so deftly that not a drop is spilled. Albatrosses continue to feed their young until they are five to six months old and almost ready to fly, and then abandon them. Thereafter the chicks, which drink salt water, may go without food for as long as two or three weeks, living on their body reserves. If they have not learned to fly and fend for themselves by then, they die. Many of those on Pearl and Hermes had already been abandoned and a man could tell almost at a glance which of them were going to live, and which not. The weaker birds would stand in one place day after day, scarcely moving, while the stronger would continue to exercise their wings preparing for their long flight out to sea.

Some of their short practice flights, however, ended in quick death. The chicks would land 20 or 30 yards offshore and while they drifted with outstretched wings sharks would drag them under. The annual feast of albatrosses had attracted to the island a large number of sharks,

Member of a species once found only on Laysan Island, a Laysan finch, shown nibbling seeds of setaria grass, is one of a growing colony introduced to Southeast Island on Pearl and Hermes Reef in 1967. The bird's right leg has been banded for identification. The island's only land birds, Laysan finches feed on insects and grass seeds. In choosing nesting grounds, they favor the dense matting of eragrostis grass on the island's sheltered side.

among them reef whitetips and tigers, which sometimes swam so close to the beach that their bellies appeared to rub the sand. A few years ago on Midway, sailors from the naval station caught a 16-foot tiger shark and strung it up on a pole to take its picture. After a couple of bushels of wet feathers had oozed out of the shark's mouth the sailors cut it open and found 13 young albatrosses inside.

Among the birds coming home to feed their young there were a number of boobies, so called because of their apparent stupidity, although that may not be quite the word to apply to them. The three species on Pearl and Hermes have a persecuted, frantic look that fits well with their names—the blue-faced booby and the red-footed booby, which are white, and the brown booby. The adults are about 18 inches tall and appear to be hard-working conscientious birds. By day they toil in their watery vineyard, dipping into it for squid and skimming over it to catch flying fish, and when they have a full basket for their chicks they try to get it home without being hijacked. They fly low, as though trying to escape the notice of the piratical frigate birds, but this is not much use. The frigates plunder them anyway.

Frigate birds, also called man-o'-war birds, are nearly as large as albatrosses although lighter, blackish in color and with wingspreads that approach seven feet. They have long, deeply forked tails, which in flight they open and close like shears. They are absolute masters of the air, remaining aloft indefinitely by riding currents, although they can also perform acrobatics and can put on a handsome turn of speed. When the boobies and tropic birds come home loaded late in the day, the frigate birds dive down on them and sometimes even grab them, forcing them to cough up their catch. Before the falling fish or squid can hit the water the frigates swoop down and gobble it up. Luckily most boobies carry more than one fish. In *Birds of Hawaii* ornithologist George C. Munro quotes an observer who is "positive that [the booby] always gives up a flying fish to the frigate, retains a squid for its young and a flying fish for itself." Whatever the case, the look of the boobies is not so much one of stupidity as of extreme exasperation verging on lunacy.

Frigate birds have their own problems. I watched one commit a midair robbery and take the fish home to its own chick. The frigate glided in, braked, hovered over the nest and then collapsed on it like a broken umbrella. After countless generations of airborne existence the legs and feet of frigate birds are atrophied, weak and useless except for perching. The birds cannot walk. When they land they must come down on a spot with some elevation, however slight, so that they can take off again without the aid of an upward push with their legs. Their great wings can make the most of the smallest updraft, but if they chance to land on a flat place on a calm day they must do a great deal of flapping and floundering before they can become airborne once more.

After dinner Marvin Cunningham, the Navy hospitalman, said that he had found a dead seal, and we walked over to have a look at it. The animal had been dead for a couple of months and there was no longer much odor. It was on the coral-reef side of the island, lying in a few inches of water in a tiny protected cove. Small waves, only a few inches high, had been lapping at the carcass and had neatly separated most of what remained of the flesh from the bones, so that Cunningham's task was mainly to gather them up and put them in a huge plastic bag. The action of the waves had detached some of the smaller bones and teeth from the skeleton. Cunningham searched carefully for them in the water, meanwhile talking about the unusual characteristics of seals.

Seals can dive to remarkable depths—a few have been caught by accident on fishhooks as far as 500 feet or more under water. One reason for their remarkable swimming ability is that most seals are so streamlined; they have no protuberances anywhere. The sex organ of the male is recessed and can be thrust out through a slit in the body when needed. To assist in this the seal has a baculum, or penis bone, that is also found in some other mammals, although not in the primates. It is not firmly attached by ligaments to other bones and thus it can readily become separated from the rest of the skeleton. In the case of Cunningham's seal this had already happened and he looked right and left for the bone in the shallows. "We can't send an incomplete skeleton to a museum," he said.

"God forbid," said a coworker, joining in the search.

At length Cunningham found the bone, which resembled a small ivory pencil, and put it in the plastic bag with the others. When he got the skeleton back to Midway Island he would put fresh water and detergent in the bag, and after some soaking, scrubbing and drying it would be ready to pack and ship.

Night, in contrast to the shattering dawn, seems to fall slowly in the mid-Pacific. It takes the stars a long time to drill holes in the sky. When it was dark Kridler made another patrol of the island. On the beach, barely visible against the sand, hundreds of little nocturnal ghost crabs glided back and forth. The flimsy tower with its guano-covered jerry can loomed like a scaffold. The sooty terns, which fly all night calling out their other name, "wideawake, wideawake, wideawake," swooped low overhead. As we approached the grassy center of the island Kridler stopped, listening. At first I could hear only the noise of the terns but then beneath it emerged a hair-raising sound, exactly like the sound of men and women, barely conscious, in agony. There were long-drawn-out feminine moans answered by masculine groans; wordless noises of heartbreak and grief; mournings, wailings and low lamentations. Certainly no other birds, and probably no other living creatures except humans, make such sounds. It was a colony of tunnel-digging shearwaters. They were singing.

In the morning Kridler and Cunningham set out to tag some seal pups. Hawaiian monk seals come ashore on Pearl and Hermes and other refuge islands throughout the year. Like humans, they are fond of wriggling on the sand until they have made a comfortable pillow and bed, where they doze in the warm sun. They are trusting creatures who have no enemies but man on land, and in the sea only the shark. A man can approach within four or five feet of them before they show any alarm, and even then they merely grumble about being disturbed and do not become belligerent. Females with pups will roar and try to bite anyone who threatens their pups, but this is not very surprising. The faces of the seals seem wise and pensive, with drooping whiskers and sad eyes. They appear to be weeping, and in fact they are. Unlike most mammals, seals have no tear ducts to drain off internally the fluid that lubricates their eyes. Instead, the fluid overflows externally, rolling down their cheeks in streams of seeming sorrow.

When seal pups are born they weigh about 35 pounds and are covered with beautiful glossy black fur, for which they would be clubbed to death if hunters could get at them. They grow at an incredible rate, drinking huge quantities of milk, and may reach weights of 200 pounds within six to seven weeks, after which they are weaned. Once on their own, they shrink to perhaps 100 pounds and begin an orderly growth until they become eight feet long and weigh 650 to 700 pounds. They moult their black baby fur six to seven weeks after birth, eventually becoming soft grayish brown above and light gray on their stomachs.

Kridler and his coworkers have been tagging seal pups since 1966 and have become very adept at it. There were a half-dozen pups on the beach with their mothers and he tagged each one in a matter of three or four minutes. Cunningham would distract the mother, waving his arms, jumping and shouting, while Kridler slipped in behind and quickly fastened a tag in the webbing of the pup's hind flipper. During this operation one of the pups became so far separated from its angry parent that it seemed safe enough to pick it up. I held the pup in my arms for a few moments, looking at its friendly unsuspicious face, and put it down when a big tear welled out of the corner of its eye. The pup hurried off to join its mother and the two immediately touched noses, which is apparently the seals' way of reassuring each other.

After the last of the pups had been tagged, we waited on the beach for the Navy helicopter from Midway to pick us up. An adult seal was swimming lazily about 50 feet offshore and Kridler was taking pictures of it. It was then that we saw the shark's fin cutting through the small waves, fast, in a straight line for the seal. Within seconds there was a thrashing in the shallow water where the two had met.

We wear, all of us, the old mammal school tie. Our blood is warm. We rarely think, until we see and become emotionally involved in a fight between a fellow mammal and a damned shark, just how strong our loyalty is. I glanced at Kridler, who was trying vainly to get pictures of the underwater struggle. He was yelling encouragement to the seal and so was I. We shouted until we were hoarse, both of us prejudiced, bloodthirsty mammalian chauvinists to the core.

What can a seal do against a shark? I had read that porpoises had been known to fight sharks. They form a ring around their enemy, and while a porpoise on one side of the ring makes a diversionary movement, another on the opposite side dashes in and rams the shark with the top of its head. In short order they batter the shark to death. But a lone seal? For an instant as I stared into the water I thought of *The Threepenny Opera* by that outstanding German mammal, Bertolt Brecht, and the translation, "When the shark bites with his teeth, dear/ Scarlet billows start to spread. . . ."

But there were no scarlet billows. God knows what the seal did to the shark, but after a few wild flurries the shark turned tail and swam off, beaten. The seal continued to laze along in the water, parallel with the beach, and then hauled itself ashore about 50 yards away. There was not a mark on her, or him. It is too much to think that the seal understood our cheering, any more than it understood the gigantic bird that soon came rattling down, swallowed us, and flew away.

A Teeming Speck in the Ocean

PHOTOGRAPHS BY DAVID CAVAGNARO

Far off the course of the ships that ply the Pacific, a mere speck in the ocean when seen from a passing jet, Pearl and Hermes Reef ranks high on any list of the world's most isolated places. Since 1822, when the wreck of the whalers *Pearl* and *Hermes* gave it its name and put it on the map, relatively few people have set foot there. The nearest landfall is Midway, 100 miles to the northwest. And although the reef is officially one of the Hawaiian Islands, Honolulu lies over 1,000 miles southeast.

But if human beings find Pearl and Hermes off the beaten path, other creatures do not. From the surrounding sea—itself incredibly rich in fish —seals and turtles lumber ashore; albatrosses, frigate birds and a dozen other winged species come wheeling in. All these visitors derive their sustenance from the ocean, but must touch down on dry land to fulfill critical parts of their life cycles. Pearl and Hermes Reef well serves their purpose, thanks to its very isolation and security—it has been part of the Hawaiian Islands National Wildlife Refuge since its creation in 1909.

Pearl and Hermes is not one reef but a series of them—a small atoll —forming a 15-mile-wide circle of coral around a lagoon whose waters fill the site of a sunken volcano. Most of the atoll lies below the surface of the sea; the notable exception is a kidney-shaped 31-acre tract of coral and sand known as Southeast Island, which stands only 12 feet above sea level at its highest point.

Southeast Island, where most of the photographs on the following pages were taken, is no paradise for the creatures that tenant it. The climate is mostly hot and dry; the island is steadily whipped by trade winds, tempered only occasionally by brief tropical showers. Salinity poses a constant threat of dehydration. The only plants that survive are grasses and vines that retain a large quantity of water in their leaves. Though scrawny, they provide a dense matting that helps to anchor the thin blanket of sand on the coral.

Each in its own way, the species that use the island as a base adapt to its living conditions. The birds, for example, have learned to tip their beaks up to catch a life-sustaining sip of rain; some use the plant matting as nesting places. Whatever their distinctive habits, seals, turtles and sea birds alike return periodically to the island to court, breed, nest, hatch, raise young—and thus perpetuate their kind.

A helicopter view of part of Pearl and Hermes Reef reveals its three distinct environments. In the foreground is the shallow lagoon, a lighter hue than the deep ocean (background). The third component, coral, appears in the form of a barrier reef, causing a white line of breakers, and as sand on Southeast Island, seen jutting into the lagoon.

A SCHOOL OF MANINI SWIMMING OVER PORITES CORAL

Life and Death in the Lagoon

The lagoon of Pearl and Hermes Reef is less than 10 feet deep in places, yet its shoals harbor a huge and diverse population of butterfly fish, parrot fish, starfish, squid, sea urchins and the ever-present black-striped manini (left). About nine inches long when mature, the manini belongs to the surgeonfish family, so called for the scalpel-like spine they use as a weapon of defense. Like the manini, which feeds on algae, most of its neighbors are also grazers, sustained by the detritus that drifts down through the underwater coral reefs, which are built up of the skeletons of tiny creatures such as porites and pocillopora.

Off limits to fishing and to the oystering once pursued there, the lagoon shields its own against all but their natural foes. A swooping sea bird nabs a fish venturing near the surface; doom also lurks in the form of larger fish—ulua and tiger sharks —that invade from the ocean via breaks in the barrier reef. The shark, omnivorous in its tastes, will make a pass at anything alive in the lagoon —seals and turtles in transit, an underwater photographer—but will settle for mouthfuls of the little lagoon dwellers.

In these harsh but necessary relationships between predator and prey, the waters of Pearl and Hermes Reef help preserve the delicate life-and-death balance ordained by nature, free of the upsets that human interference would bring.

MONK SEAL DEFENDING ITS PUP AT A VISITOR'S APPROACH

A Secluded Shore for a Seal Nursery

The Hawaiian monk seal, named for the cowl-like skin fold at the back of its neck, is only one of two species of seal that live permanently in tropical waters. (The other is the elephant seal.) The monk seal is faring particularly well at Pearl and Hermes Reef and all through the Hawaiian Islands National Wildlife Refuge —in conditions not shared by its kin elsewhere. In the Mediterranean declining numbers of the species have been driven back to a few small islands by man's encroachment, and in the Caribbean a lone pair of monk seals was last seen in 1949.

Even the Hawaiian seals were hunted to near-extinction by 19th Century sealers for their fur, meat and oil. By 1900 the monk-seal population in this area of the Pacific had dwindled to less than 100. When the Hawaiian wildlife refuge was established, they acquired a new lease on life, and now number about 1,500. Pearl and Hermes, with its smooth, sandy, isolated beaches, is one of their principal pupping grounds.

Monk seals mate once a year, but the cow bears young—a single pup —only every other year. This curious circumstance results from the fact that mating takes place soon after pupping time, but cows that have just given birth cannot conceive until the breeding season is past; since their pregnancy spans 11 months, they produce offspring in alternate years—a natural and automatic form of population control.

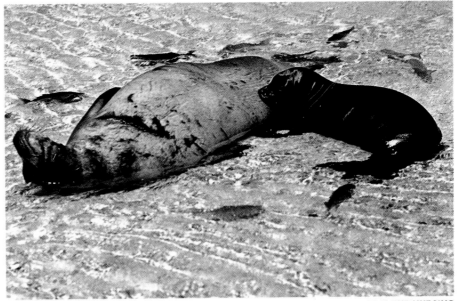

A SEAL PUP NURSING

A YOUNG ADULT RELAXING ON THE BEACH

The Behemoth of the Beach

On any given day the coral sand beach at Southeast Island may be host to half a dozen or so giant green turtles. Having fed at sea on algae and seaweed, they come ashore to sleep—sometimes for days.

The turtle population on the beach increases somewhat from May to July as females arrive to lay their eggs. While they nest only every third year they do so on a grand scale, each depositing 400 to 500 eggs in the process. After seven weeks of incubation in the gentle heat of the sand, hatchlings make an instinctive dash for the lagoon, running a gauntlet of predatory frigate birds. Once in the water, they are prey to sharks and *ulua;* only two per cent of them reach maturity.

Despite this low rate of survival, a turtle herd can maintain or even increase its numbers because those that do survive can live a century or more. Their longevity depends to a certain extent on their wanderlust, or lack of it. Green turtles have been known to roam the Pacific for distances of as much as 600 miles. The more they travel the more they are likely to end up as turtle meat, a gourmet delicacy. The state of Hawaii has no closed season on turtle hunting, and no restrictions on the number or size that may be captured. But the secluded waters of the wildlife refuge provide the turtles with reasonable security against poaching, and currently about 1,000 of them enjoy its protection.

ABOUT 300 POUNDS OF GREEN SEA TURTLE, HEAD ON

A SPHINX MOTH REPOSING ON SETARIA GRASS

A Precarious Foothold for Plants and Insects

The fact that there are plants and insects at all at Pearl and Hermes is a miracle of nature. Vegetation is vital to the islands of the atoll because it anchors the sand and provides nesting shelter for many sea birds. Yet prevailing conditions conspire to thwart the growth of all but the hardiest plants. Fresh water is available only from occasional tropical showers. Average tides rise two feet, washing over the mostly flat ground and dappling it with salt.

Seeds borne by the trade winds and the birds take hold only if they are of plant species that are endowed with fleshy leaves to store water and hairy surfaces to retard evaporation. Setaria grass is one of the handful of plants that have managed to establish themselves and another, perhaps the most successful, is the puncture vine. In 1931 only one of its seedlings was reported on Southeast Island; today it is a mainstay of higher ground there, which it covers with a dense matting.

Among the few insects that have triumphed over the vicissitudes of life on the atoll are the miller moth and the sphinx moth. A particularly remarkable adaptation was made by the sphinx moth. It is equipped with a long tongue to collect the nectar deep inside trumpet-shaped flowers —none of which grow on Southeast Island. As a result, it has learned to feed on the puncture vine's unfurled buds, which resemble the sphinx moth's favored trumpet blooms.

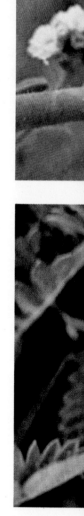

A SPHINX-MOTH CATERPILLAR

PUNCTURE VINE IN FULL BLOOM

A MILLER MOTH ON A PUNCTURE VINE

FLEDGLING ALBATROSSES START LEARNING TO FLY

A Serene Haven for Sea Birds

Legions of sea birds *(left and over-leaf)* have turned Pearl and Hermes into one gigantic rookery. By the tens of thousands, albatrosses, terns, boobies, tropic birds, shearwaters, noddies and other species claim just about every square inch of available nesting space. The shearwaters, in fact, raise their chicks in burrows underground, thus creating a double-decker kind of hatchery.

Because the adult birds feed themselves and their young on marine animals such as flying fish and squid, there is perpetual swarming overhead as they commute between water and nest. A human visitor can take few steps without the risk of being buzzed by an incoming tern, sinking knee-deep in a nesting burrow or crushing a newly laid egg. In fact, he can even reach up and pluck a bird right out of the air.

In all the apparent chaos there is, however, some order. Each species of bird stakes out a different area for its nesting ground. On Southeast Island, for example, black-footed albatrosses tend to hang around the beach; the Laysan albatrosses favor the grassy stretches farther inland. Sooty terns flock by the tidal basin; white fairy terns perch separately on craggy coral. Blue-faced, or masked, boobies prefer the bare coral beach; their red-footed cousins build their nests on higher ground amid the puncture vines. The shearwaters, in a sense, have the best of it: an underground kingdom all their own.

A NODDY TERN BROODING IN ERAGROSTIS GRASS

A WEDGE-TAILED SHEARWATER IN ITS BURROW

MASKED BOOBIES AND CHICK

A RED-TAILED TROPIC BIRD

A FAIRY TERN RESTING ON CORAL

A RED-FOOTED BOOBY WITH ITS FLUFFY YOUNG

Converging from every point on the horizon, sooty terns head back for Pearl and Hermes Reef at sunset after a long and vigorous day

of ocean fishing. Their stomachs are replete with squid and small fish, which they will regurgitate and feed to their waiting nestlings.

5/ The Swamp on the Mountain

Most beautiful, most blessed Kauai.
Serene she rests, rising from the sea
To lift the leaf-bud of her mountain Waialeale
To the sky— ANCIENT HAWAIIAN CHANT

The raindrop that struck John Sincock on the forehead came at him from a great distance, perhaps 2,000 miles or more horizontally across the north Pacific from the general direction of San Francisco. It did not start out in life as a raindrop, of course, but as an invisible waft of warm humidity like the breath of a girl whispering in a man's ear. However, by the time it reached John Sincock it had become liquid, was tearing along at perhaps 30 or 40 miles an hour and struck him smartly about an inch above his right eye.

The raindrop would never have hit him if it had not been for an array of coincidences. If John Sincock had not been a wildlife biologist; if he had not been searching for birds of ineffable rarity; if the trade winds had not been blowing briskly; if the topography of the island of Kauai had not been just what it is; if his work had not taken him to the top of Mount Waialeale; if.... But the drop *did* hit him, so it is less worthwhile to muse about what might have been than to consider how the drop flew with pinpoint accuracy all that distance and collided with his brow.

The trade winds blow from the general direction of North America out to the Hawaiian Islands and beyond them, mixing with other winds, to the Philippines and China. As they pass over the water the trades become laden with humidity. When the air becomes excessively damp it rains at random on the sea. The low islands of the Hawaiian chain, Midway for example, depend upon such scattered showers. The low islands cannot reach up and snag passing clouds; they must passively accept whatever rainfall they are lucky enough to get, which may be only 15 to 20 inches in a year. But the high Hawaiian islands have mountains on them, and therein lies the meteorological rub. The mountains grab the clouds, so to speak, and wring them out like sponges. The rainfall is unbelievable. John Sincock was standing on the rainiest place on earth.

The trade winds approach Hawaii from the north-northeast or northeast. When they strike a mountain they must rise to pass over it, and as they ascend into cooler air their moisture condenses into rain. Maximum rainfall occurs at an altitude somewhere between 4,000 and 7,000 feet; above that, the fall tapers off because the winds are less moist. The lower slopes of Mauna Loa on the island of Hawaii are very damp indeed, with patches of dripping fern jungle; but its 13,680-foot summit is a stone desert. And the rainfall occurs mostly on the windward side of a mountain; to leeward it is arid. However, these are only general principles to which there are always exceptions.

The shape of a mountain, the aspect it presents to the oncoming wind, also affects the amount of rainfall and where it comes down. There are places in Hawaii where the northeast trades are opposed at right angles by *pali,* or cliffs, running southeast. A perpendicular opposition of this sort is formed by the Koolau Mountains on the island of Oahu. The *pali* rise in places as much as 1,500 feet; when the wind encounters those cliffs head on it rushes upward with terrific force. At one point often visited by tourists on the Pali Highway the updraft is so strong that the bus drivers jocularly advise their passengers not to try to commit suicide by jumping off the cliffs because their bodies would only be blown back up. That is not strictly true, but smaller objects such as coins do sometimes return in the upcurrent. Not far from the lookout point there is an upside-down waterfall: as the stream flows over the cliff the water often falls up instead of down. Raindrops too are blown upward. Instead of landing on the windward side of the mountains most of them fall slightly to leeward of the summit ridge.

On the island of Kauai, Mount Waialeale places similar steep cliffs in the path of the trades, but the situation is compounded by a couple of factors. The summit of Waialeale is nearly a mile high (5,080 feet), reaching up into the middle of the cool zone where maximum rainfall occurs. It also happens that some long valleys, coming in from the side and narrowing upward, accelerate and funnel the wind toward the top of Waialeale. As a result, tons and tons of water fall there all the time.

On the beaten-down, bastinadoed summit region no vegetation can grow much more than a foot high. In many places there is only bare, sticky gray clay from which the water runs off as fast as it falls, giving rise to a dozen streams that radiate downward to make Kauai what it is called: the Garden Island. Just to the northwest, leeward of the summit, there begins an irregularly shaped, wooded plateau, about nine miles by two or three, known as the Alakai Swamp. It is in the Alakai that the rare birds live, and it is there that John Sincock was walking when he was hit by the raindrop that had his number on it.

It has long been known that it is very wet on Waialeale; the top of the mountain is almost always covered by a boiling mass of rain clouds like the head of an old politician slumbering under towels in a barbershop. At infrequent intervals, usually in the early morning, the clouds part long enough for a helicopter to nip up to the summit carrying Sincock and a companion or two, perhaps a few interested visitors or a team of men from the U.S. Geological Survey who go there to read the rain gauges.

Although men have been keeping track of rainfall elsewhere in the world for centuries it was only in 1910 that the U.S.G.S. began its efforts to find out what it amounts to on Waialeale. In that year an engineer and some helpers managed to place a 50-gallon galvanized can near the summit after carrying and rolling it up through the Alakai Swamp. The Hawaiian rain gods smiled and spat in the can. It overflowed. Next year a gauge that would measure nearly 12 feet of rainfall was installed, and the gods chuckled and filled it up. In 1915 another gauge, a whopper capable of recording 25 feet, was somehow hauled up to the summit; the gods laughed aloud and slapped their thighs and the gauge overflowed. By this time the engineers were beginning to glimpse the size of the problem, and in 1920 they installed the mother of all gauges. Essentially it too was only a metal can but it was as big around as a windmill tank. It had a small opening at the top and it could record 990 inches—more than 82 feet—of rainfall. The gods stopped laughing and settled down to do a little serious raining but, perhaps because they were getting old or overconfident, they were unable to fill the tank in one year. The engineers rejoiced and at last began to collect some accurate figures. However, they had overlooked a detail, as engineers sometimes do. They had forgotten to install a spigot at the bottom of the tank so that it could be easily drained. In order to empty the tank it was necessary to tip it over; the tank soon buckled, began to leak and became useless.

In 1928 a reinforced, bottom-draining 900-inch gauge was lugged up
the mountain and installed, and the struggle was over. The gauge served
until 1949 when, in the first use of helicopters for that purpose, a new-
fangled instrument was flown to the summit. Today an occasional hardy
hunter of pigs or goats still fights his way to the mountaintop on foot,
but most men who have any business up there go by aircraft. The era
of manhandling gauges through the swamp is gone, and small loss. The
task was almost unbelievably brutal. Indeed, even the task of carrying
a heavy weight *down* from Waialeale was difficult in the extreme. In
1948 a U.S.G.S. engineer died of a heart attack about 300 yards from
the summit; although he had six companions they could not muster the
strength to drag his body any distance. So they tied it up in a tree to protect it from pigs, which would have eaten it, and went to seek help. It
took a party of 16 men three days to carry the body down.

What *is* the rainfall on Waialeale? The National Weather Service in
Honolulu computes the average at 486 inches, well over 40 feet, per
year. In the record year of 1948 there were 624.1 inches, a foot of rain
every week. (New York City averages 44 inches a year; San Francisco,
20 inches; Phoenix, 8 inches.) Partisans of various localities, notably
those of a place called Cherrapunji in the hills of Assam in India, dispute the idea that Waialeale is the rainiest spot on earth. However,
their arguments do not hold water. It does rain in Cherrapunji—900
inches were once recorded there in a year, and 150 inches in five days.
But the big rains of Cherrapunji occur during the monsoon season; at
other times it is relatively dry, so that the yearly average is only 450
inches. That is 36 inches less than the yearly average on Waialeale,
where it rains heavily in all seasons. Actually, in measuring such prodigious downpourings it is not possible to be more than approximately
correct. The wind on Waialeale often blows the rain horizontally across
the summit, affecting the amount caught in the gauge. If the gauge were
moved or perhaps screened, the catch would be greater or less. The situation is the same in Cherrapunji, Luzon, Nigeria, Tahiti and indeed in
another of the Hawaiian Islands, Maui, where as many as 578 inches of
rain have been recorded in a year on the summit of 5,788-foot Puu
Kukui. In any case let us agree that Waialeale is as wet as any place on
the planet and let it go at that.

It must be admitted that the raindrop that struck John Sincock on
Waialeale, even though it had his number on it, was not a very special
raindrop. Sincock had been hit by 247,047,276 other drops, more or

less, all addressed to him c/o General Delivery, Alakai Swamp, where he spends a lot of time. He is a government man employed in the Endangered Species Program, Bureau of Sport Fisheries and Wildlife, U.S. Department of the Interior. Before taking a look at the swamp through Sincock's eyes it is worth taking a quick look at Sincock himself. Like other government employees encountered in this book—Eugene Kridler refusing to cheat on the number of transects he walked on Pearl and Hermes Reef, or Donald Peterson looking down the throat of a volcano —Sincock is a good man. In the army he would be walking the point, the one who leads a squad on patrol and gets shot at first. Behind him there would be a constantly widening train of fat PX clerks and golf-playing generals, but Sincock would be out on the point or, in this case, thrashing through the swamp.

Sincock's work, which is to him a great if often hazardous pleasure, is to search for rare birds and find out all he can about their lives and habits. In this pursuit he has passed five years on Kauai and has made scores of expeditions, almost always alone, into the Alakai Swamp. He knows the place as well as any living man and has even become grudgingly fond of it, his old adversary. A few years ago on the occasion of his second marriage he flew to the wild wet summit with his fiancée and a minister and the ceremony was performed up there. In appearance Sincock is remote from the cartoonist's impression of the vaguely effeminate bird watcher. He is a strong, uncommonly handsome dark-haired man in his early forties; in the old days in Hollywood central casting might have typed him as a white hunter.

Sincock does not spend much time on the rain-battered summit of Waialeale because that is not where the birds are, although he often pauses to look at the ruined stone foundation of a small temple built there long ago by the Hawaiians. The rain gods and a good many others—one ancient chant refers to "the four hundred thousand elves, the countless host of sprites, rank upon rank of woodland gods"—once inhabited or visited the top of the mountain. Today there are some Hawaiians who believe the gods are still there, perhaps in greater number than before. Like the native birds, the gods have sought refuge from civilization by fleeing to higher and lonelier places. When Sincock passes the temple he invariably sees offerings of coins placed on the stones or tucked in chinks, many of them put there by true believers. He would not dream of pocketing the money but recently he picked up a coin to see how old it was. The date on it was 1971.

Ohia trees weave a tangle in Alakai Swamp, 4,000 feet up in the center of Kauai; they are soaked by more than 400 inches of rain a year.

The windswept, treeless area of tussocks, dwarfed plants and gray clay, an open bog or mountain barren, extends for about a quarter of a mile downhill from the summit. Descending, Sincock enters the Alakai Swamp, which stretches off to the northwest. There the rainfall tapers gradually to amounts the mind finds easier to accept, perhaps 20 feet a year on the average, although Sincock once survived a day in the swamp when one of the rain gauges (several are in place now) recorded some 40 inches in 24 hours. "Swamp" is the term universally applied to the place but that is more a matter of convenience than of fact. The Alakai is a high plateau, bounded on three sides by cliffs, with an altitude of about 4,200 feet—well above the range of the fearsome *Culex* mosquito. There are a few flat areas in it and even some little pools, but generally the terrain is sloping. In several places it has been deeply gashed by the streams which have their origin nearby, with the result that there are dizzying ravines and knife-edged ridges. "There are places," Sincock says, "where I can walk along a ridge top that is only a few feet wide with a drop-off of 500 feet on both sides." The ravines carry off the rainfall rapidly, draining the swamp much faster than one might expect. A layer of peaty muck covers much of it to a depth of perhaps a foot, and here and there a man can sink to his waist in it, but the Alakai is nothing like the Okefenokee.

It is very easy to get lost in the Alakai. When it is not actually raining the air is full of thick white mist. The sky is toadbelly gray, the color of a January afternoon, rarely offering a glimpse of the sun or stars. The mainlander's idea that moss grows thickest on the shady (north) side of trees will be of no help in orienting him here. Light green moss grows luxuriantly on all sides and branches of the trees, coating and upholstering them to incredible thickness. A man may grasp what appears to be a sturdy moss-covered branch as big around as his forearm, squeeze it, and see water spurt in all directions while a cold stream pours down inside his sleeve. The branch beneath the moss may be no thicker than the wire in a coat hanger.

With plastic tape Sincock has marked a couple of tracks or trails for his own use, and there are a few well-nigh invisible paths known only to Hawaiians and perhaps to the gods of white mist gliding through the white fog, but an alien in the Alakai would not last long. There are tales of men who ought to have known better, hunters who have vanished leaving no trace except rifles that turned to thin streaks of rust on the peat. "On the mainland," Sincock says, "the general rule when you are lost is to follow a stream until it gets you out somewhere. But here if you follow a stream it will only lead you to a high waterfall pouring over a precipice. You have to follow the ridges, not the streams." It is useless to follow tracks used by animals; often worse than useless. "Once when I had been in the swamp for about a week I was down on my stomach in the muck, crawling under a fallen tree, when I came face to face with a pig. He was so close I could smell his breath. Meanest goddam pig I ever saw, about 300 pounds, with big yellow tusks. One of us had to get out of the way, so I started to back up to oblige him. But do you know, I looked worse and smelled worse than the pig did, so *he* backed up to get out of my way." Sometimes Sincock encounters goats in the Alakai, huge (for Hawaii), ugly creatures that weigh as much as a grown man. Because they spend all their lives walking on mud and peat, with no hard surfaces to keep their hooves in trim, their feet are splayed almost to the size of saucers.

The swamp is covered by a mixed forest dominated by red-flowered *ohia*. In their extremely adaptive fashion they are able to grow to maturity, 11 or 12 inches tall, in the summit barren. Farther down among the ridges and ravines they may reach 30 to 40 feet although the average is less, well below the heights of 100 or more they attain in favorable locations. The knee-high forms are called *ohia makenoe*, little *ohia* of the mist. Second among the trees is an endemic species called *lapalapa*, which is found only in the high, wet ground of the Alakai and the rainy heights of the Koolau range on Oahu. The *lapalapa* has several curious characteristics. When any part of the tree is bruised it emits a strong odor of carrots; its wood will burn when green, a providential circumstance that may have saved a few lost souls in the near-freezing temperatures of the swamp; and *lapalapa* leaves, somewhat like those of the quaking aspen of the mainland, are constantly in motion even in breezes so slight as to be imperceptible to men. The tree's name is related to the Hawaiian *hula*, whose performers were divided into two groups—the *olapa* (agile ones) and the *ho'opaa* (steadfast ones). The *olapa* were young men and women who could best illustrate the grace and beauty of the human form by dancing, while the *ho'opaa* were older people who handled the heavier musical instruments and played their parts while kneeling or sitting. "The *hula* you are likely to watch in night clubs or on hotel terraces," Sincock says, "are pretty sad corruptions of what was once an important art form. To the Hawaiians it combined poetry, religion, drama and dance, opera and literature. It had practically no relation to the sexy hip-shaking you see today." Whatever the case, the *olapa* dancers and the moving tree can claim some kinship.

Sincock encounters all manner of improbable plants in the swamp, but as an ornithologist, not a botanist, he studies them mainly as they relate to birds. Thus when he passes an *ape ape* (pronounced *ah-pay ah-pay*) he merely blinks in astonishment and moves on. The plant is slightly shorter than a man, with huge kidney-shaped leaves as much as three feet or more in diameter. They serve admirably as umbrellas. The plant's rhubarb-like stalk, perhaps six inches thick, can be cut with one swipe of a machete.

When he first began to search for rare birds in the swamp, Sincock tried to catch them in Japanese mist nets for the purpose of banding them and checking them for diseases. These nets are woven of extremely fine nylon threads, almost invisible at close range, and measure about 40 by 10 feet. They are stretched between trees in areas where birds, funneled there by the surrounding terrain, are likely to fly. Striking the nets, the birds drop into longitudinal pouches from which they cannot easily escape. "Mist nets may be excellent in dry country," Sincock says, "but in the Alakai they quickly become covered with dew, like huge spiderwebs, and the birds can see them. I *have* caught a lot of birds in the nets, but seldom a really rare one, and I don't use them much any more."

Although he does not employ the bird-catching method used by the old Hawaiians and other woodland people elsewhere, Sincock has a grudging admiration for its practicality. The Hawaiians merely smeared twigs or scaffold-like artificial perches with sticky substances made of viscous tree sap, gum, pitch or whatever was available, and when the birds alighted they were caught. The Hawaiians often ate songbirds, perhaps as many as four-and-twenty at one sitting in the manner of English royalty, but their most interesting use of small birds was to pluck their feathers to make brilliantly colored capes, full-length cloaks and ornamental helmets *(right)*. These beautiful objects rivaled, perhaps even surpassed the cloaks of ermine and sable, velvet and cloth of gold once made for European and Russian monarchs. Captain Cook, who was given some cloaks and helmets on his first visit to the islands, considered them very elegant and remarked that "the surface might be compared to the thickest and richest velvet, which they resemble, both as to the feel, and the glossy appearance."

The predominant colors of Hawaiian cloaks were red, from the *iiwi* and *apapane* birds; yellow, from the *o-o* and *mamo;* black, from var-

The royal emblems of an 18th Century Hawaiian chief included this handsome helmet and cape covered with the feathers of birds of the Alakai Swamp —the apapane, o-o and iiwi. The feathers—bright reds and yellows —were tied to mesh underlinings that were finely woven from vine roots.

ious birds, and more rarely, green, from the *ou*. The feathers were tied in tiny bunches and applied in overlapping rows, somewhat like roofing shingles, to a base of fine netting. The cloaks were worn only by chiefs and kings on ceremonial occasions and during battles—a few successful warriors thus accumulated several cloaks from their fallen enemies. The making of a large cloak required many years and an enormous number of feathers, which were supplied by the common people as part of their taxes. A cloak that belonged to King Kamehameha I, now in the Bishop Museum in Honolulu, contains some 500,000 golden feathers taken from at least 80,000 birds. In this case the birds were now-extinct *mamo*, a species endemic to the island of Hawaii, which were dark blue-black with a few yellow feathers on their thighs and above and below their tails. The birds were captured at the beginning of their molting season, when perhaps a dozen of the most desirable feathers were plucked out and the *mamo* were released to grow new ones. The *iiwi* and *apapane* were a good deal less fortunate. They had so many red feathers that they could not have survived plucking, so they were first killed, then plucked and eaten.

The destruction of birds to make featherwork had little relation to their extinction or dwindling in number. Today both the *iiwi* and the *apapane* are fairly common in John Sincock's territory and he has no great concern with them beyond the pleasure he derives merely from their presence in the wild. The birds of particular importance to him are so rare that some of them have been seen only three or four times in this century. Most of them are *Drepanididae*—honeycreepers *(page 87)*—in the Alakai Swamp but there are several others elsewhere in Kauai that Sincock worries about. One of them is the *koloa*, a mallard-like duck once common on most of the Hawaiian islands. Today he encounters a few of them scattered along high mountain streams and occasionally spots one in an irrigation ditch or reservoir. He thinks about 2,500 of them are still alive on Kauai, and that this population is barely holding its own. There are also about 1,500 Hawaiian stilts, handsome black-and-white birds about 18 inches tall with long, pink reedlike legs. They live in coastal sloughs and lagoons that are constantly being eyed as landfill projects and thus, because the value of Hawaiian waterfront property is on a trajectory similar to that of Apollo 17, their survival is not necessarily assured.

In its habits the most unusual bird in Sincock's region, and no doubt among the most unusual in the world, is the *ao,* a sea bird known in Eng-

Cladonia skottsbergia, a delicate lichen, grows in the Alakai Swamp amid glossy-leaved Broussaisia arguta, a ground cover.

lish as Newell's Manx Shearwater and in Latin as *Puffinus puffinus new-elli*. It is pigeon-sized, glossy black above and pure white underneath. At one time it was fairly abundant in the major islands but by about 50 years ago it had become very rare. Like other shearwaters it nests in burrows, and it is thought that on Hawaii, Maui and Molokai it had been wiped out by mongooses, which could get at it in its nest. On Kauai, however, small numbers of *ao* continued to be seen, particularly on autumn nights when they crash-landed on illuminated highways, buildings and football fields. After landing they seemed unable, even though uninjured, to take off again.

It did not seem unusual to Sincock that the *ao* might be dazzled by light or that, like other sea birds downed on land, they should have difficulty in regaining flight; what excited him was the idea that somewhere on Kauai they might have a nesting site. No one had seen an *ao*'s burrow, egg or chick in many years, and if there was indeed a nesting colony it was doubtless in a place so wild that no naturalist had ever been there. It was possible, Sincock thought, that the birds could still breed in some remote area because Kauai, alone among the major islands, has no mongooses. One widely accepted explanation of this is that a shipment of the creatures, destined for rat-catching service in Kauai's cane fields, actually reached the island some 70 years ago but was kicked overboard by an angry man whose finger had been badly bitten when he stuck it into the crate. Another version of this story is that a few citizens of Kauai, fearful of the harm mongooses might do, organized a Mongoose Party along the lines of the Boston Tea Party. In any case, there are no mongooses on the island to devour the eggs and young of ground-nesting birds.

Sincock found an *ao* nesting site by following an odd scrap of information offered by a local pig hunter. While searching for his dogs after a hunt in a state forest reserve the man had found them coming down from the top of a 1,400-foot ridge east of the Alakai Swamp, and had been surprised to see that the dogs had black and white feathers in their mouths. Hmm, thought Sincock, imagining what might be up there. He soon arranged for a helicopter to drop him on top of the ridge, accompanied by naturalist Gerald Swedberg from the Hawaiian State Division of Fish and Game. "There was a pretty thick canopy of *ohia* trees on parts of the ridge," Sincock says, "and everywhere there was an impenetrable stand of *uluhe* fern about nine feet deep. The helicopter couldn't land, so we jumped. We hacked a trail along the top for about a quarter of a mile and then we began to hear *ao* calling from their burrows, dozens of them.''

There were eggs, nestlings and adult birds in the colony, but Sincock and Swedberg could make no accurate count of them. "The ridge sloped off at about sixty-five degrees and it was very wet and slippery. Not a good place for climbing." After nightfall the adults in the burrows were joined by their mates, which had been fishing far out at sea and were returning with stomachs full of squid. "Some of the homecoming birds came down in the damnedest way," Sincock says. "They would circle overhead in the dark, making a loud, nasal sound that combined jackass braying and crow calling, and then—I assume deliberately—they would crash into the tops of the *ohia* trees and tumble down through the branches onto the jungle of ferns. After that they would claw their way down to the ground and start hunting for their burrows. Sometimes it would take a bird half an hour to find its nest."

Sincock and Swedberg watched the *ao* for several days and nights, concluding that there were perhaps 500 of them in the colony. Early one morning in the first light of dawn Sincock saw the silhouette of an *ao* against the sky and found the answer to a question that had been puzzling him. "How do the birds get back up into the air? Well, the wind really comes whistling up the face of that ridge before sunrise, and all the birds have to do is climb up through the ferns, flap their wings once or twice, and they're flying."

The rediscovery of the nesting grounds of Newell's Manx Shearwater was worth an article in *The Condor,* one of the foremost ornithological journals in the United States. Eventually Sincock will have another article, or perhaps several, on what he has been doing up in the Alakai Swamp for five years. In its learned, scientific way *The Condor* will not be interested in his personal hardships. Once, while intently following the call of a bird, he fell 30 feet into a ravine and smashed a leg so badly that the thought of gangrene and death flickered through his mind. He bound the leg with the plastic tape he uses to mark his trails, dragged himself out into an open place and lay down in the rain, hoping that sometime the sky would clear and a helicopter might come looking for him. By great good luck he was rescued after only two days, and after a couple of months he was able to walk without crutches. Today he carries flares and smoke bombs in the swamp but their value is perhaps more psychological than real. Sometimes the clouds press down on the ground for weeks at a time.

In winter it is bitterly cold in the Alakai. "I've been told that it snows up there," Sincock says, "although I've never seen it myself. The temperature drops into the low forties or high thirties, and in the rain and mist you can convince yourself that maybe you're going to freeze. Once I got so cold that I crawled into my little one-man tent and lit six candles I had with me. I was lying on my back like a corpse at a wake and I must have passed out for a little while. When I woke up it was raining like hell outside but, if you can believe it, the canvas floor of the tent was on fire from the candles." He doused the flames with rainwater and went back to sleep.

Sincock has verified, by personal observation, the existence of four exceedingly rare bird species in the Alakai—the *puaiohi* (small Kauai thrush), the Kauai *nukupuu*, the *ou* and the *o-o*. (Perhaps it is worth mentioning again that Hawaiian names did not sound laughable to the Hawaiians who invented them. The Hawaiians would have been convulsed, however, by such terms as robin or sparrow.) The most significant of Sincock's observations concerns the *o-o*, pronounced *oh-oh*, which he first saw on May 26, 1971. The bird, *Moho braccatus*, is small and generally dark in color, slaty brown and black, with one striking feature—its thighs are rich golden yellow. It had last been sighted in 1963, and before that only a couple of times since 1900. After he had located the home territory of the *o-o* Sincock was able to observe the bird on several occasions, and soon found that there were three pairs of them in the vicinity. Two pairs were nesting in cavities in *ohia* trees, a discovery that seemed of importance to him. There were few such cavities available, as far as he could see, and he began to wonder what might happen if there were more. Accordingly he made 30 nesting boxes and in May 1972, he nailed them up in trees in various parts of the swamp. He did not expect the birds to use them—if they were to use them at all—until the boxes had become suitably weathered and natural in appearance. Perhaps, he thought, in about a year. . . .

Sincock keeps returning to the Alakai, watching and waiting, making notes, pursuing bird-calls up and down ridges and through dripping entanglements of ferns. He often slips and falls, gets lost in the mist and finds himself on the brink of cliffs. He walks with a barely noticeable limp and says that his leg is well healed and hurts only when it rains.

6/ The Enigma of a Tree

It is almost as hard to tell a man what it is like to find out something new about the world as it is to describe a mystical experience to [one] who has never had any hint of such an experience. J. ROBERT OPPENHEIMER/ *THE OPEN MIND*

On this thoroughly explored planet almost all the larger species, from whales to watermelons, have been discovered by now. Scientists do find new creatures and plants every year but as a rule the discoveries are small, caught in the fine mesh of entomologists' or marine biologists' nets or observed growing in the shade of a pebble. In Hawaii the chances of encountering large new species are better than in Cincinnati, but few people expect to find anything as big as a tree. It is not likely that a plant of that size can have escaped all the professional botanists and informed laymen who have combed the islands.

Thus it was more than a little surprising to hear what the botanist, a man named Derral Herbst, was saying. Herbst, like my friend John Sincock the biologist, lives and works on the island of Kauai. We had fallen into a conversation about Hawaiian species, and in an unassuming way Herbst said that he and a fellow botanist, L. Earl Bishop, of the Honolulu Botanic Gardens, had recently discovered a new one.

Of what sort?

Herbst said that it was a tree.

A tree. I was sure I had heard him correctly and was so startled that the only reply I could make was that I hadn't heard people talking about it or seen any discussion of the discovery in the papers. It seemed, at least to me, that it was a fascinating piece of news. He shrugged. No reporters had come to inquire about it, and he is not the sort of man who would call them up and tell them. There is nothing unduly suspicious or secretive about him; he merely sees no reason to answer questions no one has put to him. Ultimately the news would find its way into a proper botanical publication, where it might be spotted and possibly direct attention to him. But that would be a long time in the future. In order for a new plant species to be accepted by scientists a description of it must be written in Latin and that, together with amplifications in a modern language, must be published in a botanical journal of impeccable standing. (The scientific tradition of writing in Latin today persists only in the field of botany. English is the universal language of the other sciences.) Such journals are glacial in their editorial movement. It sometimes requires months for a paper to get from one office to another across a six-foot hall. Herbst himself, when it comes to plant descriptions, is fairly glacial too.

"You have discovered a new tree and no one knows about it?"

"Well, of course, a few people. Other botanists."

I asked Herbst if he would be willing to show me the tree, and he said that he would indeed. "Earl Bishop and I discovered it only a few weeks ago, and I have seen it only once myself. It's down in the bottom of Waimea Canyon. We can easily walk there and back in two days." He had only two conditions: that I omit the Latin name that would be given to the tree, and that I avoid so detailed a description of its location that it might be found by a lunatic with an ax.

Derral Herbst, a South Dakotan in his mid-thirties who obtained his Ph.D. at the University of Hawaii, is the resident botanist at the Pacific Tropical Botanical Garden in Lawai, Kauai. The garden is being stocked with what seems likely to become the most comprehensive collection of tropical plants in the United States, to be used for research in conservation, nutrition and medicine. Herbst spends part of his time in the garden and part of it searching for new plants in Hawaii and elsewhere in the Pacific. As we drove toward the canyon he told me something about his tree. He is a long way from the mid-continental prairie but still speaks with a quiet matter-of-factness that covers any excitement he may feel about the discovery. It is a flowering tree that belongs to the genus *Hibiscadelphus,* which is confined entirely to the Hawaiian Islands. The genus contains only a few species—Herbst's tree is the fifth —but it is a very interesting one that illustrates somewhat painfully how slender a hold on life many Hawaiian plants now have.

The word *Hibiscadelphus* was invented more than 60 years ago by the American naturalist Joseph Rock, a master of ornithology, botany and zoology who led expeditions into western China, Tibet and Cambodia on behalf of Harvard and the National Museum. In the early 1900s in Hawaii, Rock observed that there were three species of trees, two on the island of Hawaii and one on Maui, that at first glance appeared to be hibiscus but turned out to be quite different. Their flowers, instead of opening into the familiar broad, showy blooms of the hibiscus, were closed or furled even at maturity, curved tubes perhaps two inches long and half an inch in diameter. Because the trees were related to the hibiscus but distinct from it, Rock established them as a new genus called *Hibiscadelphus,* or brother of the hibiscus.

Rock saw his first species of *Hibiscadelphus* around 1910 while collecting botanical specimens with a friend, W. M. Giffard, and named it *Hibiscadelphus giffardianus.* Its flowers were deep magenta on the inside and grayish green outside. The tree itself was many-branched and low, perhaps 18 to 20 feet in height, with a trunk one foot in diameter. It was growing in the Kipuka Puaulu not far from Kilauea Volcano and was the last survivor of what may once have been a large number. "Unfortunately the tree," wrote Rock, "is the only one in existence. It is unique among all Hawaiian plants, and the author is sorry to relate that nothing has been done to protect it . . . it will succumb to the ravages of cattle, which inhabit a great many of our native forests."

The tree died in 1930 but shortly before its death some seeds were taken from it and planted on Giffard's estate several miles away. In 1936 the National Park Service reported that only two or three young trees were alive, "waging a losing fight against what is probably too damp a climate." Having come that close to extinction, the species was saved by transplanting and careful nursing and today a few score specimens exist in guarded cultivation. The second of the three species that Rock knew, *H. hualalaiensis,* was also found on the island of Hawaii on the slopes of another volcano, Hualalai. In 1912 he saw as many as a dozen individuals; a few still survive in the wild, protected from cattle by fences that may not last much longer. The tree has also been propagated, however, and exists in a few botanical gardens. The third of Rock's species, which he named *H. wilderianus* after another friend, Gerrit P. Wilder, once grew on the island of Maui. Here again Rock found only one tree, with young flowers that were yellow within and greenish yellow outside. Before it died Wilder himself collected seeds from the tree but succeeded in raising only one plant, which apparently perished before maturing. Since there is almost no chance that others have survived in the wild, the species is regarded as extinct.

Member of a rare Hawaiian genus of trees, a Hibiscadelphus giffardianus displays a fully mature bloom on a delicate branch. One of just five species belonging to the genus, giffardianus is nearly extinct, surviving only under closely protected cultivation. It is most obviously distinguished from its four Hibiscadelphus kin—named for the resemblance of their blooms to those of the hibiscus—by the shape, size and direction of its bracts, the leaflike structures at the base of the flower.

The fourth member of the remarkable genus was found—or rather, recognized—not in the wild but in the collection of dried plants in the herbarium of the Bernice P. Bishop Museum in Honolulu. It was placed in the collection in the 1860s, mistakenly classified as a hibiscus, but in 1920 a reexamination by the botanist Charles N. Forbes revealed it for what it was. Forbes named it *H. bombycinus*—the latter word means "silky" and probably refers to the fuzzy or hairy aspect of the tree. No specimen of *H. bombycinus* is known to survive; this species too is thought to have disappeared forever.

I asked Herbst if his discovery also consisted of a single tree. "No," he said. "There are six of them, growing fairly close together." For the past 10 minutes his car had been climbing steadily up the ridge road along the western rim of Waimea Canyon. At an altitude of about 3,000 feet he pulled the car off the road, locked it and we set out to walk down the Kukui Trail into the canyon. Although in places it is a trifle steep, as though it had been laid out by a shingler of Gothic roofs, the trail is an easy one and affords several magnificent views.

Waimea is often called the Grand Canyon of the Pacific, a remark that is not as pure chamber of commerce as it sounds. The two are somewhat alike in character, if not in size, and it is startling to come upon a gorge like Waimea on a small subtropical island. Although it is only 14½ miles long it is about 2,800 feet deep; its steep many-layered walls are beautifully colored in the reds and ochers, blues and purples of the Grand Canyon itself; and here and there within it are erosion-carved shapes reminiscent of Arizona. However, Waimea receives more rainfall than the Grand Canyon and thus, except where its brightly painted slopes are too stony and steep to support it, contains much more vegetation. Waimea lies just to the west—and below—the high mountaintop swamp of the Alakai. Sparkling water pours down from the swamp into the canyon in thin never-ending streams with free falls of as much as 200 feet at a time.

We had descended only a short distance, following a path shaded by trees, when Herbst paused and pointed to a tangle of undergrowth. "Bush violet," he said. "*Viola tracheliifolia.*" Pushing its way up out of the undergrowth, and partly supported by it, arose a woody stem, or trunk, about six feet high and at least an inch in diameter. Attached to it were shiny green leaves and pale bluish-white flowers readily recognizable as those of a violet. "It might be 10 or 12 feet tall if we straightened it out," he said. "It has to lean on other plants to stand up."

The violet was arborescent, or resembling a tree, as an adolescent re-sembles an adult. Arborescence occurs in several Hawaiian species, as it does among the plants of other oceanic islands such as the Galá-pagos, where sunflowers become trees 30 or 40 feet high. The ancestors of arborescent plants came of course from the mainlands, where their descendants still grow as relatively small, soft-stemmed herbs, while on islands many of the descendants have become tall and woody. There are assorted explanations for this startling behavior, having to do with the sequence in which the plants arrived in Hawaii and exactly where they took hold. The forebears of the bush violet, for example, may have found a place available for them where there were no overshad-owing forest trees or shrubs and may have taken advantage of the sit-uation by gradually growing larger and larger. (With some conspicuous exceptions, the seeds of forest trees are generally heavier than those of violets, and perhaps for that reason take a longer time to travel.) It would have been a fairly normal evolutionary process, a fulfilling of the now-hackneyed old proposition that "if a niche opens up in nature, something will arise to fill it."

It is hard not to think of the blushing, six-foot violet of Hawaii in an-thropomorphic terms. It is an ambitious plant. No doubt the ancestor of that violet opened its blue eyes and gazed with astonishment at the un-inhabited landscape. "Hoo, boy!" it said. "Where are all those big, bullying trees?" Then it seized the main chance and began to grow as fast as it could. After 200,000 years it had become long and lank and could prop itself up on one elbow. After 500,000 it could get to its knees. After 700,000. . . . But suddenly the tall forest trees arrived, green trumpets blaring in the sky, and assumed their overshadowing place. The violet, which could almost but not quite stand up without help, leaned on a bush and murmured something that sounded like "Oh, shucks!" while a small blade of grass, which had timidly remained the same size during all those years, whispered, "Better luck next time."

We went deeper and deeper into the canyon and after a descent of near-ly half a mile reached the Waimea River at the bottom. It is a small, slow river that can be crossed at many points by stepping and jumping along the smooth gray boulders in its bed. We followed the river for some distance, disturbing a black-crowned night heron that flew, perched and flew grudgingly ahead of us. Although there were recent footprints of men and horses in the sand, we saw no one. It was very quiet and the air was cool and still.

Mile-wide Waimea Canyon, called Hawaii's Grand Canyon, harbors a newly discovered species of Hibiscadelphus tree.

In midafternoon we came to a side canyon, the Koaie, that entered Waimea on the right. Herbst said the tree was up there. We entered the smaller canyon, pausing after a few minutes to drink from Koaie Stream. The water was tea colored, rich with particles of vegetation washed down from the Alakai Swamp, and tasted clean and sweet. When we stood up after drinking and put on our packs again I looked at my watch: 3 o'clock. Unless something went wrong we would reach the tree in about an hour.

The side canyon was half a mile wide at its mouth but steadily narrowed as we went farther into it. The tall cliffs of reddish weathered lava on both sides were so nearly vertical that only a few small plants, dangling from cracks and crevices, clung to them. But down where we were walking, the trail ran along a talus of fallen rock covered with rich earth in which many trees were growing. There were *wiliwili*, which have claw-shaped flowers ranging in color from pale red through orange and yellow to chartreuse. There were forest trees called *lama*, whose hard, reddish wood was used by the old Hawaiians in building *heiau*, or temples. Among them stood shiny-leaved coffee trees, long since escaped from cultivation, and big plants of sisal, also gone wild, with five-foot, 10-pound bayonet leaves and flower poles as much as 30 feet high. The predominant trees were *kukui*, the ground beneath them thickly covered with bony-shelled, grayish-black nuts about the size of walnuts. Another name for the *kukui* is candlenut; the oil-rich kernels were burned by the Hawaiians for illumination. A row of them would be strung on the stiff midrib of a coconut leaf to make a candle that was leaned against a stone. Each nut would burn for two or three minutes and then its neighbor would be ignited. In the evenings children were assigned to keep replacing the candles as long as light was wanted. Until recently there were still a few elderly Hawaiians who spoke of a light bulb as an electric *kukui*.

The path wandered up and down, sometimes rising far above the stream and sometimes dipping fairly close to it. The talus narrowed and widened. In places it had been terraced by the aboriginal Hawaiians to make platforms for houses. They were built of uncut stones, rounded boulders put together with what must have been great labor. The vanished people, lacking other means, moved big rocks mainly by muscle —archeologists conclude that the Mookini Heiau on Hawaii, one of the largest temples in all of the islands, was built by 15,000 men standing three feet apart, who passed stones a distance of nine miles from their source to the building site. Most of the house platforms in the canyon were scarcely recognizable, their stones shoved apart and scattered by trees growing up among them. Still it appeared that there had once been a fair-sized settlement there. The remains of a five-terraced *heiau*, 180 feet high, stand against the cliff.

The trail, passing close to the old platforms, probably followed the path used by the Hawaiians centuries ago. There was nowhere else to put one. The trees of course were different but the contour of the land, offering not much choice as to where a man could walk, very likely had changed only a little. There were so few level campsites that when we came to a flat place 20 feet wide under a big *kukui* tree I suggested to Herbst that we return there at the end of the day.

He glanced at the Hawaiian stonework nearby and grinned. "You're not afraid of *akua?*"

Akua are spirits or ghosts. They wander everywhere in the islands and are thought to be fond of haunting the ruins of old houses and *heiau.* I said I had always wanted to see a ghost and had gone out of my way to hunt for them but had had bad luck. Wherever I had looked for ghosts, in attics and cemeteries, haunted houses and canyons, they had never allowed me to see them. Ghosts had no faith in me.

We went on walking. The thought of Herbst's tree was always somewhere in my mind. If he had said that we would have to climb 800 feet straight up the canyon wall to reach the tree I would have started looking for ways to do it.

It struck me that we had been making our way along the trail for at least an hour but the hands of my watch had not moved much. They seemed frozen at 10 minutes past three.

"What time is it?"

"About five after four."

The watch was running but the second hand was barely moving, creeping along at one-third speed or even less. It appeared that it was taking three or four minutes to go once around the dial. It was the best watch I had ever had, a gold electric watch powered by a little battery the size of a dime. It had always been remarkably accurate, within one or two seconds a day. I had owned it for four years. Only 30 days ago it had been cleaned and a new battery had been put in. Batteries are good for about a year. I set the watch at five minutes past four to match Herbst's and we moved on.

He walked ahead of me on the narrow trail. The tree would be on the right-hand side, he said. He hoped I would not be disappointed in it. It had finished flowering by now, and in any case the flowers were not very dramatic. He spoke like a man who is very proud of a beautiful daughter but feels obliged for modesty's sake to point out that she has a couple of freckles.

We went on for another half mile. Herbst slowed his pace, seeming to be puzzled, and at length he said, "I think somehow we may have walked *past* it. Let's go a little way more to make sure, and then turn around." Soon we reached a place where we could descend to the stream. After we had rested for a few minutes on the rocks, drinking the sweet water, he said, "Yes, we're past it. I don't know how I could have missed it, but I did."

We turned and began to go back over the trail. There was no use in my trying to look for the tree because I would not have recognized it, but Herbst gave me a description of its setting—the slope, the rocks, the way the ground fell off steeply on the right, a fallen sisal pole—and I looked for that combination.

After a few minutes he glanced at me over his shoulder, grinning again. "Do you think it's one of those things that appear only once every hundred years?"

It was profoundly quiet in that place. No birds sang and no breeze stirred in the trees. Once we heard the bleat of a goat somewhere on the cliffs overhead but there was no other sound except that of our own footsteps.

"It can't be far," he said. "This part of the trail is very familiar."

I stopped to retie the lace on one of my boots and Herbst walked on ahead, around a corner and out of sight. In a minute he reappeared, his fist raised. "Found it!"

The *Hibiscadelphus* trees were on a very steep, shady slope among boulders and ledges. *Wiliwili* and *kukui* overtopped them, cutting off much of the direct sunlight. Herbst pointed to a particular *Hibiscadelphus* and said, "That's the type tree, the one we'll describe."

In establishing a new species botanists select for description a representative individual, a "type specimen," having the characteristics by which others of its kind may be recognized. As we pulled ourselves up the slope toward it Herbst pointed out the five others nearby, all of them within a radius of 50 feet, standing among taller trees. Two were immature and three, reaching up through the shadows toward the light, had thin, leggy trunks. The type tree was more compact and better shaped. It was about 20 feet tall, like the other members of the genus de-

A new species of Hibiscadelphus tree whose existence was not even suspected before 1972 was discovered in a small canyon on the island of Kauai by Dr. Derral Herbst of the Pacific Tropical Botanical Garden. Until Herbst's find, botanists believed that all species of the Hibiscadelphus genus were highly specialized and existed almost exclusively on the island of Hawaii. The Kauai discovery suggests that Hibiscadelphus is the frail relic of a genus once widespread and thriving throughout the islands.

NEWLY DISCOVERED HIBISCADELPHUS (FOREGROUND)

FULLY OPENED BLOOM

LICHEN-COVERED BARK

SPENT BLOOM AND BRACTS

scribed long ago by Joseph Rock, with a trunk perhaps five inches in diameter at the base. There was a main crotch only a couple of feet up from the ground, and above that the tree branched and rebranched as gracefully as a small elm. The bark was smooth and dark gray, the leaves roughly heart shaped, three or four inches long with toothed edges. They were widely spaced on the branches, like ornaments, five or six inches apart. I found myself counting them and when I had ticked off a few dozen on one large branch I estimated that there were only about 600 leaves on the entire tree. The flowers had all disappeared. Later Herbst showed me one that he had collected on his first visit and placed in a bottle of preserving fluid: tubular, curved, yellow-green on the outside and yellowish within. Later still, weeks after I had returned to the mainland, Herbst sent me the opening sentences of the Latin description. "Remember," he wrote, "botanical Latin is a breed unto itself." The description began: *Arbores sex coronis rotundatis cinerascentibus usque 5 m. altas truncis 5-8 cm. diametro novimus. Ramuli novelli internodiis 0.5-10 cm. longis tomentulo pilorum stellatorum vestiuntur.* Beneath this he affixed a translation: "We know six trees with rounded grayish crowns up to 5 meters high and trunks 5-8 cm. in diameter. The young branches, with internodes 0.5-10 cm. long are clothed with a felt of star-shaped hairs."

I sat on a rock and stared at the tree while he climbed up and down the slope searching for others. He seemed not to expect to find any more, and did not. When he returned I asked him how old he thought the type tree might be.

"Impossible to tell, really. If I had to guess I'd say it was twenty-five or thirty. It doesn't look like much, does it? I mean, nurseries all over the world aren't going to start propagating it like mad."

I felt as though someone had spoken ill of *my* daughter and started to say, "Now, dammit, it's . . ." when I realized that it was scarcely necessary to take the tree's part in talking to Herbst, of all people.

We climbed down to the trail. The second hand on my watch was still almost invisibly dragging itself along. The watch now said 10 after four and according to Herbst's the time was quarter past six. "Do you suppose ghosts don't like gadgets like this?" I asked. If I were an old Hawaiian *akua*, and someone came into my canyon wearing a gold electric watch, I would treat him badly. A man like that might be capable of putting up a big plastic hotel.

"Possibly they don't like mechanical things in general," Herbst said. "Twice in the last year when I've been driving through Knudsen Gap in

the middle of the night alone, my car has stopped running and I've had
to walk. Knudsen Gap is supposed to be a good place for *akua*."

"How did it stop? No gas? No ignition?"

"It just stopped. When I went back next day it ran all right."

Herbst does not believe in ghosts any more than I do. We dropped
the subject. I wanted to explore one part of the canyon and he had it in
mind to look at another. We separated, agreeing to meet in about an
hour at the place where we had stopped to drink from the stream.

Dusk comes early and fast in the bottoms of narrow canyons. From
down there the stars are visible sooner than they are from the rims. It
was the unexpected glimpse of a star that made me realize how far the
day had ebbed. There was still some light left when I reached the place
where we were to meet, but Herbst was not there. I sat down to wait
for him. There was nothing to do except cut the corner off a plastic bag
of dehydrated beef stew, pour in water from the stream and let it soak.
I doubted that the *akua* would admire that very much, either.

Herbst seemed to be taking a prodigious time to get there. Soon it
would be too dark to move around. In fact it was already almost too
dark. Then I remembered that we had drunk from the stream not once
but twice. Now I was deep in the canyon and he was waiting for me
down near its mouth where we had first stopped. We should have had
a better understanding.

It seemed worth an effort to try to reach him but after only a few minutes of hurrying along the narrow trail I had to slow down. As the darkness deepened I looked for a flat spot to lie down for the night. Soon I
came to the *Hibiscadelphus* trees, or at any rate to a place on the trail
not far from them, and found a level patch of ground about six feet by
three between the trail and a big rock. Home.

The night was not yet full black. In the shadows I could see, very
dimly, the type tree on the slope above me. I ate the cold beef stew and
stretched out flat. I was not directly in the trail but only about a foot
away from it. Goats and wild pigs used the trail and for a moment I wondered about them. Goats are timid and no problem, but I was not sure
about pigs. I had heard that big boars will sometimes go after a man
and I did not care much for the notion of tangling with a 250-pound pig
in the dark; but there was not much to be done about that except
squeeze up against the rock and get as far off the trail as I could, so the
pig would have plenty of room to get by.

I awakened three or four times during the night and looked by habit at the luminous dial of the watch. I could not believe what the hands said but the watch was still running—it makes a faint humming sound like the dial tone in a telephone. Aside from that ridiculous noise, which can be heard only at a distance of an inch or two, there was not one sound in the canyon. Each time I awakened I became increasingly conscious of the *Hibiscadelphus* tree on the slope above me. So powerful an aura of life was emanating from the tree that I could feel it. Somehow the tree was establishing itself as an individual presence up there in the dark. I could sense its life, as a blind man is said to sense upon entering a silent room that someone else is there.

When I think about it today I try to convince myself that the case was really the other way round: I was only attributing the supernatural presence to the tree because I felt strongly about it, the best of only six on this planet. After incalculable years of evolution, millions of unknown sunsets and sunrises, the species had at last come to the end of its line. There is something deeply sad and touching about the last living thing of its kind standing with its back against the wall. But of course the species will not die now—Herbst has seeds from the tree, they have germinated, and he is watching the young plants closely.

Before dawn two jungle fowl, a long way off toward the head of the canyon, began to crow. They were brought to the islands by Polynesians long ago, escaped, and reverted to their original wild state. Jungle fowl have regained the power of vigorous flight although, like pheasants, they rarely fly long distances. The cocks are small and quite beautiful. Their hackles may be gold, bodies steel gray with russet bands, tails long, arched and black and white. The two cocks crowed alternately and the sky turned from gray to rose.

The canyon was filled with morning mist. I climbed the slope to the tree, putting my hand on it to keep from sliding back. A magical air of life like the mist flickered round it. Touching the bark, I imagined a thousand tiny pulses within the tree. I could sense its roots in the earth, curling around buried stones, weaving in the ashes of long-quenched cooking fires, drawing up moisture that passed through the trunk to the topmost leaves and vanished in the brightening air.

With all my heart I wished the tree well. I even looked to see if there was anything I might possibly do to help it. But there were no strangling vines or parasitic plants growing on it that I could remove, or any rocks farther up the slope poised to slide down on it, that perhaps I could shove aside. I took a leaf from the tree and put it carefully in my pocket, went down the slope, put on my pack and set out to find Herbst.

Nothing had been walking along the trail during the night. I broke a good many fresh spiderwebs as I passed, and noticed some that were so low to the ground that a pig would have broken them too. Several giant toads, larger than a man's fist, had taken up positions of ambush on the trail and beside it, waiting for breakfast to come wandering past. The toads are not native to the islands but to Mexico and South America. They were imported to deal primarily with sugar beetles and the very plentiful cockroaches. Occasionally they also eat Hawaiian centipedes, imported too, which attain lengths of seven or eight inches and can give a man a bite he will remember for 13 years.

Herbst was waiting for me some miles away beside the trail. He knew that I would have to pass him on my way out. No, he hadn't given much thought to our failure to meet on the preceding evening. In fact, he said cheerfully, he supposed the failure had been deliberate on my part. Since I seemed to like the wilderness so much he thought I had probably wanted to be alone in it.

It was 8:30 by Herbst's watch. Mine was about five hours behind. But the second hand seemed to be moving briskly again so I set the watch and we began to climb out of Waimea Canyon. It is not really an arduous climb but it does discourage conversation. In two and a half miles the trail ascends nearly twice the height of the Empire State Building. Beneath the weight of his pack a man feels very physical, indrawn, his mind turning over slowly. He does not solve many problems except where to put his feet.

We stopped to rest fairly often, and after a couple of hours I compared our watches. Mine was running normally again. It is still running normally to this day, with the same battery, and has not faltered once. It seemed to me that a speck of dirt must have gotten into the mechanism, impeded it for several hours, and then worked itself loose. As I plodded up the trail I was sure that much the same thing had happened to Herbst's car when it had mysteriously stopped during the night.

Near the end of the climb I turned to look down in the direction of the tree. I could not even see the mouth of the side canyon where it was growing but I could feel its presence down there. Today, 5,000 miles away, I feel it still.

Isolation on a Far Shore

PHOTOGRAPHS BY DAN BUDNIK

For some visitors, the Na Pali coast on the uninhabited northwest face of the island of Kauai evokes a sense of timelessness. Photographer Dan Budnik, who studied Na Pali's rugged profile from the air, from the sea and on the ground, came away with an impression of time in its most rudimentary meaning. Being at Na Pali, he reports, was "like being at the beginning of the world—or the end."

A walk along an 11-mile strip of this sea- and rain-washed shore afforded Budnik a microcosmic view of the entire Hawaiian archipelago. The coast takes its name from the Hawaiian word *pali,* meaning steep cliffs, like those that make up a good part of the coast *(opposite).* Some of them, composed of lava from volcanoes long extinct, drop from heights of 3,000 feet to the ocean and penetrate deep below its surface; here and there they are pierced with tunnels that once channeled molten lava, or are overhung with arches carved by the pounding surf, like the site shown on pages 178-179. The cliffs vary in color from gleaming blue-black to dull russet, depending on the mineral composition of the lava and on changing reflections of the sun's rays from sky and sea.

In some places the path along the coast opens on beaches of inviting white coral sand carried in by the surf from eroding coral reefs offshore. At other places, the way skirts beds of football-sized rocks *(page 177).* Still other stretches of the shore adjoin slopes of lava, so softened and broken by weathering that it can crumble to cinders underfoot, and must be avoided.

Where the path turns inland it follows a number of valleys—some as hemmed in as grottoes, others wide and spacious as amphitheaters. The earth is lush with exotic bird's-nest fern, thin-trunked, scarlet-flowering *ohia lehua* trees and sandalwood trees with purple blossoms. Waterfalls flash rainbows and carve gullies in the mountainsides.

Not even traces of a past civilization could diminish Budnik's feeling of wilderness isolation. When in the interior he came on stone walls built by Polynesian settlers some 1,200 years ago, he was struck by their failure to conjure up a picture of human habitation. "How different from Robert Frost's notion that 'good fences make good neighbors,' " Budnik says. "These walls, far from closing you in, seem, like the very vegetation among which they stand, to grow right out of the earth."

PLUNGING SEA CLIFFS AT KAILIU POINT

A TIDAL POOL ON KALALAU BEACH

KUKUI TREES IN THE NUALOLO VALLEY

OHIA LEHUA TREES CLINGING TO A VALLEY SLOPE

THE NA PALI COASTLINE FROM KEE BEACH TO KALALAU

MAIDENHAIR FERNS AND BRACKET FUNGUS IN HANAKAPIAI VALLEY

BIRD'S-NEST FERN NEAR THE HANAKAPIAI RIVER

A VALLEY WATERFALL, INLAND FROM HANAKAPIAI BEACH

RED HILL, RUSTY WITH IRON OXIDES, ABOVE KALALAU BEACH

SURF-ROUNDED LAVA COBBLES ON KALALAU BEACH

WAVE-CUT OVERHANG AND CORAL SAND AT KALALAU BEACH

Bibliography

*Also available in paperback.
†Available only in paperback.

†Buck, Peter H., *Arts and Crafts of Hawaii*. Bishop Museum Press, 1964.

Carlquist, Sherwin, *Hawaii: A Natural History*. The Natural History Press, 1970.

Day, A. Grove, *Hawaii and Its People*. Meredith, 1968.

*Day, A. Grove, and Carl Stroven, *A Hawaiian Reader*. Appleton-Century-Crofts, Inc., 1959.

Degener, Otto, *Plants of Hawaii National Park Illustrative of Plants and Customs of the South Seas*. Edwards Brothers, Inc., 1945.

Emerson, Nathaniel B., *Unwritten Literature of Hawaii: The Sacred Songs of the Hula*. Charles E. Tuttle Company, Inc., 1965.

Feher, Joseph, *Hawaii: A Pictorial History*. Bishop Museum Press, 1969.

†Gosline, William A., and Vernon E. Brock, *Handbook of Hawaiian Fishes*. University of Hawaii Press, 1960.

Handy, E. S. Craighill and Elizabeth Green, *Native Planters in Old Hawaii*. Bishop Museum Press, 1972.

Hawaii, A Guide to All the Islands. Lane Books, 1969.

†*Hawaii's Birds*. Hawaii Audubon Society, 1967.

Herbert, Don, and Fulvio Bardossi, *Kilauea: Case History of a Volcano*. Harper & Row, 1968.

†King, Judith E., *Seals of the World*. British Museum, 1964.

*Kuck, Loraine E., and Richard C. Tongg, *Hawaiian Flowers & Flowering Trees*. Charles E. Tuttle Company, 1958.

Luomala, Katharine, *Voices on the Wind*. Bishop Museum Press, 1955.

Macdonald, Gordon A., and Agatin T. Abbott. *Volcanoes in the Sea*. University of Hawaii Press, 1970.

Malo, David, *Hawaiian Antiquities*. Bishop Museum Press, 1951.

Maxwell, Gavin, *Seals of the World*. Houghton Mifflin, 1968.

Munro, George C., *Birds of Hawaii*. Charles E. Tuttle Company, Inc., 1960.

Neal, Marie C., *In Gardens of Hawaii*. Bishop Museum Press, 1965.

Rock, Joseph F., *The Indigenous Trees of the Hawaiian Islands*. Privately published, 1913.

Stearns, Harold T., *Geology of the State of Hawaii*. Pacific Books, 1966.

Tomich, P. Quentin, *Mammals in Hawaii*. Bishop Museum Press, 1969.

*Wenkam, Robert, *Kauai*. Sierra Club, 1967.

Wenkam, Robert, *Maui*. Friends of the Earth, 1970.

Westervelt, William D., *Hawaiian Legends of Volcanoes*. Charles E. Tuttle Company, 1963.

†Zimmerman, Elwood C., *Insects of Hawaii*. University of Hawaii Press, 1948.

Acknowledgments

The author and editors of this book are particularly indebted to Robert Wenkam, Honolulu, Hawaii, and Richard E. Warner, Foundation of Environmental Biology, Berkeley, California. They also wish to thank the following: Winston Banko, U.S. Bureau of Sport Fisheries and Wildlife, Hawaii National Park, Hawaii; Robert Bone, Honolulu, Hawaii; Sherwin Carlquist, Horton Professor of Botany, Claremont Graduate School, Claremont, California; F. Raymond Fosberg, special adviser in tropical biology, Smithsonian Institution, Washington, D.C.; Bryan Harry, Superintendent, Hawaii National Park, Hawaii; Derral Herbst, Botanist, Pacific Tropical Botanical Garden, Hawaii; Sidney S. Horenstein, Department of Invertebrate Paleontology, The American Museum of Natural History, New York City; James E. Kaina, Hawaii Visitors Bureau, New York City; Tom Kaser, Honolulu, Hawaii; John I. Kjargaard, Department of Entomology, University of Hawaii, Honolulu; Eugene Kridler, U.S. Bureau of Sport Fisheries and Wildlife, Hawaii; A. Jackson Lynn Jr., The Nature Conservancy, Arlington, Virginia; Larry G. Pardue, The New York Botanical Garden, New York City; Donald W. Peterson, scientist in charge, and the staff of Hawaiian Volcano Observatory, Hawaii; Don Reeser, Park Biologist, Hawaii National Park, Hawaii; John L. Sincock, U.S. Bureau of Sport Fisheries and Wildlife, Hawaii.

Picture Credits

Sources for pictures in this book are shown below. Credits for pictures from left to right are separated by commas, from top to bottom by dashes.

Cover—Fred Stimson. Front end papers 2, 3—David Muench. Front end paper 4, page 1—Dick Schmidt. 2, 3 —Dan Budnik. 4 through 9—David Cavagnaro. 10, 11—Robert Wenkam. 12, 13—Dan Budnik. 18, 19—Maps by R. R. Donnelley Cartographic Services. 24, 25—Robert Wenkam. 28—The New York Public Library. 30, 31—Aaron Dygart. 35—Richard Warner. 36, 37 —Donald W. Peterson. 38, 39—David Mowat, Hawaiian Volcano Observatory, U.S. Geological Survey photo by Gordon A. MacDonald. 40, 41—Robert Wenkam. 42, 43—David Muench, Robert Wenkam. 44, 45—Dan Budnik, Robert Wenkam. 46, 47—Rick Grigg, David Cavagnaro. 54, 55—Georg Gerster from Rapho Guillumette. 58, 59 —David Cavagnaro. 64, 65—Hawaiian Volcano Observatory, W. E. Ferguson—David Cavagnaro. 68 through 79 —David Cavagnaro. 85—Robert Wenkam. 87—Richard Warner. 90, 91 —Robert Wenkam. 95—Robert Wenkam. 99 through 105—Dan Budnik. 108—Map by R. R. Donnelley Cartographic Services. 110, 111—David Cavagnaro. 115—David Cavagnaro. 121 through 135—David Cavagnaro. 140, 141—Dan Budnik. 144—Culver Pictures. 146—Dan Budnik. 152—David Cavagnaro. 155—John Zoiner. 159 —Rick Golt. 165 through 179—Dan Budnik.

Index

Numerals in italics indicate a photograph or drawing of the subject mentioned.

LOTUS BLOOMS AND FOOT-WIDE PADS NEAR BAYOU LAFOURCHE

AFTER A RARE SNOWFALL IN A CYPRESS SWAMP

SQUADRONS OF BLUE GEESE AGAINST A WINTER'S NIGHT SKY

CYPRESS KNEES AND A CARPET OF DUCKWEED

A SOUTHERN BAYOU CLOGGED WITH WATER HYACINTHS

MOONLIGHT ON MARSHLAND NEAR THE GULF OF MEXICO

FOG-SHROUDED MORNING IN THE ATCHAFALAYA SWAMP

LIFE WORLD LIBRARY
LIFE NATURE LIBRARY
TIME READING PROGRAM
THE LIFE HISTORY OF THE UNITED STATES
LIFE SCIENCE LIBRARY
GREAT AGES OF MAN
TIME-LIFE LIBRARY OF ART
TIME-LIFE LIBRARY OF AMERICA
FOODS OF THE WORLD
THIS FABULOUS CENTURY
LIFE LIBRARY OF PHOTOGRAPHY
THE TIME-LIFE ENCYCLOPEDIA OF GARDENING
THE AMERICAN WILDERNESS
THE EMERGENCE OF MAN
THE OLD WEST
THE ART OF SEWING
FAMILY LIBRARY:
  THE TIME-LIFE BOOK OF FAMILY FINANCE
  THE TIME-LIFE FAMILY LEGAL GUIDE

THE BAYOUS

THE AMERICAN WILDERNESS/TIME-LIFE BOOKS/NEW YORK

BY PETER S. FEIBLEMAN
AND THE EDITORS OF TIME-LIFE BOOKS

The *Author:* Peter S. Feibleman was reared in New Orleans, and drew on boyhood memories as well as more recent explorations in writing this book. He has contributed two books to the TIME-LIFE Foods of the World series, *American Cooking: Creole and Acadian* and *The Cooking of Spain and Portugal.* His novels include *Strangers and Graves, A Place Without Twilight, The Daughters of Necessity* and *The Columbus Tree.* He has also written for the theater, films and television.

The *Cover:* Bald-cypress trees, characteristically festooned with Spanish moss, are mirrored by the still surface of Lake Dauterive, one of a number of lakes along the Atchafalaya River flood plain, in the heart of southern Louisiana's bayou country.

Contents

A Meeting Place for Rivers and the Sea

The waters of half a continent churn south through Louisiana in the formidable currents of the Mississippi and its tributary, the Red River (both shown in white). On the way they feed countless smaller waterways, known in this part of the world as bayous. Neighboring states have bayous, but, as this map demonstrates, Louisiana is quintessential bayou country.

In the northern half of the state most of the terrain is dry and hilly (areas with elevations above 150 feet are indicated by deeper green). In Louisiana's delta region, where the Mississippi and its main distributary, the Atchafalaya, meander to the Gulf of Mexico, the land is mostly flat and mostly wet, with many fresh-water swamps and open, sunlit salt marshes. (Both are marked by blue dashes.) Louisiana's Indian and French heritage is richly recorded in the names of towns and waterways.

The bayous themselves are shown on the map as solid blue lines, as are the Atchafalaya, the smaller rivers and man-made channels. Wildlife refuges and public parks and forests are outlined in red, while a line of blue dots traces the Intracoastal Waterway, an inland route for small boats.

RGIA PACIFIC
DLIFE MANAGEMENT AREA
CHICKASAW

CITIES SERVICE
WILDLIFE MANAGEMENT
AREA

COULEE NATIONAL
WILDLIFE REFUGE

ROE

RUSSELL SAGE
WILDLIFE
MANAGEMENT
AREA

TALLULAH   20   **VICKSBURG**

CALDWELL WILDLIFE
MANAGEMENT AREA

JACKSON

55

MERIDIAN

20

M I S S I S S I P P I   **ALABAMA**

59

55

AHOULA
ONAL
LIFE
GE

CONCORDIA WILDLIFE
MANAGEMENT AREA

NATCHEZ

SALINE WILDLIFE
MANAGEMENT AREA

HATTIESBURG

RED RIVER WILDLIFE
MANAGEMENT AREA

GRASSY LAKE WILDLIFE
MANAGEMENT AREA

THREE RIVERS WILDLIFE
MANAGEMENT AREA

G BAYOU
IFE MANAGEMENT

WEYANOKE   **TANGIPAHOA**   **BOGALUSA**   59   **MOBILE**

ZEMURRAY WILDLIFE
MANAGEMENT AREA

1

THISTLEWAITE WILDLIFE
MANAGEMENT AREA

10   **PASCAGOULA**

PORT
ARRE
OUSAS   190   **BATON ROUGE**   55   **PONCHATOULA**   **BILOXI**

Mississippi   _Sound_

HENDERSON   10

**BREAUX
BRIDGE**   **BUTTE
LA ROSE**   ST. TAMMANY STATE
WILDLIFE REFUGE   PEARL RIVER WILDLIFE
MANAGEMENT AREA

YETTE
MARTINVILLE   1   Lake
Maurepas   _Lake_   10

Pontchartrain   BONNET CARRE WILDLIFE
MANAGEMENT AREA
NEW IBERIA   _Atchafalaya
Basin_

FERSON
AND   90

**AVERY
ISLAND**   CHITIMACHA
INDIAN
RESERVATION   Lake
Cataouatche   **BILOXI WILDLIFE
MANAGEMENT AREA**

**NEW
ORLEANS**   Lake
Borgne   _Chandeleur
Islands_

rmilion
Bay   W.
Cote Blanche
Bay   **BERWICK**   **MORGAN
CITY**   90   SALVADOR WILDLIFE
MANAGEMENT AREA   Lake
Salvador   _Sound_

Breton   BRETON NATIONAL
WILDLIFE REFUGE   _Gulf_

Marsh
Island   E. Cote Blanche
Bay   90   **HOUMA**   1   BOHEMIA
WILDLIFE
MANAGEMENT
AREA   _Sound_   _of_

POINTE AU CHIEN
WILDLIFE MANAGEMENT AREA   23   DELTA NATIONAL WILDLIFE REFUGE   _Mexico_

RUSSELL SAGE
WILDLIFE
REFUGE

ISIANA STATE
DLIFE REFUGE   Pointe au Fer
Island

Barataria
Bay   _Mississippi Delta_   **VENICE**   North Pass   N

Grand Terre
Is   Pass a Loutre

GRAND ISLE   Northeast Pass

Caillou
Bay   Timbalier
Island   WISNER WILDLIFE
MANAGEMENT AREA   S. E. Pass

Isles Dernieres   PASS A LOUTRE
WILDLIFE MANAGEMENT AREA

1/ The Liquid Land

It is a place that seems often unable to make up its mind whether it will be earth or water, and so it compromises. HARNETT T. KANE/ *THE BAYOUS OF LOUISIANA*

Imagine that you are traveling behind a flock of snow geese as they wing south from Canada along the Mississippi Flyway toward the Gulf of Mexico. Follow them into Louisiana and you will recognize the bayou country by its look. Seen from the air, the land appears to be crisscrossed by a lacework of waterways that twist and turn, lashing back and forth. Here and there the lakes, rivers and creeks, the swamps, marshes and smaller patches of dark liquid seem to fill up—to grow solid in some mysterious way—until they turn into vast stretches of dry land rooted with trees, soft with flowers, swathed in grasses.

Move farther south with the wild geese as they look for a place to land; earth that seemed solid appears to melt from under its lush vegetation until it becomes water again. Still farther, the whole country seems to congeal into an amorphous substance whose texture is neither liquid nor solid, but an odd combination of both. Along the Gulf Coast, where the geese will touch down for the winter, streams branch out, disappear, reappear, coincide, mesh, forming a vast patternless pattern that looks, from high above, as though a sheet of dark glass had been shattered in a hundred different directions.

In all, Louisiana has about 3,500 square miles of water surface. Some of that total is accounted for by such enormous lakes as 41-mile-wide Pontchartrain in the east and 15-mile-long Calcasieu in the west, and, most notably, by the lordly Mississippi, which courses from the north of the state to its southernmost tip in a path half a mile wide and 569 miles long. But of the smaller waterways that interlace Louisiana like veins, the most numerous and the most fascinating are the bayous. There are scatterings of bayous in Arkansas, Mississippi and Alabama, but only in Louisiana are they so rife that the state can justly be called bayou country. The term derives from *bayuk,* the Choctaw Indians' word for creek; presumably they passed it on to the early French settlers, who gave it a euphonious lilt. Today geographers use "bayou" to describe a watercourse that serves as a distributary, or natural outlet, of a river. Louisianans prefer to be less precise. Following the Choctaw example, they apply the word to almost every kind of watercourse, whether it is a distributary or a tributary, whether it begins or ends in a river, a lake, a swamp or a marsh.

An exact count of the bayous of Louisiana would be almost impossible. A change in the course of the Mississippi or a flood may cause new bayous to form or old ones to disappear; moreover, many of the smaller ones have never been named. As if to make up for the oversight, those that have been labeled often bear such delightful identities as Bayou Go to Hell, Bayou Funny Louis, and Bayou Mouchoir de l'Ourse (meaning Handkerchief of a She-Bear). But nameless or not, most bayous are simply short creeks. Some, to be sure, are more than 100 miles long and at certain points as wide as a broad river. Yet even these, at other points, become so narrow that mosses hanging in branches on either bank meet in the air above the water.

The bayous are most thickly concentrated in southern Louisiana, in an area roughly the shape of a huge triangle. The apex lies 100 miles north of the Gulf of Mexico, where the formidable Atchafalaya River diverges from the Mississippi. The base is the entire sweep of Louisiana coastline, southeastern corner to southwestern corner, along the Gulf. But every other section of the state—northwestern, northeastern, central—has its bayous as well, in settings that vary markedly according to the terrain and that dispute the Hollywood-fostered image of a prototypical bayou. A bayou may indeed be—as the moviemakers have pictured it—a dark stream closed in by a jungle-like swamp; but it may also look very different.

In the hill country in the northwestern part of the state, for example, a bayou may lie at the base of a 300- or 400-foot eminence—a mountain by Louisiana standards—whose crest is dominated by trees alien to a watery realm. Because in this area the mean water table (the level to which the earth's subsurface is saturated with water) lies 10 to 60 feet below ground, hardwoods like red oak and hickory—which cannot tolerate wet roots—flourish on the heights of the hills. Below the hardwoods are towering pines and dense underbrush, and it is only on the banks of the bayou that water-loving willows and cottonwoods are to be seen. Standing at the top of one of these hills, looking down on its three-storied forest to the bayou far below, a visitor quickly abandons any preconceived notions he may have held about bayous.

He will recapture them, however, as he moves south from the hill country. Gradually the land flattens, turning into a pancake world in which the only significant rises are the natural ridges, called levees, that occur along the banks of rivers and streams. Often the land dips below the water table to become swamp; in this setting, cypress and tupelo-gum trees predominate, and the bayous that thread through the green gloom confirm the romantic image. Along the Gulf Coast, they take on yet another look. In this area of marshland trees thin out; mostly the bayous are fringed with grasses and are wholly open to the sky.

As varied as the settings of the bayous are the movements of their waters. The lively currents of most bayous in the hill country hardly differ from those of larger rivers. But in lower Louisiana the bayous seem to flout hydrological convention; the aura of strangeness that many people sense about a bayou derives in part from this phenomenon.

Early French colonists, who ventured into the swamp wilderness beyond their settlements, wrote back to the mother country about the mysterious bodies of water they had come upon. A bayou, they reported, was "sleeping water," a "dead" stream with no discernible current, altogether a dangerous place for a boatman to find himself. Concerned less with scientific inquiry than with the problems of daily survival, the settlers could not know that "sleeping water" might be the result of a change in the course of the river that originally had fed the bayou. Along the coastal fringes, where fresh and salt water mix, the movements of bayous also appear to defy any rules. Near the Gulf they cannot be said to "run" at all. Instead, they move at their own slow pace in their own manner—and in no definite direction. All day a bayou may flow almost imperceptibly east, emptying into a lake. Then in the evening the bayou will reverse its course and flow westward, draining the same lake. Mysterious as the turnaround seems, it does have a reason: it is a subtle response to changes in the water levels of nearby estuaries that are linked to the flooding and ebbing tides of the Gulf.

To understand the apparent willfulness of the bayou's behavior, it is necessary to know something about the forces that bear upon the land itself. The bayou country is a place where earth and water wage an endless struggle. Its deceptive calm is that of an Eden where time seems to stop; where breezes waft, easy and warm, through great trees and swaying mosses; where streams are gentle; where the humid air appears to magnify the colors of nature; where nearly everything that moves, moves slowly, and where nothing promises to happen—until it happens. Until, that is, the wind rises and this land of slow motion becomes a place of sudden violence. The bayou country is a place of extremes where death mingles with life, in the form of water lurking through the land and over it as well, always posing a lethal threat.

The focal point of the tug of war between land and water is the delta area, where the Mississippi River meets the Gulf of Mexico. By definition a delta is a nearly flat plain through which the diverging branches of a river run as it nears its end. Many people think a delta is carved by a river, as it continuously cuts new channels on its way to the sea. Actually the reverse is true—a delta is built up, not torn down, by a river.

As a river flows on its course, it picks up a burden of sand, silt and clay. The amount of sediment it can carry depends not only on how deep and broad its waters are, but also on how swiftly they move. An enormous river like the Mississippi, running swiftly where the continent is high, carries along with it half a billion tons of sediment a year. At its very end, where the river's fresh water meets the salt water of the Gulf, its velocity is reduced almost to zero and it is forced to drop its silty burden. The waters of the river spread into the sea through distributary channels in a kind of fan shape, like the Greek letter Δ (delta), spreading the sediment in an arc. The currents of the Gulf further distribute the sediment in an even broader sweep. Over the centuries, sediment accumulates to form land masses laced with distributaries that extend the delta farther and farther out into the Gulf.

In the last million years, the location of the Mississippi Delta has changed with the coming and going of each ice age. While the glaciers that covered the continent did not reach as far south as the Gulf of Mexico, Gulf waters—like those of other seas—nourished the glaciers, in the form of water vapor that turned to snow and then to ice. As the great freeze continued, no water returned to replenish the oceans, and the sea level dropped. The reverse occurred when the climate warmed and the glaciers melted: the sea level rose. These rises and falls were no minor matters; each could measure as much as 450 feet, drastically shifting the shorelines. In the last ice age, which ended about 10,000 years ago, the sea level of the Gulf dropped so that the Louisiana coastline extended 50 to 100 miles farther south than where it is now. With the return of warmth and the retreat of the ice, rising Gulf waters flooded northward to a point about 100 miles inland from today's Louisiana coast. By about 3,000 years ago, when the sea level stabilized at its present height, the modern, postglacial Mississippi delta system, starting at what is now the juncture of the Atchafalaya and Mississippi rivers, was already 3,000 years old.

In the process of carrying sediment to its mouth and building up more land, a river gradually lengthens the route it must follow to the sea. Finally it becomes so long that when its upstream banks overflow during flood stage, the rushing waters desert the usual channel and adopt another, shorter route to the sea—a route that then becomes the river's main channel. This has happened to the Mississippi many times during the last 6,000 years or so, and each time the river has shifted, it has created a new subdelta and forsaken an old one. Each time a subdelta has been created, new bayous have been born to help distribute the Mississippi's flow; and after the main channel of the river has moved elsewhere, the bayous have remained as a watery legacy.

Five subdelta regions together now make up what is called the Mississippi Delta, a great triangle nearly 150 miles at its base. The base, however, is anything but straight-edged; the river's restless shiftings, depositing its burden of sediment here, there and everywhere, have produced a series of overlapping, irregular lobes. The subdelta where the Mississippi now flows—Louisianans call it the true delta—has a shape geographers describe as a bird's foot. Curiously, the name has remained apt even though the delta has been extending at the rate of about 200 feet per year. On late-19th Century maps, it resembled an eagle's foot with a narrow shank and four sharp talons. Today it has filled out along the edges and looks more like the webbed foot of a duck.

In the "true" delta, land is encroaching on the Gulf's domain. Along the rim of the subdeltas that the river has abandoned, the Gulf in the main is winning its battle with the land; that part of the southeastern coastline is retreating slowly and steadily into the bayous.

Along the muddy southwestern fringe of Louisiana, the struggle between earth and water has taken a different form, but one in which the Mississippi has also played a role. As the river was building its westernmost subdeltas, some of the sediment it carried washed out to sea and was borne farther west by Gulf currents. During times of storm,

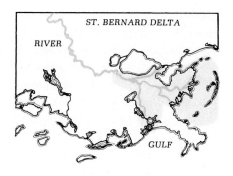

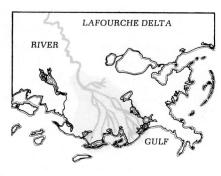

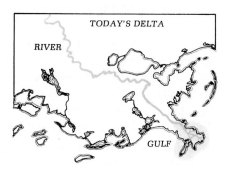

Three of the delta areas that have been formed over the centuries by the Mississippi River as it has shifted its course in flowing to the Gulf of Mexico are shown in blue on the maps above, each superimposed on an outline of modern southern Louisiana. The St. Bernard Delta began building 4,700 years ago, the Lafourche Delta some 3,500 years ago, and today's still-expanding delta about 600 years ago.

waves picked up this sediment and piled it onto the beaches in ridges that paralleled the shore. Varying from a few yards to 30 miles in length, and from 2 to 10 feet in height, these ridges formed barricades of mud, silt and shells where plants could grow, safe from salt water.

The ridges are called cheniers, from the French chêne, meaning oak, because they are places where live oaks flourish—and the clinging roots of the trees, in their turn, help to hold the land fast against battering waves. Over the centuries, as Gulf currents have brought more and more river sediment to this western shore, the coastline has crept south, ridge by ridge. A measure of its penetration into the Gulf is that in some places the parallel ranks of cheniers are 10 miles deep. But they are far from invulnerable; high winds and waves can demolish the cheniers altogether, breaking them down and spreading their substance around marshy wetlands that range as far as the eye can see.

The role of water in the bayou country does not end with its shaping of the land. Under the hot sun that beats down on Louisiana most of the year, water continually evaporates, rises, condenses and drops—contributing to rainfall that averages 4.6 inches a month. Again because of water, the high temperatures that prevail except in the brief winters are coupled with high humidity, which hovers at 70 to 80 per cent year round. The idea of high humidity is an abstraction for people who have not lived in this kind of climate; the presence of water vapor in the atmosphere is a tangible, grueling fact, especially during the summer, for those who live here. Extreme humidity reduces evaporation and the effectiveness of the body's cooling system. In similar temperatures on a desert you may be parched—in the bayou country you will be drenched.

Another result of humidity is that clouds writhe and wrinkle and swirl continually overhead as water does on the land below, making the skies among the most beautiful anywhere in the world. Most of the time the clouds are driven by the gentle Gulf winds—breezes, really. But one fact should be kept firmly in mind by any wilderness traveler in the bayou country: the sense of vast peace felt on bayou waters —the serenity that makes it seem as though the earth itself had stopped turning—that serenity can, at a moment's notice, explode into a Walpurgisnacht of the skies in which all life is endangered. For evidence there are the great live oaks of the cheniers. Winds have bent, whipped and savaged these trees so often that they have taken on extraordinary convulsed and agonized shapes. Lying at the southern fringe of the bayou country, they are like tree-demons that have been set there to warn the adventurer of what he may expect in the region round about.

Two kinds of winds are to be dreaded: tornadoes and hurricanes. Tornadoes strike the area an average of four times a year, most frequently in spring. A tornado is generally only 400 yards wide, follows a track only a few miles long, and usually travels at about 30 to 40 miles per hour, but it is the most violent kind of storm in nature. A tornado's winds, too furious to measure but estimated to reach a speed of 450 to 500 miles per hour, leave total havoc in their wake.

Even so, hurricanes are more fearsome because of the size of their swath: a hurricane can be 100 miles across, and the high winds and torrential rains around it may extend another 100 miles. From late summer through autumn, a hurricane can rise out of the sea like an aerial monster to overwhelm the land, its winds reaching speeds of 150 to 200 miles per hour. The winds and the rain are accompanied by an invasion of the sea that can flood the low-lying coastal areas with a deluge of salt water more than 15 feet deep. Farther inland, rainfall of up to 10 inches in 24 hours can cause destructive flooding without any help from the sea. Hurricanes strike Louisiana in full force on an average of once every four or five years. But when they hit, everything in their path is in danger of being ripped, torn apart, drowned and buried.

It is a remarkable characteristic of the bayou country, however, that even a killing hurricane can have a beneficial result. Silt stirred up by the storm and redistributed over the marshes by waves may enhance their fertility; more plants will grow to replace those that have died. The vegetation that has managed to survive in and around this country despite periodic natural disasters does so with a kind of wild beauty and an intensity of color; each plant or tree seems to be living at its peak during any given moment of its existence. Both the piny upland bayous and the cypress-filled swamps are dotted with color from early spring to late fall. Bright wild flowers grow like badges of bravura.

Hibiscus, wild iris, spider lilies and pond lilies decorate the freshwater marshes next to sheets and masses of the loveliest bayou flower of all, the water hyacinth—a bloom whose delicate appearance is belied by its habits. For just as a hurricane can be life-giving in this place of extremes, so the elegant hyacinth can be death-dealing.

A solid layer of hyacinths stretching from bank to bank on the surface of a bayou is an extravagant sight, like a river of orchids. Each lavender blossom—pale, with a dab of yellow on the center petal—is surrounded by bright green leaves; its roots dangle invisibly in the water below. The color of the petals shifts faintly with the light, as if reflecting the changing skies, so that the bayou seems to shimmer from lavender to dark purple and back again with the passing of a cloud. And yet the story of the water hyacinth is a story of blossoming death.

It is a flower that might well serve as a prime example of the dangers of tampering with the ecological balance of a wild area. Its story begins in 1884, during the International Cotton Exposition of New Orleans, when exhibits were shipped to the city from a great many foreign countries. Among them, reportedly, was a Japanese exhibit that featured a flowering aquatic plant that was actually native to Latin America. Each visitor to the exhibit received one of the flowers as a souvenir—an attractive bloom that looked like a water orchid. Shortly thereafter, fountains and fish pools and ponds in the city—as well as in the surrounding countryside—were filled with the blossoms.

What people did not know was that this flower was able to reproduce in ways, and on a scale, that are frightening in their ramifications. It did not grow just where it was planted, but soon began to invade the bayous. Birds and storms carried its seeds deep into the swamps, and within a few years a problem of heroic proportions had arisen.

The reproductive system of the water hyacinth is something to marvel at. It is endowed with a means of self-pollination, and can also reproduce by root offshoots. In water that moves as sluggishly as it does in the bayou country, hyacinths can double in number every two weeks. A single plant can produce 65,000 others in a single season. One acre of flowering hyacinths may contain anywhere from 50 to 800 million seeds. Although only 5 per cent usually germinate the next season, many of the rest of the seeds stay dormant. These, however, are still to be reckoned with. They may germinate any time within the next 20 years.

As many as 900,000 plants can float in just one acre of water, and what is so lovely-looking above the surface is not so gentle underneath. A mat of hyacinths eventually may become a floating island in which alligator weeds, cattails, even willow trees can grow, and the stream will be no longer navigable. Below, the vegetation is deprived of light; photosynthesis—the process by which plants use energy from the sun to produce food—is not possible. The plants below the hyacinths die. Phytoplankton disappears and with it the fish. The pond weeds on which ducks feed go—and so, of course, do the ducks.

Along with its ability to reproduce, the hyacinth's indestructibility has over the years become the theme of a sort of black comedy whose setting is the bayou country. As early as 1897, the U.S. Army Corps of Engineers was called in to destroy the plants. Then other federal agencies as well as state conservation authorities joined the fight against the delicate flower—and the delicate flower won.

The record of attempts to destroy it—attempts made on and off over the course of four decades—reads like a script written by Charlie Chaplin in collaboration with W. C. Fields. The first weapon used by the Corps of Engineers was the pitchfork. The choice was somewhat naïve. A great many of the plants were forked onto the banks of bayous; but while they were being thrown up to rot and die, others were reproducing faster than ever as the water was cleared.

In 1900, a sternwheeler was brought, at some expense and difficulty, into the bayous. It had a four-foot conveyor-belt attachment that picked up the hyacinths, chewed them into pulp, and spit them back out. The result was disappointing, and history shows that the men who were trying to get rid of the flower understandably lost their tempers—they soon turned to dynamite. The wilderness boomed with explosion after explosion. Everything in the immediate vicinity of each explosion was destroyed—everything but the hyacinths, thanks to the redoubtable ability of their seeds to sprout after long dormancy. A bayou can be completely cleared on the surface, and can stay clear for a number of years; then the seeds germinate and the hyacinths rise again—and very soon after that the bayou is once more covered by a mass of flowers.

After dynamite proved useless, a flame thrower was paddled up into the bayous. The *Louisiana Conservationist,* published by the state's Wild Life and Fisheries Commission, carried an account: "A full cone of fire, hot enough to melt a block of steel, was squirted on a hyacinth raft. When the fuel was exhausted, a frog emerged from the blackened mat and began sunning itself. The scientist using the flame thrower was even more astounded later during the next growing season. The burnt plants were not only the first to sprout but also averaged nine inches taller than surrounding plants."

After fire, arsenic was tried. Some of its loose powder got into the food of the workers at the site, resulting in the death of one man and the critical illness of 13 others. The hyacinths grew on. Finally, in the 1940s, the Corps employed a weapon that would kill the plants if not the seeds, and that would not harm men or the fish, fowl or animals that used the streams: a chemical called 2,4-D.

So now hyacinths can be kept under control to a certain extent—with vigilance and the expenditure of substantial sums—but they remain fixed inhabitants of the bayou country. They have outlasted not only

Flashing his white rump patch in alarm, a young buck hightails it through a fresh-water marsh near the Mississippi River, heading for a thicket and safety. The deer of Louisiana's marshes, a subspecies of the common white-tailed deer, have slightly larger hoofs for extra support in the spongy terrain.

several generations of men intent upon killing them, but also natural calamities like hurricanes, which may wipe out other plants but only spread hyacinths. Wherever you go in the bayous, at a turn in a stream or behind a clump of cypress, you can see a fragile lavender blossom whose petals tremble in the slightest breeze: the survival flower.

The creatures of the bayous are as profuse as the plants. Flying squirrels and gray squirrels thrive in the wooded northern bayous; chipping sparrows and red-cockaded woodpeckers nest in the pine trees, and the streams hold largemouth bass, bream and white crappie (known locally as sac-a-lait) as well as bullfrogs, harmless water snakes and less harmless copperheads, cottonmouths and eastern coral snakes. In the swampy jungle bayous farther south, white-tailed deer run, mourning doves coo, barred owls hoot from the branches overhead, and cicadas shrill underfoot. Providing a counterpoint to these sounds are the noisy munchings of gatherings of huge lubber grasshoppers, three-inch-long creatures that have presumably derived their descriptive name from the popular local term for a clumsy fellow. In the backwaters, countless little prehistoric-looking crawfish breed, along with musk turtles and snapping turtles and several species of salamander.

Farther south, in the marshes, fur-bearing animals like muskrat and nutria abound, sharing the waters with crabs, shrimp, oysters and alligators. Here the skies often teem with birds; the Louisiana coastal region is North America's greatest winter resort for migratory ducks and geese. It is also the spring breeding ground for such wading birds as the snowy and great egrets, and the year-round home of the brown pelican.

In a land where water and land themselves are forever switching places, change of any sort should come as no surprise. The changes hardest to adjust to are those that men have wrought. I have compared parts of the bayou country today with my childhood memories. Bayou Teche, for instance, in the south-central part of the state, is still beautiful. It is perhaps Louisiana's most celebrated bayou, along whose banks grand and elegant houses have stood for well over a hundred years. Nowhere else are there so many live oaks; in no other bayous do the trees grow to such size. Some have trunks nearly 20 feet in girth, wildly twisted giants whose branches stretch out into vast moss-draped tents, mingling their leaves with other trees, standing guard over the water. But the little towns I remembered along the Teche have grown into big ones over the past few decades, and there are only occasional stretches today where the banks are untamed and uninhabited.

The differences in the great swampland known as the Atchafalaya

River Basin are more vivid. The building of flood-control locks at the river's juncture with the Mississippi, and the deepening of the Atchafalaya's main channel to prevent it from overflowing, have diverted much of the water the swamp needs to maintain its level. The expansion of farming and industry, in the drained areas especially, has brought new dams, dikes and highways. As man has advanced, the swamp has retreated, leaving a trail of cypresses standing like gaunt skeletons in the parched earth. Even the sweet gum and palmetto are endangered as their seedlings are attacked by rabbits or rooted up by armadillos that are found in ever-increasing numbers as more land is drained. Fishing holes have dried up, but the white-tailed deer are flourishing, using shrubs and saplings for forage. Though the cougar and the red wolf are nearly gone, the black bear has been saved from extinction by the importation of cubs from Minnesota.

Fortunately, not all of the bayou country has been civilized yet. In the south-central part of the Atchafalaya Basin there are still places where the only movement to be seen is that of an alligator gliding through the water, or a heron swooping down on a crawfish.

Bayou Dorcheat in northern Louisiana was seriously polluted by oil-field salt and gravel washings in the 1940s and 1950s, but these problems have been largely solved; even the gravel strip-mining that persists along parts of its outer fringes has not spoiled the stream itself. And to the angler's added delight, Lake Bistineau—into which the Dorcheat empties—has been dammed, turning it from a swamp into an enormous clear-water lake. At the opposite end of the bayou country, along the coast, oil fields have indeed altered the skyline with their drilling gear, and allowed salt water to spill into fresh-water areas through man-made canals. Even so, much of the marshland remains untouched and as inaccessible as ever, and broad bands of it—totaling some 600,000 acres—are wildlife refuges.

However much they may change, the bayous remain a touchstone for anyone who comes to know them. "When you visit here, you never truly leave," they say in southern Louisiana. Something about these places becomes a part of your life and gives it added meaning. That is the truth that makes a journey into the bayou country worthwhile.

A Rivalry of Earth and Water

In southern Louisiana the bayou country is a place of innumerable subtle variations on the theme of earth versus water. Most of the land is flat, and all of it is wet or moist; what is solid and what is not is often difficult to discern.

Two rivers—the Mississippi and its major distributary, the Atchafalaya—have been chiefly responsible for shaping and defining the lower bayou country. Flowing southward toward their rendezvous with the Gulf of Mexico, they meander slowly through level land, constantly building and taking away, in the process altering both the landscape and their own channels; in the case of the Mississippi, its changes in course cause variations in its length of as much as 50 miles a year.

Both rivers roll past woods and fertile fields, swamps and marshes, here and there spreading out to linger in shallow basins choked with lush vegetation. As they go, they nourish countless bayous: streams, creeks, ponds that make the countryside a watery patchwork. At spring floodtime, when the current's measured pace becomes a roaring rampage, huge areas are inundated with the rivers' sediment-laden waters.

Eventually the Mississippi, having traveled approximately 3,800 miles from its beginning, and the Atchafalaya, having traveled some 150, encounter the Gulf. The currents and waves of this sea—the fifth largest in the world—nudge and batter the coastal fringe, and its salt water surges inland on each high tide. Here the resilient land performs the role of a buffer between river and sea, an accommodator of opposing forces. Here, too, fresh and salt waters mix in tidal estuaries and ponds, producing miles of brackish marshes that serve several functions: as a vast nursery for aquatic animals, as a home for numberless amphibians, and as a temporary residence for millions of waterfowl and wading birds. Finally, at the continent's edge, the Gulf takes over but continues the work of shaping the land—extending the coast in some places, eating it away in others.

Because the bayou terrain is so flat, a view from the air is the best way to gain a perspective on the southward progression from river to sea, from fresh to salt water. Cruising the area in a small plane, photographer Russell Munson took the pictures on the following pages—a record of a land where earth and water become almost one.

Muddy and flooded, the Atchafalaya River snakes southward, soaking the wooded areas on both sides of it. The river, which channels almost a third of the Mississippi's water to the Gulf, also shares the Mississippi's burden of sediment, depositing it liberally along the way and changing the look of the land: the long, crescent-shaped island at right is slowly being built up by river clay, silt and sand.

The Mississippi courses swiftly past the sheer face of a bank it has bitten into during a previous period of flooding. The bare soil, laced with a tangle of exposed tree roots, is evidence that the river has undercut the bank and sliced off a chunk, trees and all. New vegetation may grow to cover the denuded earth—until the next time the waters rise to attack it.

The three dry ridges rising from the flooded lowlands are natural levees built by the Mississippi. Such low ridges are formed during successive flood periods when the water overflows its banks and, with room to spread, slows suddenly and drops much of its sediment. Some natural levees have been added to by men; these remain as the river shaped them.

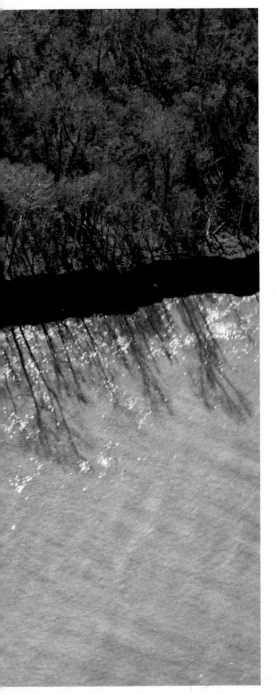

Countless thousands of pale green water-hyacinth plants blanket a pond in the 1,900-square-mile Atchafalaya Basin and inexorably invade a mixed stand of cypress, tupelo-gum and willow trees. Beautiful but pestilential, the water hyacinth grows nearly everywhere in the fresh-water bayous, clogging the waterways, choking out other vegetation and cutting off the sunlight necessary for aquatic life.

A few miles inland from the Gulf of Mexico, this marshy pond—a so-called mixing bowl—is one of thousands in southern Louisiana in which fresh and salt water blend, producing the brackish broth that fosters rich aquatic life. Fresh water enters the pond from small bayous (top and sides). At high tide, salty water enters through the sinuous tidal inlet (bottom), and the waters mix; at low tide, the blend flows out toward the Gulf.

The salt water of the Gulf, coffee colored by river sediment, washes a marsh at the brink of the southern bayou country. The briny bath nourishes a variety of vegetation. Oyster grass grows on the raised ridge at the water's edge; right behind is wire grass, a salt-tolerant marsh plant that threatens to overrun the dark patches of three-cornered grass (top left), which is favored by the muskrats and nutria that inhabit the marsh.

Tidal ponds, inlets and estuaries spangle a trackless coastal marsh in southeastern Louisiana. Their calm, protected waters, warm and brackish, constitute one of the world's finest aquatic nurseries. They also provide an abundant larder for the many creatures, such as shrimp, sea trout and channel bass, that grow to maturity here before entering the Gulf to spawn.

A ridge of solid earth, called a chenier, rises from a wet coastal marsh, providing a foothold for live-oak trees in an otherwise watery habitat. Such ridges, named after the French word for oak, chêne, may extend as far as 30 miles. They were once beaches marking the edge of the Gulf, formed by wave action that deposited a mixture of river sediments and broken shells from the Gulf's own bottom.

Sea water swirling over the Chandeleur Islands, about 20 miles off the Louisiana coast, testifies to the Gulf's triumph over land that once belonged to the bayou country. These islands were once part of the old St. Bernard Delta when it marked the mouth of the Mississippi (page 24). After the river shifted course, much of the old delta was gradually submerged in the Gulf's waters, leaving a few islands, such as the Chandeleurs, to be buffeted by the Gulf's restless waves and currents.

2/ A Difference of Bayous

*And there are the bayous — the Boeuf and the Teche,
Bayou LaFourche, and some whose names are known only
to the moss pickers and the fishermen.*

CHARLES EAST/ *THE FACE OF LOUISIANA*

There are no mountains around southern Louisiana, not even any real hills, and as a child growing up in New Orleans I had never seen the earth look anything but flat. So, one summer when Richard Breaux's father offered to take me with them for a week-long canoe trip on Bayou Dorcheat I was as unprepared for the rolling countryside of northern Louisiana as I was for the wilderness we found there. I was 10 years old at the time and, though I didn't realize it, I was about to discover the northern bayou country in the best manner possible, under the tutelage of a man who had spent a good deal of his life studying and appreciating the face of nature in Louisiana.

Springhill, the nearest town to what would be our starting point for the journey down Bayou Dorcheat, is in the northwest corner of the state; and since New Orleans lies in the southeast, it was a long way from one place to the other. I couldn't for the life of me understand why anybody would want to drive the better part of a day just to go canoeing on a bayou. On the edge of a park not far from where I lived there was a small natural canal that I knew as Bayou St. John; I had often played on its banks. All the other streams I had seen on family picnics looked more or less like Bayou St. John, only not as well manicured. So, for most of the early hours of the drive I dozed, dreaming of other, greater adventures.

At that point I had never even heard of Bayou Dorcheat, but it is a long stream and once it was a famous one. It follows a southerly course for 122 miles from Nevada County, Arkansas, through northern Louisiana to Lake Bistineau, where it empties. The lake feeds into Loggy Bayou, which then drains into the Red River, which in turn leads to the Mississippi. Until about the time of the Civil War, the Dorcheat was an important north-south waterway with sawmills and gristmills, wharves and warehouses along its banks. The virgin pine forests provided choice timber and, after they had been cut, farmers settled in. In 1873, the Red River was cleared of accumulated log jams and steamboat traffic left the Dorcheat for the Red's larger channel. As lumber companies moved away and farmers abandoned their weevil-plagued lands, the Dorcheat gradually reverted to its natural state, becoming a kind of second-generation wilderness.

As we headed toward it that day in the early 1940s, I woke from my dreams with a sense of alarm. The road was dipping up and down as if it had hiccups, and outside the car windows the earth rolled and curled in every direction. I was seeing my first hills. We had made a detour into the Kisatchie National Forest, where we could find a picnic table and an outdoor grill for roasting hot dogs.

To me the word "forest" seemed a strange name for the five- to six-foot-tall trees standing beside the road. Richard's father explained that this area had been heavily lumbered until recent years, but that with the Depression the federal government had bought up the land cheaply and was now in the process of replanting the denuded acres with loblolly, slash and longleaf pines. Because the land was assembled piecemeal, the Kisatchie consisted of six separate sections; we were in the northeast one, in the area known as the Catahoula Ranger District.

In the years since then, the sapling pines have grown into towering giants as much as 100 feet high and today's Kisatchie is densely forested, rich in game animals and birds. Even back then, we could see signs of returning wildlife. Close to where we stopped for lunch, I spotted a quail looking for seeds in a patch of burr-spangled beggar's-ticks, oblivious to our intrusion. Later Richard and I went climbing in a grove of sweet gums and red oaks; the lumber companies, interested primarily in pines, had left these hardwoods alone.

Back in the car, we headed northwest again, and as we approached the end of our drive, something about the trees along the road struck me as odd. Directly beneath the tall pines, a band of young broad-leaved trees pushed up from the soil. These were deciduous hardwoods —a mix mostly of white oaks and hickories, sweet gums and elms. A bit farther on, the hardwoods were almost as tall as the pines. Soon there was another change. The deciduous trees had taken over; the pines were nearly all gone. It was as if the first forest had been replaced by the second through some slow-motion sleight of hand.

What I was seeing was three of the stages in the development of a "climax forest"—and what to me appeared as a fairly rapid transformation actually takes several hundred years to accomplish. Whenever tamed land reverts to wilderness, as it had done here, with a new forest rising where an old one has stood, it does so in a series of steps. The successive species of trees vary from region to region, but the firstcomers are always softwoods; and the ultimate survivors, the trees of the climax forest, are always hardwoods.

In the hills along the Dorcheat, the pioneer softwood species is the prolific loblolly pine, augmented by the shortleaf pine. A single loblolly can produce 500 cones a year; each cone holds 70 or 80 seeds. After the cones open, the infinitesimally lightweight seeds are sown widely by winds, and they are able to germinate readily in almost any sunny soil, even soil that is not particularly rich. Within five years or so, the pines can turn a barren acre into a nursery crowded with as many as 5,000 five-foot-high saplings.

After the pines are established, squirrels and birds bring in acorns, nuts and seeds from neighboring hardwood trees. Hardwoods, which can tolerate shade when young, spring up quickly. Pine seedlings, on the other hand, die out if deprived of full sunlight. Over the years, as hardwoods increase in size and number, they appropriate every clearing until they crowd out the pines or kill them with shade. Occasionally a brush fire may give the pines a reprieve by destroying the understory of hardwoods while hardly damaging the pines, which are insulated by thick bark. But hardwoods are longer lived than pines, as well as better equipped to compete for sunlight; and eventually they triumph.

The northern part of Bayou Dorcheat lies in a valley of such hardwoods. Approaching the bayou, we turned off the highway onto a long series of dirt roads that led into open country. We stopped at the top of a steep slope. Below and in front of us the forested hill country of northern Louisiana lay in undulating waves of trees. Under a slate-blue sky the hills stretched away in long and secret splendor. The foreground of bright green gave way to a paler green, then in the distance to a bluegreen. Above the trees was a film of glittering dust that suffused the atmosphere with a reddish glow like visible heat. I could not imagine where the red was coming from until I looked down at the earth.

Soil that contains iron oxide is rust colored; the hard topsoil on which we were standing had a baked look, like the surface of a vast irregular brick. I gouged at it with a stick. Underneath, it was even more reddish. The look of the freshly dug soil, turned out over the ground—red on red —became, for me, the look of the Dorcheat. In the silent heat of early summer, a male cardinal flitted out of a branch overhead, brilliant in his crimson feathers—the square root of red, as if he had come from someplace deep in the earth where the color began.

A few minutes later we walked over a high roll of earth down to the bank of Bayou Dorcheat. I knew then that the streams I had seen in New Orleans bore about as much resemblance to a bayou running through wooded country as a man-made canal bears to the Mississippi. The Dorcheat was my first glimpse of an untamed bayou, and I have never forgotten it. At the water's edge a few cypresses bent gracefully over the quiet stream, their knobby knees sticking up out of the water, seemingly separated from the trunks two or three feet away. But there was none of the moss one finds in the south. Here the cypress trees were backed closely by a line of bright green pines. Beside the cypresses, a willow hung above the water, stirring in a faint breeze.

For most of its course, Bayou Dorcheat runs through the wooded hill country, and where we stood its banks rose and dipped in easy arcs until the stream curved out of sight. Beyond the cypresses and pines and hardwoods, I could see a solitary patch of bamboo, looking tropical and out of place.

We pitched camp in a small clearing near the water's edge and there, in the light of late afternoon, Richard and I played tag. On the hill that rose several hundred yards from the bayou, purple blossoms of verbena flashed, and a tangle of yellow-petaled black-eyed Susans cascaded down the slope. The hillside drew us, and we climbed it. From a height the bayou looked like a stream of molten lead cooling as the day waned. It flowed faster than the bayous I came to know in later years, but not so fast that it was dangerous for swimmers. At a turn in the bayou we could see other children, diving from a thick branch of an oak overhanging the water.

For a while we stayed on the hillside, running through the peppergrass and sour dock that lined it in places. There was milkweed too, spilling white sap when we broke stalks that stood in our path, and here and there a scattering of pink wild roses. To the west an overgrown dirt road stretched like a long red ribbon through the green, leading away from the metallic glint of the bayou. Later we went diving with the other boys. They had tied a rope to the oak branch, and we took turns swinging out over the bayou and streaking in.

When the light began to fade, we rejoined Richard's father at the campsite and ate the cold cuts and salad we had brought. The chirping of the crickets, signaling the end of day, was replaced by the singing of frogs in chorus. All along the stream the melody rose; by 9 o'clock the land itself seemed to be vibrating with the sound.

Through the years, frog song has become, for me, the sound of the bayous. Only the male frog vocalizes, using his music to attract a female, and each species sings differently. One kind or another is singing year round, but the chorus is largest from March through August. In those months one hears the deep resonant hum of the bullfrog and the *quonk-quonk* of the green tree frog; the gray tree frog sends forth a sharp *brrill-brrill,* while the cricket frog emits a rattle as clear as the noise of two pebbles clicking together.

That first night I lay awake for hours, listening to the singers and watching the bayou. Bats flew, silent as shadows in the warm air above the water, searching for bugs. When the bats disappeared I wondered what other, larger nocturnal animals—bears maybe, or wildcats—might be prowling about. Richard nudged me. In the trickle of starlight that filtered down through the branches of the tree over our heads, some sort of movement was dimly visible. Something flicked from a higher branch to a lower one—not bats but flying squirrels. As my eyes adjusted to the dark, I watched them dipping and swooping gracefully—settling on one branch, skimming off to the next—a high filigree of small black patches, like pieces of the night.

Unlike bats, flying squirrels can only glide, so all their flight patterns are downward and between dives they must run back up into the trees. Their gliding apparatus is a pair of thin, furry elastic membranes attached to their sides and legs. As a squirrel launches itself into the air, it spreads out all four legs and stretches the membranes taut. Then it adjusts the slack in the membranes to control the angle and speed of a glide. At the end of its glide the squirrel pulls its hind legs together and lands upright, on all four feet; at that point the membranes relax to their original size.

The air was full of these little acrobats and their antics absorbed us until finally sleep came. About 6 o'clock the next morning, Richard shook me. His father was fixing breakfast—fish he had caught from the

Black willows in leaf share a stand with bare cottonwoods in this aerial view of northern Louisiana bayou country. Both kinds of tree thrive best when their roots are generously watered, and are often found on river flood plains such as this nearly flat stretch along the course of a bayou.

bank of the bayou in the light of dawn. The air was misty, and the reddish earth and gray-green country looked unreal, like a photographic image emerging in a developing solution. Fried fish reestablished reality for us, and before the sun was high we had unhitched the canoe from the top of the car, were packed up and out on the bayou.

The effects of the annual spring floods had long since gone and the bayou's water had begun to evaporate under the heat of the summer sun, so that the stream presented a kind of obstacle course. Twice we hit spots so shallow that we had to lift the canoe and portage it. The portages were places where silt had piled up sufficiently to provide a fairly firm footing. In some spots cypress trees had taken root. This happens, Richard's father explained, where the silt build-up has lasted for more than a year; and once a few of the trees get started, only a very large flood can demolish the spot—silt, cypresses and all.

By noon we had paddled to a point along the bayou where it was little more than a ditch, four feet wide. We stopped to eat lunch and enjoy a bit of shade. The sun was high and blinding, though the heat was not as bad as the kind I was accustomed to at this time of year in New Orleans; at the northern end of the state the humidity is lower, and the air relatively dry.

We were sitting, half-dozing, when my eye fell on an object about 20 yards away. It looked like a hump-shaped rock—but it was moving. It was an armadillo—a small-scale version of an armor-plated truck —heading across a patch of dry place along the bank. Armadillos are not indigenous to bayou country; native to Patagonia at the southern tip of South America, they made their way northward in a trip that probably took millions of years and did not arrive in Louisiana, according to verified sightings, until 1925. They multiply so fast—each spring producing litters of identical quadruplets—that armadillos had already become a familiar sight throughout the bayou country.

A soft plop in the bayou caught our attention next, and for a quarter hour we were entertained by a family of wood ducks. From their nest in the hollow of a tree across the stream, several baby ducks had made it into the water, a little flustered, and were paddling around busily under their mother's eye. As we watched, she began to preen. She would put her bill into the feathers at the base of her tail, then use the bill to stroke her wings and body. The duck's bill serves a dual purpose in this maneuver; it picks up the oily secretions of a gland located at the tail, then distributes the oil over the wings and body. The oil water-

Fresh from a fast bath in a woodland bayou, a wood duck ruffles the exquisitely tinted feathers that cause many ornithologists to acclaim it North America's most beautiful bird. The shy wood duck lives year round in forested bayou country and owes its name to a preference for nesting in the hollows of trees instead of on the ground.

proofs the feathers; otherwise they would become waterlogged, and the duck would be unable to fly.

Wood ducks, as their name indicates, prefer a forested habitat, and they are full-time residents of the Dorcheat. Their green and reddish-brown mix of feather colors seemed perfectly suited to the landscape.

We could have admired them for hours, but the time came to go. Richard and I ran about on a last-minute errand, filling a paper sack with the blackberries that studded bushes all around. We munched on them as the canoe took us downstream. The flow of the water was more sluggish now. As we passed a willow tree, I reached up to brush at its streamers; Mr. Breaux sharply warned me to stop. Where a bayou runs so narrow that a canoe must scrape through overhanging branches, it is a good idea to keep your hands away from things. Otherwise, you may find yourself sharing the boat with a snake, jolted by your gesture from a tree where it has gone looking for a nest of bird's eggs.

In the long afternoon we paddled through swirls of current, then through places where the water seemed not to move at all. At one place stretches of the bayou, separated by silt build-ups, were so still they were stagnant. The water on the surface looked dusty—as though it had been there for so long without moving that dirt from the banks had settled over it. The water had also begun to collect a dark green scum, and even the tree shadows looked heavier here.

A shy map turtle, five or six inches long—its olive-colored shell marked with dark lines in a geometric pattern that suggests the look of a map—slid off a log and slipped into the motionless stream. It moved quickly through the water for a few seconds, then floated head up, watchful. Beyond the turtle, an object that looked like a flowering bush stood in the high reeds. Then a leg lifted, and I saw that what I had judged to be inanimate was a great blue heron; this species sometimes leaves its normal habitat in the south to visit the northern bayous. The heron stood as quiet as if it had grown out of the mud.

The air itself seemed peculiarly still. There was a sense of secrecy about this stretch of the bayou, as though things were happening that were not visible to the eye. It was not so much the look as the feel of the place that was different.

For the next two days we continued our downstream journey. The rolling hills began to disappear; flat land was more and more frequent. Since we had only a week's time, and had to paddle all the way back upstream to our starting place, we did not try to go all the way to the end of Bayou Dorcheat at Lake Bistineau. Mr. Breaux preferred to let us stop here and there, ramble the woods and climb the trees, fish—to get to know the bayou.

During our third day out, as we were gathering kindling for our camp-fire, a cooing came from high in a tree above us. I watched the branches for a few minutes before I finally saw a brownish-gray bird, sitting on its nest. It was about a foot long, with a slender, pointed tail—a mourning dove. Named for its sorrowful, drawn-out call, this species of dove is common in the bayou country. While most birds nest once a year, mourning doves mate four times, producing a total of eight eggs, two at a time. For all this, the dove population does not explode, partly because the nests are flimsy platforms of grass and sticks, unprotected from winds or rainstorms or tree-climbing predators, like snakes.

The bird we were watching could have been a male or a female; both share the duties of incubating the eggs. Richard's father guessed it was a male because, he said, the male often takes the daylight shift. Suddenly, as we stood there, the dove fluttered to the ground near the trunk of the tree. It fell in an awkward way, and for a moment lay still as if stunned; then it began to flop and hobble along in a frantic effort to get as far away from us as it could. I thought its wing was broken.

Mr. Breaux merely smiled. As we headed back to the canoe, I glanced over my shoulder. The bird's entire performance had been staged to distract our attention from its nest. Now that we had gone, it pulled its wing into shape, puffed itself out like a pouter pigeon, and immediately flew back up to sit on its eggs. Such tactics are common to many species of birds that nest on the ground with their eggs vulnerable to hungry foxes, snakes and skunks. Though the mourning dove of the forested Dorcheat can nest high on branches, it has developed the same decoying technique used by its kin in the plains and deserts of other states, where doves often lay eggs among grasses or rocks. As a means of keeping the species alive, most adult doves—even tree nesters—put on their act of helplessness whenever they sense danger to their young.

Farther south on the Dorcheat, where the red rolling hills were beginning to peter out, we rounded a curve in the stream and came upon a pair of pine trees—each probably older than a century—standing higher than any of the surrounding growth. Beside the pines in one of the countless tiny tributaries of the bayou, a white sand outcropping, as white as the sand on any beach, was visible under the broken mud-bank. Here in northern Louisiana, some 40 million years ago, had been the ancient coast of the Gulf of Mexico. The sand remained as a tes-

The stands of pine and hardwood trees that line the edges of northern bayous provide a meeting ground for four wild flowers that separately thrive in very different habitats elsewhere. Grass-pink orchids abound in bogs; jewelweed, also called touch-me-not for the way its seed pods burst open when touched, flourishes in marshes; the low-growing Carolina mallow often invades lawns, and spiderwort does as well in dry pinelands as in the moist soil near the bayous.

GRASS-PINK ORCHID

JEWELWEED

CAROLINA MALLOW

SPIDERWORT

tament to that time, and to the millions of streams that had appeared and disappeared, building up land southward into a wilderness of silt, water and green growth.

Several hundred yards beyond the two pines, the woods lay peaceful and quiet. Mr. Breaux drove the canoe in to shore. After we had prowled through the woods for an hour or so, he declared resttime, and we sat down in a clearing. But we were soon bored and restive, and Richard's father came up with another diversion. He raised his hands to his mouth, cupped them together, uttered a long, clear, plaintive cry, then lowered his hands. We waited, mystified. Nothing happened.

He was imitating the sound of a wild-turkey hen seeking a mate; it is not an easy cry to duplicate. Wild turkeys are famous for their keen hearing. A caller not only has to be accurate in the sound he makes, but must remain totally silent once he has made it. In springtime—the turkeys' mating season—the call of a single female wishing to join a tom turkey's harem carries for a great distance in the woods. On hearing it, a male will seek her out, strut, and spread his feathers. Even after the season, the hen's call may attract a curious male.

Mr. Breaux repeated the call twice more. But the quiet was broken only by the rustling of a breeze in the branches high above us and by the hard cry of a distant blue jay. I opened my mouth to say something. Mr. Breaux held a finger to his lips. The precaution struck me as silly, but I settled back.

Again he made the call; again there was no answer. My left leg was falling asleep, and I couldn't move without making some noise because I was sitting on a bed of dry leaves. I inched one knee up slowly. Richard's father frowned at me, and I decided to speak up whether he liked it or not; I was about to, when I saw something move over his shoulder, 20 yards behind him.

In the space between two red-oak trees, a big and powerful-looking tom turkey was scratching at the ground. Then he began to strut. Richard pointed, and his father nodded. So slowly that the movement was almost imperceptible, Mr. Breaux began to turn his head and shoulders. The tom, which had not seen us, stopped and looked around. Like many novice woodsmen under similar circumstances, I developed an immediate and overpowering desire to sneeze. I tried to control myself, but only partially succeeded, making a low, choked sound. The tom melted into the underbrush and disappeared from sight.

Richard's father looked at me hopelessly, and made the call again. For what seemed hours we waited in the clearing, and then another tom turkey appeared. He was larger than the first one, more deliberate in his movements. With a sort of slow-motion strut, he passed within 10 yards of where we sat and continued on into the underbrush.

That clearing was as far south as we went on the Dorcheat. Late that afternoon Mr. Breaux decided that we should begin the more difficult return trip upstream. After three days, we hoisted the canoe back onto the top of the car and left Louisiana's northern hills behind us.

I was not to see a bayou as wild as the Dorcheat for another three years. When I was 13, I had a look at a very different part of the bayou country under the guidance of my own father. This time there were no hills, no rolling country. The land was as flat as it is in New Orleans, and the trip much shorter than the way to the Dorcheat—a distance of no more than 100 miles. We headed southwest from the city on open country roads, past pale earth that seemed to grow darker and wetter as we traveled. Hackberry trees (called sugarberries in other states) were heavy with the sweet reddish fruit that Louisiana birds favor; live oaks were interspersed with the hackberries along the roadside. The white oaks I had seen rising 70 to 80 feet above the Dorcheat would have towered over these live oaks, no one of which could have been more than 40 feet tall. But what the live oaks lacked in height they made up for in breadth—stretching out their branches to make crowns 100 feet or more across. Both the deciduous white oaks and the related, but evergreen, live oaks bear acorns; but while the leaves of the white oak are deep lobed, paper thin and shaped like open hands, those of the live oak are oval, leathery textured and smooth edged.

The streams nearby were muddy, the color of milk chocolate, as if the earth had melted and begun to ooze. The clamshell roads over which we drove were white and dusty. Near the Gulf, clam and sometimes oyster shells—because they are plentiful, weigh less than gravel and are easier to haul—are used to surface everything from private driveways to secondary roads. The shells are dredged, mainly from Lake Pontchartrain, by machines that operate like giant vacuum cleaners. After the shells are deposited and spread in place, they are crushed with rollers. The bits compact quickly into a roadbed that is firm, but still resilient enough to flex with the jelly-like land beneath.

Finally we stopped at a broad stream; I got out of the car and walked up onto a levee to look down at the dark water. Lines of live oaks drooped and patches of long yellow spiked cane and green palmettos reared up from the banks like oversized hands, motionless in the shade of the trees. Waxlike leaves shone wetly, and the stream shone through them into darkness.

We were on Bayou Teche, the most elegant of all the bayous; though itself too civilized to be considered wilderness, it borders some of the least-traveled swamps of the Atchafalaya Basin. Originating near Port Baree, in the south-central part of the state, the Teche meanders south and east for more than 100 miles, curling lazily back and forth until it finally spills into Berwick Bay near the Gulf of Mexico.

Legend has it that a silver snake of fabulous proportions once terrorized the region of the Teche. When Indian warriors set out to kill the snake, they rained arrows into its body, and after they ran out of arrows used clubs on it. In its death agony the serpent cut huge grooves into the soil, which later became filled with water. The stream was known by the local Indian word for snake, *tenche,* which eventually was modified to Teche.

In the northern part of the Teche there is a long stretch of about 50 miles where the bayou is only 100 feet or so wide. Where we were walking, near its southernmost end, the bayou is twice as broad as that. On the opposite levee, we could make out clusters of dark green ferns and tall trees thickened with gray Spanish moss. The water between the banks ran slowly, dark and warm-looking under the sun. In the dusky light that pervades the Teche whatever the time of day, there are always shadows.

For the next days my father and I followed small bayous westward from the Teche through countryside that grew more and more wild-looking. A stream would go sometimes in one direction, sometimes in another; one led into a waterway so small it could hardly be called a bayou, then into a marshy spot that turned back into a larger stream. We didn't know where we were going, and yet it was as if the long walks were leading to some particular end. Anyone who has hiked through this wilderness has known the feeling. It is as if the streams are drawing you into a whirlpool of smaller and smaller circles, spiraling inward to a deep center that pulls you almost against your will.

One morning my father allowed me to wander off alone. Clumps of thorny dewberry bushes sprawled over the ground here and there, and I had to go around them. In doing so I changed direction many times, and by the time the sun was high I knew that I was lost. The streams I followed had an almost mesmerizing quality; the sluggish tempo of the bayou flow had taken over. The plants I saw seemed to grow faster than the streams themselves moved.

Once a small bird led me across a patch of clover-leaved wood sorrel through high grass to a stand of hackberry and magnolia trees. The magnolias were in full bloom, their scent so strong as to be almost overpowering. Within the dark green leaves the white blossoms seemed to be bursting. The sun was so bright I couldn't look up toward the sky for very long. Then the magnolias were behind me and I came upon a small stream. I veered to avoid stepping into it and found what I had been drawn to all along.

The end of the journey was a nameless place, a kind of arch of shadows. I stopped and looked around. Oaks and willows and cypresses on either side of the stream formed an interlocking fan above it. The water was motionless, dark brown, and the moss and leaves overhead nearly blotted out the sky. Tall reeds, a few jack-in-the-pulpits and wild dandelions lined the mudbanks. Something in the reeds stirred—a swamp rabbit. It looked at me, then calmly went back to munching.

There was a stillness, an airlessness about this place, as if the whole earth were holding its breath. Then without warning, a darkness fell. It happened so fast that for a moment I thought I had gone to sleep on my feet and lost track of time. A single wide, black shadow had blotted out the sun; the tops of the tree branches looked as though a pair of gigantic wings were hovering over them. Then there was a far-off lightning flash of dim white. Before the thunder could follow it, rain started to rattle through the leaves. Big warm drops sloped onto the earth from the black cloud above. The rain was gentle, and the dark was somehow comforting.

NATURE WALK / **Exploring the Dorcheat**

PHOTOGRAPHS BY ROBERT WALCH

At first glance, the Dorcheat gave every appearance of being a typical bayou. Its waters were moving slowly, even after several days of heavy spring rain, and ranks of bald cypress, sweet gum, water oak and other hardwoods crowded its banks. Yet an element classically associated with bayous was missing: no Spanish moss draped the branches of the cypresses. For the Dorcheat is a northern bayou.

Like other northern bayous, the Dorcheat, which rises in Arkansas and flows down into northwestern Louisiana, differs in three distinct ways from bayous in the south: it has better drainage, the atmosphere is less humid and the climate is cooler. As a result, there is less swamp area—although in spring the Dorcheat has its share—and the vegetation is not so lush. The curious thing is that none of this should affect Spanish moss. It could grow perfectly well in the northern part of the state, but for some unexplained reason only an occasional trace of it grows along the Dorcheat.

From a clearing at the bayou's edge that afforded a good view of its dark waters both upstream and down, the trail plunged into thick woods and then led upstream for about eight miles to a bridge near the Arkansas border. This part of the Dorcheat runs through a land of cattle ranches, lumbered forests and oil wells, but the river's array of animal life and its brooding, timeless aura made the human enterprises out of sight beyond the next ridge easy to escape—and forget.

Along the way this special quality of isolation was enhanced by the weather. All morning, thick spring rain clouds kept sweeping in to hang over the Dorcheat for a few moments, softening the greenery, scattering a few large drops of rain and briefly shutting off the rest of the world before being blown away by crisp gusts of wind. Then the bayou and its protective greenery would brighten in a wash of sunlight.

The thick woods along the bayou were loud with morning activity. Woodpeckers drummed their energetic beat as they drilled nest holes in live trees and combed dead trunks for meals of bark beetles, wood borers and termites. Two red-headed woodpeckers broke into a brief, furious fight; one paid for violating the territory of the other by being driven across the bayou. Overhead a turkey buzzard wheeled on the air currents, its crimson head sharply

HARDWOODS AT THE DORCHEAT'S EDGE

visible even at a distance. Also riding the currents was a pair of red-shouldered hawks. The hawks do very well for themselves at this time of year: the spring floods force many small creatures out of their natural cover onto ground where they are more vulnerable to aerial attack.

On the bank of the bayou stood a

BIRDHOUSES IN A CYPRESS

straight old bald cypress whose partially hollowed-out trunk was doing double duty as a riverside housing project. Half a dozen tiered holes in the tree, originally drilled by woodpeckers, were now being claimed as summer homes by other birds, perhaps several kinds, although on this morning only a couple of starlings were to be seen flitting in and out of their high-rise dwellings.

The old cypress made an admirable apartment house. During the scores of years it had grown beside the bayou, its leafy crown had been broken, probably a number of times, by lightning strikes or hurricanes. Exposed to the rain and weather, the interior of the trunk rotted, softened and slowly disintegrated from the top down. The tree did not die, how-

A SHY RED-EARED TURTLE

ever, since nourishment is carried to the growing parts through the trunk's outer layers. In fact the hollow trunk may have actually saved the life of the cypress by causing it to be passed over by the loggers who scour the Dorcheat in search of valuable lumber.

On a sun-dappled log a red-eared turtle pulled into its shell at the approach of potential danger. After a few moments its head reappeared, the red stripe behind each eye revealing the source of its name. Faced with the continued presence of interlopers, the turtle flipped itself with surprising agility into the water and swam off.

The trail led deeper into the woods, and suddenly there was plenty of water around—but no river. The spring rains had sent the Dor-

A BELL-BOTTOMED BALD-CYPRESS

cheat over its low-lying banks to inundate the flood plain; for miles around, hardwoods and pines rose spectrally from the calm, reflecting waters. Why was this section of the Dorcheat flooded, while downstream —and upstream too, as it turned out later in the day—the waters were contained by the banks?

Even at its swiftest, the Dorcheat never courses rapidly. It drops only about 80 feet in the 50-odd miles from the Arkansas border to Lake Bistineau just above the Red River —a descent so gradual that the bayou never builds up enough speed or power to gouge a very deep channel. But in some places, as here, a few miles south of the Arkansas border, the land is so flat the Dorcheat has practically no channel to deepen. It slows to a crawl and deposits much of its silt load. In the drier months the shallow sections of the riverbed become mud flats that require boatmen to portage their craft to the next stretch of water. But when spring rains swell the river, the portages are covered and the waters spread over the banks to creep into the forests. There they remain until the sun dries the land.

Of all the trees rising from the flood plain, the bald cypress appeared the most at home. With its huge, bell-bottomed trunk and enigmatic knees sticking up from its root system, the cypress is traditionally associated with warm, watery locales. By comparison, the loblolly pines seemed out of place, standing with the bottoms of their trunks temporarily concealed in the brown

water. Not as massive or majestic as the bald cypress, the loblolly pine nevertheless has its own grace as it rises 80 feet straight up.

The source of the name loblolly is as convoluted as the pine is straight. The word has a variety of meanings: in one sense, it is a kind of thick

A FLOODED LOBLOLLY

gruel, in another it betokens a loutish fellow, and in North Carolina it is used to describe a natural damp depression in the land where this particular type of pine prospers because its roots tolerate wet soil better than most pines.

The species is not limited to North Carolina, however, nor to damp ground. It is a relentless colonizer, a sort of weed among pines that thrives wherever its seeds can reach bare soil—particularly abandoned, burned or cutover fields. Because of this capacity for growing in neglected land, the loblolly has become one of the most common of the eastern evergreens. It is cut for lumber and cultivated for the manufacture of paper. Close examination of a low loblolly branch revealed the reason for the tree's ability to proliferate: a cluster of young male cones heavy with pollen. With the onset of sum-

mer, the cones would wither and fall off, but not before the wind had distributed the pollen widely to fertilize female cones.

The climb became steeper as a red clay ridge rose beside the Dorcheat's flood plain. Here the lower limbs of the loblolly pines were sparse. In the shade, deprived of sunlight, limbs die and fall off, in a kind of self-pruning. Only the upper branches

POLLEN-RICH PINE CONES

A RIDGETOP STAND OF LOBLOLLY

get enough sunlight to stay alive.

The seedlings of sweet gum and other hardwoods that were infiltrating the pine stand are not so choosy about sunlight. In time these tiny trees will carpet the entire floor below the pines, in shade where the pines' own seedlings have trouble surviving; the hardwoods will grow and win the competition for light. As they tower and spread their leafy branches, they will eventually triumph decisively over the pines.

Not only do the pines self-prune without sunlight, they also, in effect, self-destruct without it.

Ridges like this one were formed in an indirect way by the Mississippi River. As the silt it dumped built up the delta in the south, the weight of those deposits exerted tremendous pressure on the earth's crust. Like a massive seesaw, the land mass of northern Louisiana reacted to the weight in the south with an uplift, a geological phenomenon that formed the ridges and hills. The fulcrum for this seesaw is just above the capital of Baton Rouge in the south-central part of the state.

At the top of the ridge the sunlight glinted suddenly on the shiny green armor of a tiger beetle that was hurtling with flying leaps across the forest floor. The tiger beetle is a favorite of farmers and gardeners, not because of its handsome carapace but because it is an efficient enemy of various insect pests, such as the destructive gypsy moth. The little tiger beetles are downright voracious, in fact, and will attack creatures as large as snails.

TIGER BEETLE

COACHWHIP

MULLEIN PLANT

For a moment it even looked as though this beetle were about to tackle a snake; one long hop landed it right next to an eastern coachwhip coiled elegantly on a bed of dry pine needles. But neither creature showed any interest in the other. The beetle zoomed on its erratic course, and the snake continued to bask in the sun.

It is said that the coachwhip will curl itself around the leg of a man and whip him to death with its tail. Not true. Actually, the snake gets its name from the intricate pattern of scales that gives it an uncanny resemblance to a braided leather whip. The whiplike motion of the tail as the snake moves reinforces the name —and the legend. But rather than whipping, the snake depends for its defense primarily on protective coloration and speed.

Even so, this coachwhip caused one unnerving moment before it finally glided out of sight; its quivering tail tip struck some dead leaves and produced a sound exactly like the rattle of a diamondback.

Also getting the most from the sun was a mullein, an unassuming plant with a clump of soft, velvety leaves. In midsummer this prosaic plant sends forth a tall spike, one to two feet high, from which will bloom clusters of small yellow flowers. Mullein is a home remedy; the tea brewed from its leaves is much acclaimed as a relief for respiratory ailments. The plant also served a purpose in the days before commercially packaged rouge. When the hairy leaves were rubbed on the pale cheeks of local belles, they stimulated the blood to flow and produced a modestly lingering blush.

The trail eventually led over the red clay ridge and back down into the hardwood-dominated lowlands. The floodwaters still made it impossible to tell where the real bayou was —a shallow green pool lay in a depression among the trees. But already the spring sun was drying up the water, and in a few weeks the leaf-strewn floor would be dry again.

On a log in the forest a little cotton mouse was resting, with the haggard look of a creature that has endured many hardships. And well it might have. For during this time of flooding, all creatures, including snakes and mice, are driven into the narrowing dry zones together. With their hunting ranges reduced by the waters, the snakes are in keen competition for the mice. The mice thus live in extra jeopardy, and must be especially alert to survive.

There certainly seemed to be a lot of snakes about. In short order two more appeared—first a harmless black rat snake, then a young but deadly copperhead. As the name implies, the rat snake is a consumer of rodents; this one, initially drawn by the cotton mouse, now found it was confronted and cornered by a human enemy. Like the coachwhip, its tail vibrating among some dead leaves, the rat snake sent out an ominous —but meaningless—rattle. It lunged forward, mouth open in a display of ferocity, but the show was temporary; it moved off smoothly into the underbrush. Also like the coachwhip, the speedy rat snake is a

BAYOU OVERFLOW IN THE WOODS

nimble climber, and is likely to make its nest in made-to-order cavities of high, hollow trees.

The copperhead blended so perfectly into the background of dead leaves that only a trained eye could have spotted it from more than a few feet away. Camouflage is one of its defenses, but poison is its heavy artillery—it belongs to the same group as the rattlesnake and cottonmouth. The copperhead is known as the highland moccasin while the cottonmouth is called the water moccasin.

Copperheads are night feeders, generally lethargic by day, and this one lay coiled in its defensive posture without striking out. A trace of yellow on its tail indicated that the snake was slightly more than a year old. For the first year, the copperhead's tail is a greenish yellow, which then slowly disappears. The snake endured a cautious inspection and then, after some defensive pos-

COTTON MOUSE

DOGWOOD IN FLOWER

turing, executed a graceful retreat.

Even in the shade the late morning was warm, particularly when the breezes languished, but the dimness and humidity were evidently just right for a flowering dogwood tree, which illuminated the woods with a pastel display of tiny yellow flowers centered in symmetrical white petal-like bracts. Dogwood is an exceptional plant in that it can carry on normal photosynthesis at one third full sunlight. While other plants wither and the growth of other trees is stifled in the shade, the dogwood thrives as though it were drenched in full sunlight.

For some time the way had led through forest and flooded woods that denied a view of the Dorcheat itself. But now, just beyond a thick patch of saplings and underbrush, the bayou reappeared, flowing serenely once again within the limits of its regular channel. A perfume

COPPERHEAD

RAT SNAKE

came wafting on the wind from a tall bush of wild azalea. Honeybees were seeking the sweet nectar from its upper branches. The blossoms of the wild azalea are so fragrant, the taste of them so sweet, that it is known locally as honeysuckle, even though it is quite different from the vine plant of the same name.

way of the bridge, and cultivated land lay beyond the ridge on the other side. Noisily confirming the nearness of human enterprise, a farm pickup truck suddenly rattled over the bridge, its driver unmindful of the bayou. Civilization had intruded abruptly and shattered the mood of the time and the place.

WILD AZALEA

BLACK-CHERRY BLOSSOMS

The drooping blooms of a young wild-black-cherry tree also enlivened the bayou's edge. If it grows in a field away from the competition of the forest, the wild black cherry usually has a stubby trunk and knotty branches. But in the woods, competing for light with other trees, it may rise to a height of 100 feet with a trunk five feet in diameter.

A long, low bridge spanning the Dorcheat marked the walk's end. A county road crossed the bayou by

Yet as the dust of the vehicle's passing settled, the warm, sunny midday grew still again. The bridge afforded a wide view of the bayou and the thick stands of hardwoods along both banks. A twisted, dead branch jutted from the water, causing only the faintest disturbance in the gentle current. The bayou's wildness slowly reestablished itself; and, as if for emphasis, a woodpecker drummed its tattoo against a tree in the deep woods not 50 yards away.

THE VIEW FROM THE BRIDGE

3/ Hurricane in the Atchafalaya

*Then the Wind grew weird. It ceased being a breath;
it became a Voice moaning across the world — hooting —
uttering nightmare sounds.* LAFCADIO HEARN/ CHITA

It was years after my trips to Bayou Dorcheat and Bayou Teche, during a humid week in late summer, that I discovered the region I came to think of as quintessential bayou country, and encountered the storm responsible for giving that area a justified reputation as a place of danger —hurricane country.

Hurricane is a word that means little to those who have not seen at least the edge of such a storm. We read in the newspapers that a hurricane has struck some coast, done so many dollars' worth of damage, and passed on. Perhaps a few lives have been lost—perhaps more than a few. Often 25-foot-high storm swells, started out at sea by the winds, have raced the hurricane to the coast and are reported to have caused more havoc than the storm itself. The story appears in the papers one day, two or three at most, then is gone as the storm is gone and we think no more about it.

In New Orleans, with the Gulf Coast and hurricane country nearby, the word is a more familiar one, and a few facts accumulate around it through the years. I remembered, for instance, hearing that the great hurricane that struck Florida on Labor Day in 1935 killed 150 people and did six million dollars' worth of damage. In science class at school I learned something about how our own Louisiana hurricanes are believed to form: over the mid-Atlantic near the equator in summer, two winds coming from opposite directions may meet and start to twirl around each other in a counterclockwise motion that is accentuated by the forces of the earth's rotation. Hot moist air from the ocean beneath the winds is drawn up into the center. As this air rises and cools, its moisture condenses and throws off heat that releases extra energy into the rotating mass, making it rise and spin even faster. As more and more tropical sea air sweeps in to replace the rising air, condensation quickens to create thunderclouds around the core, or eye, of the towering ring-shaped storm. It becomes an official, full-fledged hurricane, I learned, when its internal winds reach a speed of 74 mph. Meantime the storm has started to move northwest at about 10 mph, gathering momentum and intensity.

Usually hurricanes never hit land at all, but blow themselves out at sea. When they do come ashore they can hit anywhere from the West Indies to New England; occasionally they thread their way across the Gulf of Mexico to strike Louisiana. As a schoolboy I knew that the official hurricane season for southern Louisiana begins the first of June and ends the 30th of November, and that the peak of the season is during the month of September.

Yet statistics such as these never quite take on reality. They remain as remote as a set of old road maps tucked into a cupboard. And so, when a high-school classmate asked me, one hot August, to join him for a week of fishing in the Atchafalaya swamp, I jumped at the chance. I knew there was a hurricane brewing in the Gulf, everybody did—it had been announced in the papers and over the radio—but if it struck shore at all, it was expected to hit south and west of where we were going. The enormous swamp filling the 75-mile-long Atchafalaya River Basin, which I had long wanted to explore, was nowhere near the course the storm was taking; besides, I had never heard of a storm, even a bad one, doing much damage to a place like that. The fact that a hurricane can alter its course several times in a single day didn't disturb me because I didn't know about it. Nor did I consider that storm damage to uninhabited swampland is not reported in detail for a very simple reason —no one is there to report it.

I wedged the butt of a fishing rod into a duffel bag with some old clothes, a few cans of food and a thermos of coffee, and stood on a street corner in the French Quarter of New Orleans waiting for Jim to pick me up. It was 4 o'clock in the morning; like all fishermen we wanted to get an early start. The sky was deep blue-black, the air heavy with heat, and nothing seemed further away than danger of any kind. When Jim pulled up in an old truck, I hopped in and we took off across the bridge to the other side of the Mississippi River, heading west.

In little over an hour and a half we reached what Jim called his parents' hunting lodge. A few hundred yards from the banks of a bayou, it was one of a small group of jerry-built shacks owned by city families who used them as bases from which to go fishing and frogging and crawfishing and crabbing, and to shoot squirrel and rabbit and deer. We arrived before dawn, but after one look at the line of trucks already waiting to launch boats from the makeshift dock at the water's edge, we decided to spend the day some other way and go fishing the next morning when we could get an even earlier start.

After we got the truck unpacked and made some breakfast, we turned on the radio in the shack. A news announcer said that the hurricane, still in the Gulf, was moving forward at 15 mph in a northwesterly direction, and was expected to hit the low-lying Louisiana coastal areas, not far from the Texas border, by nightfall. We turned the radio off and thought no more about it.

We spent most of the day enjoying the bird songs in the trees around us. There were dozens of warblers, among them the prothonotary warbler—a beautiful bird no larger than a canary, with slate-blue wings and a bright yellow head and breast. Jim spotted an indigo bunting, and I a painted bunting, its gaudily colored body lashed indiscriminately with rose red, yellow-green and violet blue, as if paint had been thrown at it by a drunken artist.

The gray moss overhead fascinated us too, trailing in places for more than a yard, touching the ground or the surface of the water. This moss has become so closely identified with bayous that it is a kind of symbol of them. There is something moody and dark, a sense of brooding, about its gray presence in the pervasive green. The rival French and Spanish explorers who came to this wilderness both marveled at the moss, and vied with one another in attempting to name it. The story is that the French called it, somewhat derisively, *barbe espagnole,* Spanish beard; the Spaniards countered by dubbing it *peluca francesa,* or Frenchman's wig. The French won out and today it is known as Spanish moss; its scientific name is *Tillandsia usneoides.*

Local Indian legend—which has an explanation for most things found in the bayou country—tells of a girl killed by an enemy tribe during her wedding ceremony. Her mourning family cut off her hair and spread it on the limbs of the oak tree under which she was buried. The hair then blew from tree to tree, finally turning gray, and it endures as a tribute to those who are not fated to live out their love. The facts are less ro-

Outside its nest hole in a charred tree stump, a prothonotary warbler prepares to digest its catch. An annual warm-weather visitor to Louisiana from Central America, the warbler was named by local Creoles for the yellow-garbed prothonotaries who are prelates of the Roman Catholic Church.

mantic. Botanically, Spanish moss is not a true moss; it is a member of the pineapple family and is epiphytic—nourished by air. It isn't a parasite, as is commonly believed, nor does it smother the trees it lives in. It can grow just as well in dead trees as in live ones, for it feeds only on dust carried through it by breezes. It bears tiny emerald-green flowers, like minute lilies, that cannot be seen from more than a few yards away, but carry cylindrical seed pods. The parent plant reproduces not only by seeding but also by breaking off when swayed by winds; bits of moss landing on other branches continue to grow at a steady rate, averaging about an inch a month.

Through the years Spanish moss has been gathered for many uses. The Indians clothed their infants in it, used it to bolster their reed-and-mud huts, and even claimed to cure illness with it. A sick man would be wrapped in many layers of the moss and laid on a high cane bed set over a charcoal fire topped by boiling herbs. The vapors and heat rising through the moss produced a heavy sweat in the patient, which was believed to rid his system of disease.

Jim and I spent that first evening listening to the bayou frog chorus. The green frog, locally known as the banjo frog because its voice rattles like a loose banjo string, was most conspicuous among the other croakers. One green frog sat motionless and silent at the base of a hackberry tree as we watched—its tongue darting in and out for bugs so fast that we were unaware of the movement until a delicate shimmering dragonfly, caught on the wing, lay folded and crushed in the frog's small green jaws.

We went to sleep very early and woke four hours after midnight to make breakfast and load the family's fishing yacht (an old rowboat aided by a rusty outboard motor) onto a platform on wheels that hooked to the back of the truck. While we were working, a man from a neighboring shack came by and told us of the latest radio announcement. The hurricane had veered off course and had struck the Gulf Coast earlier than expected; it was southwest of us, but no official warning had been given to evacuate our area. Still, it was best to be on the safe side, the neighbor added—you could never tell about a hurricane.

Jim and I decided not to stay out in the bayous longer than half a day. If the hurricane were to head anywhere near our vicinity, which seemed unlikely, noon would be time enough to get out of its way. While hurricane winds have been known to rise to 200 mph, the forward movement of the hurricane itself is rarely much faster than 15 to

20 mph. The storm was now almost 150 miles off, and there seemed no reason not to go fishing.

We drove the truck to the dock along a road lined with magnolia trees. A thick black predawn sky was paling slowly at the edges to ash-blue; overhead it was heavily overcast, like a dark sagging roof above the land. The air, even though sunup was an hour away, was fevered with summer. On the southwest horizon the sky briefly gleamed now and then with the ominous, soundless glow of heat lightning. The mist was heavy enough to require the use of windshield wipers. At the land-ing—a small area of earth packed with white clamshells—the rank metallic smell of the water was mixed with the fresh smell of live fish and the sweet scents of honeysuckle and verbena. We were early enough this time to beat the crowd. In 10 minutes we were on the water headed for the center of the swamp, with the outboard motor chugging comfortably at the stern. Other small fishing boats took off from the landing and disappeared quickly in the distance. The fish we were out to catch—green trout, sac-a-lait, bream—were in the small bayous that intertwined the large swamp to our west. Actually, fishing merely gave our excursion a purpose; what we really wanted was to see the swamp without parental guidance.

Above us now the trees were becoming loud with bird song. The birds were noisier than usual, we decided, because of the cloudy weather. The far bank was lined with cypress and willow trees. Jim headed be-tween them into a stream that led away at a right angle from the one we were on; we followed it for about half a mile, then took a smaller stream that forked off, then another fork that branched from that, then still another. Soon we were in a maze of quiet small bayous—mean-dering streams that seemed to lead nowhere. The dawn was coming fast, the sky clogged with clouds, an occasional break of misty blue showing through like pale smoke. High in the east, a lone heron streaked silently over the swamp. We came to another narrow stream and Jim took it. Then he turned the motor off, and let the skiff drift.

Without the chugging of the engine, in the sudden silence, we felt un-easy. Neither of us made any move to take out a fishing rod. I noticed that Jim pressed the palms of his hands over his ears and released them twice, as if to test his hearing ability. I heard nothing. The silence lay about us like a sleep. We avoided each other's eyes and sat drifting, say-ing nothing. The skiff moved more slowly, finally coming to a stop, poised over the stream.

A haze over an eerily still bayou, caused by moisture build-up in high-altitude clouds, heralds a change in the weather, possibly a storm.

The silence in a cypress swamp seems, oddly, to contain some mysterious sound. It is as if all the small ordinary noises of day were removed to make the ear ready for something else—something that can almost be heard, but not quite. Jim and I sat, straining our ears, focusing our attention on the thing we only sensed was there. All around us ripples in the water glided outward from the skiff and broke soundlessly on the mud embankments. Then some ordinary noises seemed to come back, but from a distance. A red-winged blackbird called a few raucous notes from a nearby branch, but the bird, and the branch too, seemed somehow removed from us.

Of its own accord the skiff began to move again slowly. We passed a line of water-ash trees arrayed like friendly ghosts on the bank. Jim ducked to avoid an overhanging branch, its tip supporting a small brownish wasp's nest. Alongside the boat, minuscule insects made dents and streaks in the water without ever breaking its surface. A sudden patch of mosquitoes zoomed past and slipped into the silence. Palmettos bent forward, their flat-fingered leaves limp in the heavy air. The skiff drifted, then stopped again, its bow nuzzling a knotty cypress "knee" that jutted out of the stream.

Cypress, the most abundant tree in Louisiana swamps, has an odd look: it appears to be waiting for some unforeseeable event. The tree before us, its feathery deep-green leaves punctuated by gray moss, stood like a mourner in readiness, seeming to be supported by the knees, which rose from its roots. Whether the knees do actually help the tree stand firm in its base of muck is not certain. There are various other theories as to their function—that they are exposed in order to increase the tree's intake of oxygen, or that they serve to store nutriments for it. Whatever the reason for the knees, the cypress seems indestructible. In this part of the world its lumber is known as wood eternal.

The bow of the skiff drifted off the cypress knee and we moved on, passing more cypresses and other trees as well—sweet gum, persimmon, water locust—their branches and leaves mingled in a canopy overhead. A gray squirrel, called a cat squirrel here, ran along a branch of a tupelogum tree and hurdled the stream, landing on a tree on the opposite bank. Yellow-throated warblers filtered from nests built on bunches of Spanish moss high in the tips of the branches, out of reach of all but the most intrepid of snakes.

The sky had taken on a gray, bloated look; it was a single mass of clouds swollen with light, almost too bright to look at without squinting. Jim turned his head, and I followed his glance. High up on the bank to our left lay the wreck of a skiff like ours. Only its skeleton hull and a few boards with rusty nails remained, a testament to some long-past surge of wind and water that had lifted and deposited it so far out of the stream. Jim and I decided not to fish today, but instead just tour for a while. Jim started the motor again and we turned back to one of the wider streams behind us. The main bayou—the one we had taken at our first turn—had divided and redivided so many times it was impossible to tell whether we were headed north or south, east or west. We should have brought a compass, but had neglected to do so; now we would have to rely on our general sense of direction.

It is easy to get lost in the Atchafalaya. In fact, it is a rash idea to go in at all without a guide who is so familiar with each bend and turn that he can travel in his sleep. To the two of us, 17 years old and uninitiated, one stream looked like another; we recognized the main bayou, when we finally reached it, only because of its size. A few cottonwoods and sycamores grew here along with the cypresses, and the earth itself had a verdant look. The bayou water, too, was greenish, reflecting trees like a mirror image of the swamp life above. To check our depth, Jim dug an oar upright into the water. Halfway down it stuck in mud. The soil lay only a little way beneath the surface of the water just as water lurked only a little way beneath the surface of the earth that supported the trees. The swamp was neither solid nor liquid, earth nor water, but a thickened mixture of both.

The light in the sky had grown grayer. Two great blue herons streaked by; in the darkening morning their wings appeared to brush the treetops. Then a peal of thunder sounded. The next moment a few raindrops dotted the water. I felt some on my arms and the back of my neck. Jim poled the skiff beneath the protective branches of a cypress. Neither of us minded the rain; it seemed a part of things in this wilderness. Not just water and earth, but water, earth and sky were one around us —like the roots and trunk and leaves of a single tree. We watched as the rain increased from a mass of dots to a solid sheet. Jim glanced up at the cypress branches. So far, the leaves were shielding us relatively well; we knew, though, that if the squall lasted more than 15 minutes or so, the cypress would no longer provide any protection. But rainstorms in the swamp rarely last long; they come and go with each passing cloud. The trouble was, the cloud above us could not pass. It covered the entire sky. The word "hurricane" was in our minds by now, though neither of us had spoken it aloud.

Half an hour later the rain was cascading down on our heads; our high boots were full and sloshing, our clothes clinging to our bodies. Jim pointed over my shoulder in the general direction of the clamshell dock from which we had set out. I nodded, and he started the motor and aimed the skiff into the center of the bayou. Water was rising in the bottom of the boat; I took a can and began to bail as Jim steered. Despite the summer heat, the rain felt cold, and we shivered. Ahead, the streaks of water were so thick it was impossible to see more than a few yards. Another fishing skiff loomed out of the rain and veered off to our port side. As it passed, Jim yelled, "Are you going in?" The two men in the other boat, both covered in yellow slickers, nodded. Without another word, Jim reversed direction; we turned in a tight arc and began to follow them. Then we looked at each other and laughed. If the men had not come along it would have been nothing to laugh about; we had been going the wrong way—deeper into the swamp rather than out of it.

Following in the wake of the other skiff, we relaxed and the unspoken fear we had felt turned to an exhilaration close to euphoria. Jim began to yodel under the cascading sheets of water. I joined in. We did not know that the squall, bad as it seemed to be, was only one of the small cloudbursts that sometimes precede a dangerous tropical storm; we did not know that the front edge of the hurricane, which had changed direction again, now lay only about a hundred miles to the south of us. The storm was approaching the swamp in an unerring straight line. The skiff chugged along merrily, and the branches on either bank of the bayou dipped and swayed in the pelting water as if the trees were bowing to us. The place felt safe. The look of it was extraordinary. The vast mist of the Atchafalaya rose all around us like steam, monochrome and thick, heavy and wet.

We docked at the landing, dripping and shivering, almost three hours before our noon deadline. As we maneuvered the boat onto the trailer, an old fisherman next to us wiped the streaming water out of his eyes with the back of his wrist, looked up at the gray glare of the sky, and shook his head. "You all better get out of here fast," he said, without looking at us, in the voice of a man who has spent much of his life trying, vainly, to cope with the idiosyncrasies of city folk. I said the storm didn't look that bad. "Storm?" he said, "this ain't no storm." The old man looked straight at me; his pale eyes flashed like a fish coming to the surface of the water. "You all better get out of here," he said again, in a firm, low tone. Then he turned and walked up the landing.

Back at the shack, Jim and I took off our wet clothes and rubbed ourselves down with towels. We put on dry jeans and sweaters and brewed some coffee on the ancient stove to warm us. Outside, the rain was still coming down—no slower, no faster. I told Jim what the old fisherman had said, and he scoffed. "Uncle of mine has a summer house about fifty miles northwest of here," he said, "big enough to hold up under any storm. He'll put us up if we want. If the hurricane comes, we can watch it from the house . . . maybe go out in it." I said I wondered whether we ought to chance driving there. "Hell," Jim said, swallowing a smile, "if you're chicken. . . ." I rose and packed my things quickly, and we locked the front door and ran out to the truck. Jim started the motor and we headed up a dirt road that led northwest. About 25 miles on, the rain suddenly ceased. Jim glanced in my direction and grinned. "See?" he said, cocksure. "I told you."

After three more dirt roads and another hour, we turned onto a clam-shell driveway flanked by hackberry and live-oak trees. This part of the swamp country was heavily wooded; we had seen no other building of any kind for the last 20 miles. As we pulled up under the branches of a big oak near the garage I saw a glint of dark water beyond the trees on the far side of the house where the place bordered the eastern edge of the swamp. Jim went up to the door and rang the bell while I stood in the driveway and watched the sky. Its harsh, blinding look had given way to a glow that pulsated through the unending bank of clouds. The sky dipped dangerously at the center; it gave the impression of a water-filled canvas. A distant muted rumble came from it, as though the canvas had begun to tear. Jim turned his head and stared blankly at me from the front door. "No answer," he said. He walked along the side of the house and disappeared around a corner.

I stayed where I was, watching the sky and the earth. A green chameleon slithered past my foot, its body turning dull brown as it crawled along a branch that had fallen in the rain, then changing back to green as it jumped off and went running into the wet grass. The cloud bank above the southern horizon had taken on a sickly yellowish tint. It was an eerie light for 11 o'clock in the morning. Except for the water that dripped from the leaves of the big oak and the gutter of the house, there was no sound. It was as quiet here as it had been in the center of the swamp. A window went up in the second story of the house and Jim stuck his head out. "Nobody's home," he said. "I climbed up the grape arbor. Attic window was open. Come on." His head disappeared, and after a moment the front door swung back. I followed him in. Jim

A familiar sight in the fickle skies of southern Louisiana, storm clouds menace a willow-lined channel of the Atchafalaya River.

made some joke about breaking into his own uncle's property, and we both pretended not to know that the house had been evacuated because of the coming storm.

The silence within the walls was as solid and tomblike as the silence outside. Except for the occasional cry of a bird, the world around us seemed to have died. By now we both wanted to leave, but neither of us had the guts to suggest running. I said something flip about getting out of the swamp before the swamp got us. "Where would we go?" Jim said. "Might as well sit it out here. Big enough house. . . ." He walked away before I could answer and opened the doors that gave onto a screened gallery outside.

The south side of the house faced a bayou that led into the swamp beyond; we stood on the gallery looking at the view. A grizzled swamp rabbit with bristling ears squatted on the near bank of the bayou, looking at us. Then it turned slowly and faced the southern bank. The sky in the south had turned a deeper yellow. We stood there without speaking. Jim heard the sound before I did. "Listen to them," he said. "Lord . . . listen to them."

He opened the screen door quickly and I went out after him. We stood on the grass between the house and the bayou. Then I heard the sound too. It seemed to be coming from the branches themselves, as if the swamp trees were calling out. "What is it?" I asked. "Herons," Jim said. "And blackbirds. And ibises probably, and warblers . . . all the swamp birds together."

We waited, listening to the eerie sound. It was unmistakable: the bird calls had changed. These were not mating cries, or flight notes such as those heard from a flock of geese on the wing. Instead the birds were calling all at the same time, many species at once, producing a sharp edgy sound like a wail. There was an ugliness in the collective noise, comparable to a human voice wavering on the edge of hysteria. As a child I had heard stories of the change in the sound of bird cries before a hurricane strikes, but I had never really believed them. I had not yet learned that some bayou-country legends are based in fact, and this was one of them.

An hour passed, I think, or two—my sense of time was lost. By now the noise of the birds had broken into its separate parts, gathered again into a single chorus, shattered once more, and ended. The quiet was back, and beyond the line of trees something flopped and splashed in the bayou. The grass glistened hard under a jaundiced sky. I don't know how long we stood there before the yellow turned abruptly into the color of copper. Then the wind started.

At first it did not seem bad. It came in from the east; leaves fluttered, and the grass bent. Then the light deepened, and the wind left as quickly as it had come. Jim nudged me hard and pointed excitedly. A cougar was slinking along the high limb of a tupelo gum, its body gleaming like a bar of gold caught in the copper glow of the sky. It leaped to the branch of another tree, and from there to the earth, the slow majestic arcs of its movements magnified in the humid air. For an instant after touching ground it froze, motionless; then it was gone. We did not see it bound off into the underbrush or slink behind a tree; it merely vanished from sight. Cougars are rare in the swamp; I had never seen one before, I have never seen one since. The last image of it remained like a brand on the retina, and I stood staring at space for a long time. I could still see the hot gold shape of the cat that was no longer there, when the wind came back.

The second gust was longer, but not much harder than the first; the interval after it was shorter. The third gust brought the rain. I started to go inside, but Jim grabbed my arm; he wanted us to wait and watch the storm as long as we could from outside. I had read enough to know that high winds, accompanied by heavy rains, usher in the most dangerous period of a hurricane, and I wasn't as entranced as Jim was by the prospect of the beauty of the coming storm. I was more inclined to see what could be done about making the house safer than it looked. Evidently Jim's uncle had left hurriedly when the storm changed its course; no storm shutters were up and only two windows had been taped. For a while we stayed outside watching, as time after time the trees across the bayou bent, seeming almost to double over. Moss bounced in the branches. Small objects and bits of things began to blow over the water, as twigs, leaves, pieces of bark and birds' nests broke loose.

Inside the house, I found a roll of tape on a window sill, and began to make an X across each pane of glass to prevent it from shattering. After a while Jim came in and helped me. His face looked flushed; his eyes glittered as if in fever. Many animals, humans included, work themselves up to a high pitch in the face of a hurricane; apparently, the body makes ready to protect itself with an extra dash of adrenaline. I wondered if the cougar that had vanished faster than my eye could follow had felt the same strange excitement. Jim and I worked silently, taping the panes of glass, listening to the wind rise. The tape ran out before we had finished with all the east windows on the ground floor of the house; we left the windows on the west unprotected. There was not much we could do about it. Jim went to the kitchen to check the food supply, and I went to latch the outer screen door, which was flapping loudly back and forth on the gallery. The gusts of wind were violent now. The rain fell, not with an even slant as it had before, but in fierce curls and streaks, hissing and lashing like whips of water through the trees. As I opened the inside door to get to the screen door, I saw a full-grown raccoon at the gallery railing staring at me. At first I thought it had huddled there to get out of the wind; then, from the angle of its head and the peculiar slant of its shoulders, I realized that its neck was broken. Probably it had crawled from the hackberry tree nearest the house to the roof and had been blown off trying to get to the gallery. Beyond the house the wind ripped savagely at the moss in the trees. Some moss came loose and streaks of gray flew over the grass like torn pieces of sky. I shut and latched both doors and went back to help Jim in the kitchen. "You were right," he said. "I guess it's coming to get us."

By now the wind was a fierce, endless shriek, rising and falling. Every so often something hit the roof or a side of the house, and the whole place seemed to shudder on its foundations. Through the kitchen window I saw a large, bulky dark object lumbering with difficulty against the wind, across the space between the gallery and the bayou. On its lee side, protected at least partially from the wind, was a much smaller but equally bulky-looking object. "Black bears," Jim said. We watched as the female and cub disappeared in the lashing streaks of water. The rain was so heavy we could no longer see the bayou, and the wind was coming stronger all the time.

The woods all around were being shaken, as if some giant invisible rage had unleashed itself on the bayou. Trees bent their branches wildly in every direction. A few small animals skittered across between them, too fast to be identified; leaves and vines twisted high in the air. Something struck the roof with a force that reverberated like an earthquake in the kitchen, and the lights went out. The wind screamed in the half-dark; debris began to collect on the outside of the windows, to be blown away and collect again in the next vicious gust. A burst and a loud shattering of glass from the living room told us that the tape had not worked for all of the east windows.

Then, with a violence that seemed methodical, the wind rose higher. Beyond the trees, the bayou was a shapeless dark mass of water with waves and whitecaps, and the mass was approaching the house. Already the near line of cypress and tupelo gum and hackberry were in water halfway up their trunks. The swamp seemed to be growing, feeding on the fury of the hurricane, threatening to whirl the house and everything it contained into the wilderness of air, water and land. Jim darted across the kitchen and looked outside at the truck. I could tell what he was thinking. "We couldn't make it," I said. He shrugged. "We'll try," he said, "if the water comes much closer."

We stood and watched as the churning lake that had once been a bayou came toward us through the trees. "If it reaches that hackberry," Jim said, looking at the tree trunk nearest the gallery, "we'll start." We kept our eyes on it, and 20 minutes later the water was lapping over its roots. "Let's go," Jim said. I found a rope in a cupboard and Jim tied it to his waist. I held one end so that I could anchor him and pull him back if necessary while he tried to make it to the truck. The noises were at their wildest now, first on one side of the house, then on the other; the scraping of swamp debris sounded as though the storm were clawing at the walls. Jim opened the front door and I tightened the rope behind him. Then through the lashes of rain I saw that there wasn't any point in his getting to the truck. The big oak in the yard had been snapped like a pencil; it was lying half on top of the truck, half behind it. In the deafening wind we had not even heard the tree fall. I pulled hard on the rope and Jim fought the wind to make it back the four feet he had walked. In those four feet I thought he might be going to die. The wind slammed him against the house, and the rope grew so taut I was afraid it would cut through him. But at last he got inside and shut and bolted the door—as if a door, or a bolt, could have any effect on a storm that might destroy the house as easily as the oak outside.

The kitchen and living room were ankle-deep in muddy water by now. We grabbed armfuls of canned goods from a shelf, along with a can opener, and ran upstairs. We sat in one of the bedrooms away from the windows and watched. There wasn't much else to do but wait and hope. Then, as if a giant cleaver had descended from the sky and cut off all sound, the wind stopped.

The rain no longer fell. Calm came so suddenly that neither of us knew what to make of it. For a moment we sat where we were, Jim on one twin bed, I on the other, staring into space. Then we jumped up and opened the windows.

Outside, the swamp, the entire wilderness, was as still and soundless as a vacuum. No trees, not even the moss, swayed. What had once been a bayou, and was now a lake surrounding the house, was speckled with drops falling from leaves and soaked branches. The air was heavier than ever and there was a choked feeling to it that made it difficult to breathe. "The eye," Jim said. "We must be in the eye."

We ran to the top of the stairs, then stopped. The water had come up to the third step. There was no point in trying to get out of the house any more—there was no way to leave and no place to go anyway. We went slowly to a window and looked out. The swamp was a glittering maze of broken branches, leaves and swollen water. The last drops shone like jewels in the scene of silent devastation. I remembered reading that especially along the coast the worst danger in the aftermath of a hurricane came from snakes that try to climb onto high ground or even the rafters of partly submerged houses to escape the encroaching water. We were already flooded, and the flood would get worse, and I wondered about the snakes.

Before that problem, we would have to face the second half of the storm. It would be at least as bad as the first, I knew. We sat on the window ledge and looked below us. In the rain gutter a pileated woodpecker lay smashed and dead, its body twisted, one wing bent double under it. The gutter itself had been torn loose; half of it stuck out from the eaves like a long broken bone. The silence was complete. We had been shouting in order to hear each other during the first part of the storm. Now the ticking of a bedside clock clucked out of the room behind us, sharp and loud, the only noise for miles around. It was marking the minutes until the eye passed and the far side of the hurricane struck.

We watched the wreckage in the wilderness and waited for the wind.

The Spell of the Swampland

The storied bayous of literary tradition, those shadowy places of still water, Spanish moss and mystery, really do exist, and they are as numerous as the very different-looking bayous of Louisiana's hill country and of its marshes. Like those waterways, the poetic bayous have acquired their special character because of their particular setting—the swamps that cover vast areas of the south-central part of the state.

One such area is the Atchafalaya Basin, a great soggy expanse along the 150-mile course of the Atchafalaya River. Another is the sprawling region, about 60 miles northwest of New Orleans, where the Blind River and other streams interweave in a tangled skein. These low, flat swamplands are alluvial—built up and molded by river waters that have overflowed their natural levees and, through the millennia, have deposited an immeasurably huge cargo of particles of solid matter.

Regularly nourished by water and sediment, this alluvial soil is among the richest anywhere in the world. Vegetation in the swamps grows wildly, engulfing everything—and as it decays it further enriches the muck that nurtured it. The wealth of plant food attracts a variety of animals. Though none are exclusively swamp dwellers, they take easily to the environment. Many are aquatic, or at least amphibious, but deer and other land mammals also cope well with the watery surroundings.

The swamp bayou reflects its setting in all aspects. The prodigal vegetation encloses it in dim, leafy, vaulted chambers, an inner sanctum where the sun seems an intruder. The water of the bayou moves faintly and sluggishly, fluctuating in depth from time to time. Some of the water is pure and sweet, though often stained the color of dark tea by the bark and fallen leaves of trees growing in it. Some bayous are muddy and thick with sediment, others are covered from bank to bank with plants (right).

Both the swamp bayou and the terrain in which it lies represent yet another of the ambiguous compromises between earth and water that characterize much of the rest of Louisiana. Where there is solid land in the swamps, it often bears the mark of man—roads, houses and fishing shacks. But in the deeper reaches, where a boat is the only way to get around, a primeval world prevails, discovered yet inscrutable, accessible but supremely detached.

A quiet stream, overhung with Spanish moss and carpeted with vegetation, exemplifies the classic swamp bayou. The lush green carpet on the water's surface, at first glance seen as scum or slime, is actually a delicate mosaic of the tiny leaves of duckweed, one of the world's smallest flowering plants.

A Splurge of Riotous Growth

Except for its dark waters, the element that most shapes the Louisiana swamp is its luxuriant vegetation, at once beautiful and ugly, airborne and earthbound, fragile and indestructible. Mosses, vines, trees, air plants, water plants, algae, ferns assault every surface, screening the bayous, disguising each contour and defining every vista.

Lord of all is the bald cypress, rising smooth-trunked and stately from the water, with its strange gnarled knees standing nearby like dwarf sentinels. The seeds of the cypress need water-saturated soil to germinate in, and the wood is extremely durable and resistant to rot, which makes the tree admirably suited to swamp conditions—and also makes it coveted for the construction of houses, picket fences and coffins.

Crowding the cypresses at water level are water hyacinths, which grow floating on the surface and spread irresistibly wherever there is water and enough sunlight. High above, the air plants, too, seize on anything that offers a foothold. They need no roots in the ground, getting nutrition from dust particles and the moist air, and they seek nothing from their host trees except support.

The air plants, or epiphytes, include tree orchids and resurrection fern, but unquestionably the foremost is Spanish moss. Not a moss at all, it hangs everywhere in poetic festoons, ethereal and haunting, the hallmark of the swamp.

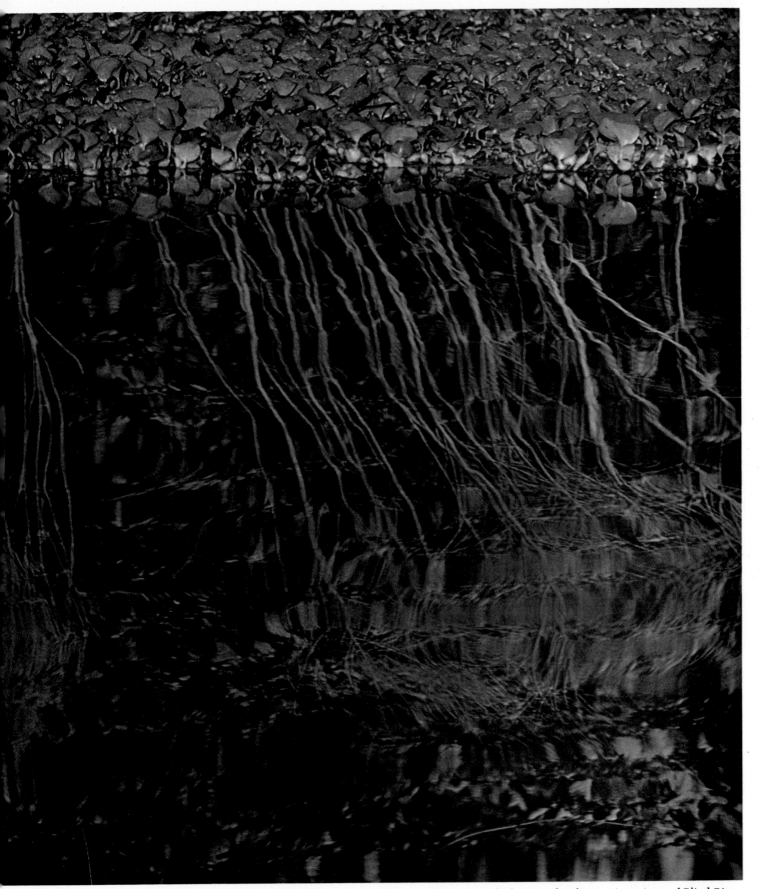

Coffeeweed stems, rising from the bank beyond a bed of water hyacinths, are reflected upside down in the shimmering mirror of Blind River.

Vines of Virginia creeper, fan-shaped palmetto leaves and green ash trees compete for space on the crowded bank of an Atchafalaya bayou.

Hardy butterweed adds yellow splashes to a layer of duckweed.

An aggressive water hyacinth displays a blossom of gentle hue.

Resurrection fern grows green again after turning brown in a dry spell.

Cypress knees, outgrowths of submerged roots, form a rampart for a pair of giants.

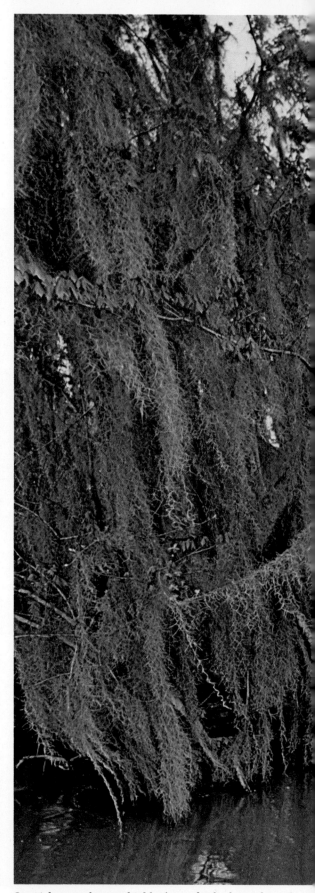

Spanish moss hangs thickly from the limbs and trunks

of swamp trees, which it uses only for support. Tiny grayish scales on the surface of the stems give the ubiquitous air plant its ghostly color.

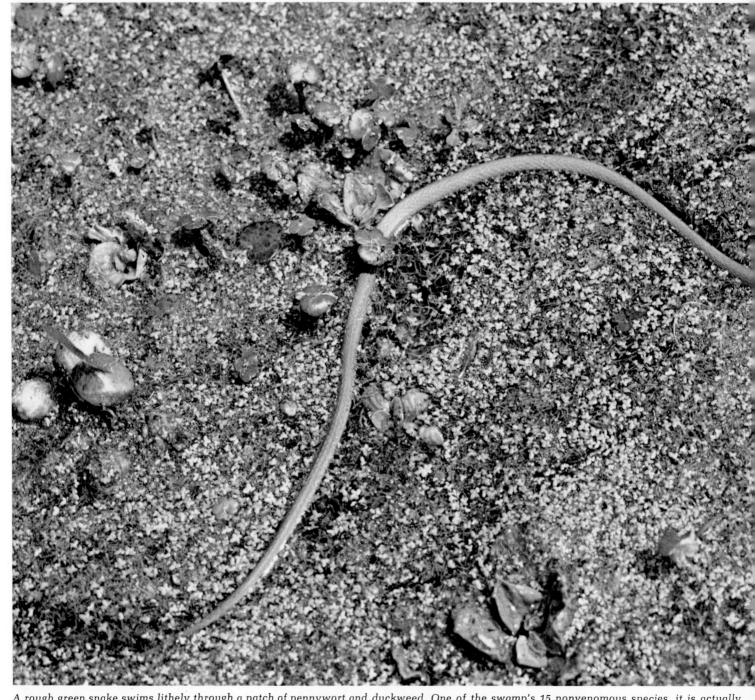

A rough green snake swims lithely through a patch of pennywort and duckweed. One of the swamp's 15 nonvenomous species, it is actually

less at home in the water than in the trees, where it spends much of its time hunting insects.

Creatures of Stealth and Silence

The animals of the swamp are sensed more than seen. Leaves quiver, a bush rustles, the bayou water ripples—the eye has to be quick to catch the signs, for they are quickly gone. Many creatures are exquisitely camouflaged, like the rough green snake at left, and blend superbly with their surroundings. Some spend most of their time partly submerged, like the alligator that lies with its dark, corrugated head just breaking the surface. Others are nocturnal and move silently under the protective cloak of darkness.

Reptiles, birds, mammals—all are in the swamp, each where it fits best. There are fewer birds than in the open marshes, but still ample numbers. The staccato *quock* of the stubby black-crowned night heron is a familiar echo in the swamp, and even the space-loving great egret comes to fish and sometimes nest there. Small mammals such as squirrels and swamp rabbits find haven where there is solid land. For the water lovers, of course, the places of shelter are almost limitless, and the bounty beyond compare. The shy otter and the gregarious raccoon feed on fish, crawfish and young amphibians; the raccoon's diet includes insects, small birds and plants as well.

Rarest of all mammals in the swamp are the bobcat and the black bear. Though they are almost never seen any more, the swamp affords them a last refuge against the pressures outside the wilderness.

Its coat glistening, a rarely seen river otter suns on a safely isolated log.

A black-crowned night heron stalks a meal.

Baby raccoons, about two months old, cluster on a moldering tree stump.

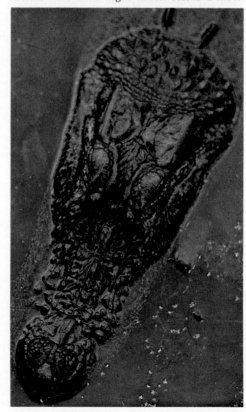

An alligator pokes its snout out of the water.

A white-whiskered nutria plows purposefully through a duckweed-spattered pond, alert to peril from its chief swamp predator, the alligator.

A monarch butterfly, passing through the swamp during its springtime migration to the north, pauses among butterweed blossoms.

Flyers and Hoppers and Crawlers

Too small to dominate but too numerous to be overpowered, the insects of the swamp fill every possible niche with their trillions. Whatever the species, the insects are a basic food source for birds, fishes, reptiles, spiders and one another. Every year, for instance, hordes of mosquitoes provide a spring feast for dragonflies, which in turn make meals for birds and frogs; midsummer swarms of young lubber grasshoppers are good eating for everything from egrets to alligators.

In their turn, the insects act as scavengers, feeding on dead animals and on vegetation that would otherwise choke the swamp. Among the most assiduous are the fierce fire ants, whose colonies go at their task with a purposefulness that brooks no barrier (overleaf).

The ants and most other insects are permanent swamp dwellers; but the black and orange monarch butterfly is a visitor. One of the few types of butterflies that migrate, the monarchs travel to tropic regions in great swarms in autumn; on their way back north in spring they return as individual travelers, alighting here and there in the swamp.

Not actually insects, but heavily dependent on them for food, are the swamp's many kinds of spiders. One of the more extraordinary is the fishing spider, which makes the most of its environment through a knack for walking on water and eating small fish as well as insects.

A fishing spider, which kills its prey with poison injections, lurks on a water-lettuce leaf.

A lubber grasshopper, grown to a formidable two and a half inches, rests between leaps.

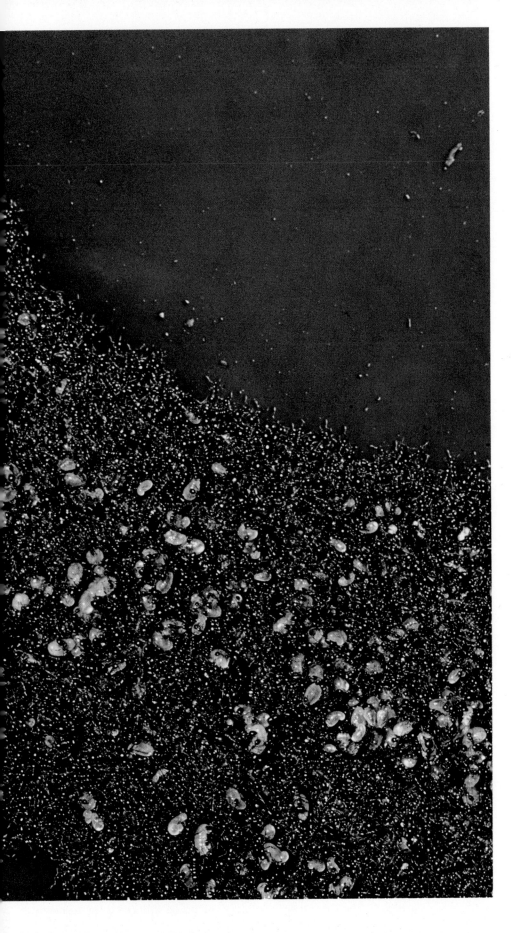

A column of fire ants, flooded out by
high water, crosses the surface of a
shallow bayou in search of dry land.
Though they are not aquatic, the ants
are so light that their mass does
not break the water's surface tension.
Those tightly packed in the center
carry the white pupal cases of their
young while the whole formation is
moved along by the current or a breeze.

As an early-morning autumn mist creeps over a cypress swamp in the Atchafalaya Basin, a solitary great egret waits on a log. Immobile, it

watches for an underwater movement or surface splash that will betray the whereabouts of its next meal—a young bluegill sunfish, perhaps.

4/ Violence and Aftermath

Over their heads the towering and tenebrous boughs of the cypress/ Met in a dusky arch, and trailing mosses in mid-air/ Waved like banners that hang on the walls of ancient cathedrals.   HENRY WADSWORTH LONGFELLOW/ EVANGELINE

There is no clearer way to understand the special nature of the struggle for survival in the bayou country than to see the area, and its inhabitants, under some form of stress. Jim and I began to understand it all too well as we waited for the second half of the hurricane to strike. We knew it must come and the animals seemed to know, or sense, it too. Amid the devastation, nothing moved. In the airless eye of the storm we waited, silent, like the swamp around us.

The house in which we had sought refuge stood surrounded by a boundless lake strewn with pieces of bark, branches, leaves, moss and the trunks of fallen trees. As we watched, a red maple that rose tall and strong 50 yards from the house appeared to stir. It shuddered in its leaves, was still, shook again, and began very slowly to dip to one side. With a sound like a grunt it toppled, disappeared beneath the water, then surfaced to float with the rest of the debris left by the storm. A young otter swam frantically out of its sunken branches. We stared at the dead maple. In the wake of the first terrific winds, its roots torn from its trunk, it had stood for several minutes as though still alive, like a soldier who has been shot but does not immediately fall. The lifeless tree seemed a bad omen in the gleaming yellow of the windless sky. Drops of water glittered over everything in sight. No animal ventured into the open; instinctively none trusted this long silence. The swamp stretched out, poised and rigid.

The winds came back as abruptly as they had left. We stationed ourselves near the inside wall of the big upstairs bedroom, facing away from its windows. Through the windows of the smaller bedroom across the hall we could see into the claw of the storm. The first half of the hurricane had come from the east. Now, from the west, the whips and lashes of air and water resumed. With an audible shiver the swamp began again to twist under a slashing sky. Branches and broken roof shingles scraped and bounced above us. An explosion from below announced the cave-in of another wall of windows on the first floor.

Twice an animal of some kind clattered over the house, its screeches cut short as the wind took its life. The first sound was the wailing of a cat—a cougar, perhaps, or a bobcat. The second was louder and more shrill, and whatever was making it struck the chimney with a hard dull blow. A flutter of something large, white and feathery streaked down past the far windows. "Egret," Jim said. "It's funny—they almost never get caught—not in the open sky." Then, staring through the windows, he added, "There is no sky."

Through the sheets of rain that blew against the glass, the view outside was distorted and mangled, as if the heart of the swamp had burst from the force of the pressure above it. The moss in some of the cypress trees pointed straight up. A lash of gray slapped the house, and in the far bedroom two panes seemed at first to tremble, to stretch, then to melt into the room. Slivers of glass shone for an instant in a long spurt of water. Then thin rivulets rolled across the floor toward us, driven through the empty squares that had been the panes. The house had started to disintegrate into the moaning wind, which seemed to be in mourning for itself.

Suddenly, when it seemed that the house could not hold out much longer, the walls shuddered—like the maple tree in the instant before it fell—and just as abruptly the moaning ceased. But the wind began again, resurged to buffet the west side of the house in a last lethal burst, fluttered, and left. The rain continued to fall, but almost listlessly now, a wet shroud hanging from the sky, swinging back and forth above a swamp that had been turned into an open grave.

Ten minutes later we ventured out of the room to the top of the stairs. But even as I started down, Jim grabbed my arm and pulled me back. The level of swamp water on the first floor had risen nearly a fourth of the way up the staircase. Stretched across the last visible step was a trio of snakes, each about three feet long, with triangular blackish heads. Cottonmouths. One of the creatures opened its mouth, revealing a pinkish-white inner membrane that did indeed look like cotton. "We may have to wait quite awhile," Jim said.

He went back to the bedroom and I stood staring at the snakes. It was not the first time I had seen cottonmouths, for they are common in the bayou country, the most numerous of the six poisonous species of snakes found in Louisiana. Now, however, I could not stifle the wild hope that these invaders were not cottonmouths after all, that they belonged to one of the 33 harmless species to be found in the state. I studied them carefully as they lolled on the stairs below.

Each had about a dozen dark, wide crossbands, olive brown in color. The underside of the tail and the rear of the belly were black. I could see the loreal pits just below and in front of the eyes, and the vertically elliptical pupils. Clearly the snakes were cottonmouths, dealers in a poison for which Jim and I had no antidote anywhere within miles—crucial hours away.

The snakes appeared to be on the stairs to stay. And even if we could get past them, their presence inside the house promised that there would be many more snakes in the water outside—a formidable obstacle between us and the nearest dry land. Swimming through the flood would not help; snakes can and do bite underwater.

Snakes! Both Jim and I were wearing boots of a soft leather that could easily be pierced by their fangs, the elongated hollow teeth through which the venom is discharged to kill prey. Fangs grow in pairs, one on each side of the mouth, and there are usually several smaller sets in reserve, moving frontward as they grow. To ensure the sharpness of its bite, a snake changes fangs every two or three weeks; as the front fangs grow blunt or break off, the set behind them will move into position.

People unaware of the phenomenon have sometimes discovered it the hard way. Sometimes a bayou visitor traps a baby snake and removes the fangs—with the prudent use of pliers held in gloved hands —intending to raise a harmless and unique pet. The pet, of course, turns out to be anything but harmless.

Jim came back with a half-consumed can of beans and I spooned it up, my eyes still fixed on the stairs. One of the snakes had moved a step higher. I remarked that the water was rising, too. Jim nodded. "Won't come up much farther," he said, "but it won't need to."

I followed him to the bedroom windows and looked out. A vast drowned world lay around us. I had heard about the deluge of saltwater waves that accompany hurricanes in coastal areas. But a flood

A highly unusual sight in the bayous or anywhere else, a hanging honeybees' nest is suspended from a branch in the Atchafalaya swamp. Honeybees usually build their combs in the crotch of a tree or in a hollow of the trunk; this colony was probably forced to relocate to emergency quarters by a natural disaster that ruined the original nest.

caused only by wind and rain was something I had neither seen nor heard about, short of the Old Testament.

There was still some wind, as if an afterthought of the hurricane. A shrub went bobbing past the house. It was a buttonbush, common in the swamp, its dark green leaves gleaming around the little balls of white that give the plant its name. It seemed alive, bouncing gaily along in the flood. As it dipped behind a partly submerged cypress trunk, something else caught my eye. What appeared to be a mound of black earth was drifting, heavily and slowly, on the far side of the trunk; I could not make out what it was until I saw a small black bear cub, perched above it on the trunk. The cub descended, tentatively prodded the body of its mother with one paw, then climbed back about a third of the way up the tree waiting for her to respond. "It'll leave her," Jim said, "when it gets hungry enough." Some time later we noticed that the cub had at last deserted the corpse of its mother and gone off foraging through the water for food.

The night came, soundless; even the frogs were quiet now. Jim and I sprawled on the twin beds of the big bedroom. We dozed fitfully. At moments one or the other of us would get up and move restlessly about, prowling the second floor of the house and trying to remember to avoid the stairs. With the morning the sky, cloudless and crystalline blue, gleamed brighter than I had ever seen it, as if the storm had polished the arch of blue above us as sand polishes stone. The Spanish moss hung straight and still in the trees, over a flood that had lowered somewhat overnight. Here and there the water's glassy surface was broken by surreptitious movements, too tentative to be identifiable but unmistakably the work of living things. From between two tupelo-gum trees came the dark brown furry back of a nutria, swimming determinedly northeast; the animal seemed to know where it was going. A plop in the water just ahead of the nutrias signaled a fish jumping.

As we sat on a window sill surveying the scene, Jim jumped up, frowning. "I'm going to have another look inside that chest," he said. During the night, he had gone rummaging through every box and drawer in both bedrooms and in the attic, looking for anything that might prove useful to us in getting away from the flood. Now he ducked into the attic and emerged a minute later carrying a pair of torn but heavy hip boots. Jim had rejected them during his first search because the soles flapped and water would seep in through them. "Water doesn't matter," he explained, "if I can get as far as the garage without being bitten by anything. There ought to be a rowboat. Everybody who owns a house around here keeps a skiff of some kind."

He took a broom from the hall closet and went to the top of the stairs. Two of the cottonmouths had gone during the night, but one was still there. One poisonous snake was just as bad as three, as far as I was concerned; but Jim took a metal book end from the small bedroom and aimed it down the staircase. It struck four or five steps above the snake and bounced down loudly. The snake slithered off into the water. Jim started down, moving the broom in a wide arc ahead of him, sweeping and stirring the surface of the water. When he reached the bottom step, the muddy water was well over his knees, about two inches short of the top of the hip boots. "I think I can make it," he said, and slogged out the door. I ran back to the window and watched him heave through the water toward the garage, still swinging the broom. Once he flipped something out of his path. "Snapping turtle," he called. "The water here's like thin mud . . . feels as if the earth's melted."

Half an hour later we were both sitting in the small skiff he had found in the garage. He had poled the boat over to the door of the house, as near to the stairs as he had been able to manage, and I had half-slid, half-flown down the stairs to join him, sopping wet but unmolested by snakes. I began to row as Jim fiddled with an outboard motor that refused, of course, to function. Around and above us, the vines of trumpet creepers dangled, torn loose from the branches. A few of their orange blossoms had survived—flashes of color in the moss. We passed the body of an opossum floating belly down. I turned it over with an oar. It was clinging to a branch as though, even in death, it felt safer that way.

Two water snakes crisscrossed ahead of the boat, and beyond them a big bullfrog jumped from a rise of earth onto a torn lily pad that had no stem and was too soft to hold the frog's weight. It tried to jump back, but the pad sank so quickly that it was forced to swim. I watched as it made its way back to the rise of earth, moving heedlessly past one of the snakes. The bullfrog's careless disregard of its traditional predator was curious.

Then I noticed something even more curious. Two other animals were waiting on the rise for the flood to ebb. A bobcat and a large swamp rabbit were sitting only a few feet apart, as unconcerned by each other's presence as the frog had been of the snake. The frog positioned itself between the bobcat and rabbit, and all three creatures stared fixedly at the flood. As we drifted past, not one of them took any notice of us.

A company of brown pelicans drifts lazily along a coastal waterway after feeding. The state bird of Louisiana, and once as common there as cypress and the water hyacinth, the pelican is now an endangered species, seriously threatened by heavy pesticide concentrations in the fish it eats.

In the immediate wake of a flood, a kind of truce may prevail among the shocked animals. For a few hours, for a day and a night, enemies are not enemies; there is a pause in the killing. Then, as the shock wears off, hunting resumes, with more risk than ever to the small creatures that have been dislocated by the floodwaters and can no longer escape into the safety of a familiar burrow or tree. Exhausted by the ordeal of the storm, wood rats, squirrels, opossums, even birds become such easy prey that their populations—already diminished by the hurricane—are further reduced.

Our skiff drifted from shoal to shoal, touching a sunken log here, ricocheting gently off the top of a cypress knee there. Jim had given up trying to fix the motor. He pointed over my shoulder. I turned in time to see a white-tailed deer, a full-grown buck, on a rise in the distance. He was rubbing his antlers against a tree trunk. The antlers, which had started growing in February or March after the old set was shed, were fully developed by now, some six months later, and the skinlike "velvet" that covered the tines was beginning to dry up and peel off. As the velvet shrivels, it makes the antlers itch so that what looks like a polishing operation is actually a way for the deer to scratch himself.

We rowed around for hours near the house in a kind of trance, letting the boat drift when an occasional current took it, feeling our way in an uncertain world that glistened freshly. Life was reaching up through the flood. The reaction to the effort for survival imbued each plant or animal with a surge of energy that was almost visible. The clear blue sky provided a brilliant backdrop to the scene that remained untarnished throughout the day. In the humid stillness a great bubble of sunlight capped the earth like a natural hothouse, and all living things stretched open inside it. By midafternoon the swamp was in motion. It crept and tingled around our skiff, oddly sensual in its reaffirmation of life. The surrounding wetness acted like a magnifying glass. Each cypress leaf or streamer of moss looked larger than before. Each edge of a plant, each color, stood out—etched, vivid. Jim said, "It's like being inside a diamond."

It was late afternoon before we remembered that our purpose in taking the skiff had been to leave the flooded area. Our families would be worried; we knew we ought to contact them by nightfall. We rowed past the flooded house in the direction of the road we had driven on to get there. At last patches of dry land appeared ahead. When the water under us was shallow enough, Jim stepped out and grounded the skiff. I got out after him and we moved slowly, single file, through the slosh, each of us carrying an oar that we had taken along as a precautionary weapon. Jim, moving ahead of me, spotted a cottonmouth on a log; reflexively, he lunged at it with his oar. The snake struck his leg almost lazily, fastening its fangs in his right boot; they did not, however, pierce through the rubber. Jim yelled at me to get around to his other side; he remembered not to reach down with his hands, and the snake slid off the boot and curved away into the water.

As we walked on, I thought about Jim's reckless attack on the snake, odd behavior for someone so knowledgeable about swamp creatures. In time, I was to realize that Jim had been in a state approaching euphoria. Just as men and animals become more alert in an emergency, so the letdown afterward and the promise of escape can have the opposite effect; behavior grows careless. In the end it was luck more than anything else that got us out of the flooded area soon after sundown. With the disappearance of the light, the truce among the animals seemed to end. From the edge of the swamp, in the darkness, we could hear far-off cries, and directly above us a screech owl shrieked.

During the weeks that followed, I found myself needing to return to the place Jim and I had seen during the hurricane—as though my sense of the world would remain incomplete until I saw the swamp with its balance returned. In the fall I drove back. This time I went alone. From the bank where the house stood, the bayou appeared peaceful and quiet. Jim's uncle had been at work on his battered property. He had boarded over the windows he had not had time to reglaze, and the fallen oak and the old truck crushed by it had been cleared away.

The woods around the house were strewn with branches and vines, brought low where they would provide forage for the swamp rabbits and deer. The hurricane had not taken a significant toll of the swamp rabbits, I knew; even when only half-grown, they swim well enough to reach floating pieces of wood and ride out the storm. New litters would quickly compensate for the young that had drowned.

Deer, needing sturdier supports for use as rafts, probably had not fared so well. In the long run, though, the deer population would benefit from the blowdown of succulent tree tips, mistletoe, greenbrier and poison ivy. Where high winds had leveled acres of timber, underbrush would soon sprout in profusion to provide future generations of deer with both food and fawning cover.

Here and there beside the bayou a whole tree lay rotting, already a host to the mushrooms that deer relish. Scattered along the banks of the stream were dead fish. Some had been tossed up in the hurricane it-self. Others had died a slower death later, as leaves accumulating and decaying in the water used up the oxygen. Except for a few gray squir-rels twittering near the grape arbor, I noticed no other animal survivors.

Even the squirrels might disappear from the place if they ran out of food. The hurricane had whipped away much of the trees' seed crop —the acorns, hackberries and pecans on which the squirrels depended. I had heard tales of the migrations of gray squirrels: hundreds of them, of all ages, moving through woods and swimming across waters in a mass exodus from a territory where their population had outrun the local food supply.

The orphan bear cub was nowhere to be seen. Most animals of the swamp, including the black bear, are secretive nocturnal creatures, and only special or dire circumstances, such as a hurricane, will drive them into the open during daylight hours. The cub, the bobcat and the cou-gar that Jim and I had seen in August could have been holed up somewhere not too far away, sleeping by day to hunt by night, or they could have moved on to a less-damaged part of the swamp. Bears can survive as vegetarians if they have to; but wildcats must have meat, so that when a hurricane kills the small animals and birds on which they feed, they often leave for another territory, making their exodus singly rather than in hordes the way squirrels do.

There was loneliness in the swamp now. I left quickly and drove sev-eral miles to where a patch of pine trees spread their shade across a sandy slope. I took a book and a blanket and stretched out to read. It was one of those gentle, humid days that make the earth feel safe, and it was hard to remember that the ugly violence of a hurricane had passed here so recently. I dozed for a while, then woke and lay still, looking for animals in the trees above my head. I saw none.

But, on the earth next to me, something coral red glinted and moved. I turned my head slowly, hoping that the thing beside me would not no-tice the movement. The muscles in my neck cramped from the effort. Finally, my face lay at an angle that allowed me to see the coral-red ob-ject. It took what seemed an age before I understood what it was that I was looking at.

First I thought that it must be a flower. Then I saw that it was not a flower but the circular base of a plant, no bigger than an inch across, from which rose a single, thin stem. It was the base itself that was coral colored, shaped like a starfish with many legs; each ended in a

Balanced on its spindly perch, a Louisiana heron looks all neck, wings and legs. But when fishing in its native marsh it is, like other wading birds, extremely efficient. It stands in the water, extends its wings and pirouettes, casting a shadow that both attracts its aquatic prey and cuts down surface glare to make the prey more visible; the heron's long neck and bill are well designed for snaring the catch with a quick darting thrust.

round pod covered with hundreds of minute tentacles that appeared to be in motion. At the tip of each tentacle was a single drop of a glittery, sticky-looking substance that gave the whole base the look of a meticulously fashioned jewel. Caught in one of the pods was an ant; it was raising its legs one by one in a frantic effort to release itself from the crystal drop of mucilage. As it struggled, the drops of moisture grew larger. The pod in which the insect was by now hopelessly stuck began very slowly to close. Tentacles from below and outside the pod curved upward until the ant was buried inside.

I sat up fast and looked around. There were about 20 more of the plants—sundews, they are called—behind the one next to me. Two were closed; the others lay open, their delicate coral tentacles spread out, waiting to trap, devour and digest any insect that came along. Twice more insects lighted on the surface of the plant pods, only to be caught in one of the drops of liquid.

There are 90 varieties of sundews around the world, all of them worth watching. After a while, I took a key from my pocket and touched one of the pods. Nothing happened. I prodded it—still nothing happened. The syrupy drops at the tips of the tentacles did not increase, nor did the plant stir. It was not until much later, when I came across something Charles Darwin had written, that I understood why. In 1875, reporting on his own observations of sundews, Darwin said: "After feeding the leaf pods [with] insects, beginning actions of digestion took place. Then on other leaf pods sand, then glass, then artificial insects were placed; however, the plant would not react to the foreign matter. The plant knows! It appears to sense that these materials are not food it can utilize. The leaves won't curl, the tentacles do not react, and no juices form. Amazing!"

The bayou country provides a hospitable home for the sundew, as well as for another insect eater: the pitcher plant. Both grow in acid bogs or sandy places whose soil does not provide enough nutrients—nitrate and phosphate in particular—to support most other plants. The pitcher plant, which hybridizes so often that it is seldom easy to differentiate among its nine species, is no less amazing than the sundew, and has a splendid diversity of colors. The most common are the purple and the crimson pitcher plants. The purple variety has a flower of reddish purple, thinning to an orange or rose color the nearer to the Louisiana coast the plant grows; its leaves are mottled yellows and reds. The crimson pitcher plant has bright red flowers, about three inches across, with leaves veined in red and white. Added to the flamboyance of color is the remarkable shape the leaves take. As they grow—as much as two feet in the case of the crimson variety, no higher than eight inches in the purple variety—the leaves curl together to form a cone, much like a trumpet in shape, closed at the bottom and flaring open and wide at the top. The cone serves as a receptacle for rain water, a fact that led the early Spaniards in Louisiana to liken the plant to a pitcher—the name it has borne ever since.

The pitcher plant not only holds water, but secretes a sweet liquid inside its cone that attracts insects. Unlike the "active" sundew, the "passive" pitcher plant does not move to capture its prey. When a beetle or an even larger insect starts down inside the cone, it encounters partway a lining of infinitesimal white hairs, as slippery as they are invisible. No longer able to sustain a foothold, the insect slides toward the liquid at the bottom of the cone. Even if it is able to stop its fall, it cannot climb back up, for the hairs all point downward to form a barrier. Sooner or later the insect will plunge into the liquid, drown, decompose and be digested. Its skeleton remains stored deep inside the cone. A different ending awaits the insect devoured by the sundew. Its skeleton is released by the plant to be blown away on the first passing breeze.

For hours that afternoon I watched the sundews. Growing on relatively high ground, safe from flood, they were among the tiniest survivors of the summer's disaster. The most delicate-looking life in the bayou country often proves to be the sturdiest.

I caught another glimpse of bayou life during that solitary outing. As dusk approached, I spotted a raccoon rummaging for food in a shallow stream. Raccoons, as even suburban dwellers know, will eat anything they find on land, including the garbage at the back door. But here in the watery wilderness the raccoon is the consummate fisherman, expertly scooping up fish, frogs, crawfish and salamanders with its slender-fingered paws. So ingrained is its association of water with food that a captive raccoon may wet even a sugar lump before eating it. For years zoologists attributed such acts simply to the raccoon's desire to wash its food, and indeed the scientific name for the raccoon is *Procyon lotor*—*lotor* being Latin for "one who washes." But more recently the raccoon's behavior has been recognized as merely a way of re-creating the conditions under which it naturally finds food.

As I watched the raccoon deftly fishing for its supper, I thought of the other common nocturnal hunter of the bayou country, the opossum. The contrast between the two is interesting. The raccoon's

Beyond an array of cypress knees, a toppled bald cypress lies and rots—victim of a violent storm that shook the Atchafalaya swamp.

wiliness is legendary; it can outsmart a pack of the best-trained hound dogs. The opossum, on the other hand, puts on a show that deceives no hunter. It does not try to run when cornered, but feigns death—"plays possum." It falls limp, clamps its eyes shut, lolls its tongue; even its heartbeat slows down. But what it may lack in persuasiveness it makes up for in fertility. There can be as many as 18 babies to a litter, and two or even three litters a year. Possums are marsupials—relatives of the kangaroo. They are born underdeveloped, about the size of bees, and —like baby kangaroos—they spend their first month or two inside their mother's pouch, clinging to her nipples. Often, during this period some of them perish for want of nourishment; a female possum has 11 or 13 nipples, and if she has produced a large litter the demand for her milk outruns the supply. The survivors venture from the pouch when they reach the size of mice; for a while, until they can manage on their own, they have a distinctive mode of getting about—traveling on their mother's back, their toes clinging to her fur.

I was tempted to stay in the pine grove studying the raccoon at the stream and hoping that a possum—or perhaps a bear—might appear. But as the light faded, prudence prevailed. I got into my car and drove back to the bustle of the city.

A few months later, in early winter, I went back to see how the wild creatures of the Atchafalaya had recovered from the ravages of the August hurricane. This time I was on the west bank of the river, where the swamp begins. I had been hiking for more than an hour and had paused to rest when I saw a white-tailed buck, the points of his antlers glistening. This was mating season—a period that lasts in Louisiana from early December into late January.

White-tailed deer are polygamous; several bucks frequently stalk the same doe. When rivals meet, a battle follows with each buck using his antlers to shove the other away from the doe, to gore his rival or throw him to the ground. The antlers are defensive tools as well; although the tines may be as sharp as those of pitchforks, they are arranged in a basket shape that serves to ward off blows. Actually, the worst peril for the rival bucks is the possibility that their antlers will become firmly interlocked; then both deer starve to death. As long as the rut—the period of sexual excitement—lasts, each buck prowls alone, staying with one doe for just a few days before running off to look, and fight, for another. Only afterward do herds of males and females congregate peaceably again.

I sat motionless and watched as the buck moved from tree to tree. In his winter coat of thick gray hair—in the blue, hunters call it—he was camouflaged, quite difficult to see against the background of dark tree trunks. Then, without thinking, I lifted my hand to scratch my knee. The buck stiffened, bent his head, lowered his upraised tail so that it no longer showed the "white flag" of fur on the underside—and melted into the underbrush. For a long time I sat waiting; the buck did not come back. When the day waned and the sun turned red through the cypress leaves, I decided to leave. But first I took off my belt and tied it to a branch of the tree under which I had been sitting, to mark the place.

Early the following autumn I went back to the west bank of the Atchafalaya River. After more than a day of searching, I found the tree with my belt still tied to it. I sat down again to wait. No buck appeared. But as the afternoon progressed I saw a doe behind the trees, poised and delicate, incredibly elegant, followed by a small fawn. The doe still wore her lightweight reddish summer coat; the fawn was nearly three months old and beginning to lose its white polka dots. Her first fawn, I thought. Except for the first birth, a doe usually bears twins. Heedless of my presence, the doe and the fawn went on eating greenbrier from a patch behind the tree line, and I kept my eyes on them until they disappeared, still browsing.

A heavy plop in the river and a flutter in the branches overhead reinforced the message that creatures were thriving underwater and in the sky as well as on the land. The air and the water cling to the earth in this place—each separate, yet each part of the whole—each a matrix of life in some form. Another spring, another summer, had come and gone. The bayou country lay calm and gentle, the hurricane of the previous year now a distant memory.

The Hospitable Marsh

As the land of Louisiana stretches south toward the Gulf of Mexico, the dark swamp bayous of towering cypresses and dangling Spanish moss give way to a vast and virtually treeless area of marshes stippled with ponds and coarse grasses. From afar these wetlands, flat and open to the sky, appear monotonously unchanging. Nothing much seems to be going on except for the rhythmic swaying of grasses moved by the wind blowing off the Gulf.

The appearance is deceptive. The nearly five million acres of marshland bordering Louisiana's coast, extending inland from 10 to 60 miles, sustain an intense year-round concentration of plant and animal life. Blessed with bright sunshine, thick black soil and protected brackish waters, the marshes provide as extensive a nursery and haven for fish, crustaceans and water birds as can be found anywhere on the continent. More than 100 species of fishes either spawn or live in the marshes. Nearly a third of all North America's species of birds are either permanent or winter residents; birds whose breeding habitats are a continent apart come together to feed in this hospitable place.

Differences become softened here, where land and earth are often indistinguishable and where fresh water and salt blend in a mix that changes with each tide or wind shift. Gulf fish are sometimes found miles up the marsh bayous; salt-water and fresh-water fish often swim side by side. Animals that are swimmers at one time become overland travelers at others; prominent among them are the marshland's 170,000 alligators. Crawfish in the millions spend their early days along the pond bottoms, but as adults they often come to the surface to feed.

Even the changing seasons reflect the state of gentle compromise that characterizes the marshland. Average temperatures vary from summer to winter less than almost anywhere else in the United States, and seasonal contrasts in the look of the land are muted. But changes do occur. Each of the seasons has its own rhythm, and the differences between winter and spring are particularly noticeable. The one resounds to the clamor of invading migratory waterfowl; the other hums with the activity of new generations of animals and plants. In the meantime, during the brief transition between the two seasons, the marshland enjoys a quiet period of respite (right).

Serene in the evening light of late February, a Gulf Coast marsh bears the scars of a recent onslaught by winter visitors. The watery gaps in the foreground are "eat outs," areas where geese—abetted by muskrats—have torn up the three-cornered grass that is their favorite food. Eventually new plants will grow to close the gaps.

A Rip-Roaring Winter Resort

Winter in the marsh is a lively, noisy time filled with the whistling beat of strong wings and the raucous gabble of half a million blue geese and snow geese that have come south on their annual migration. Their arrival itself, wave upon wave over a period of about six weeks, is a sight to behold —and hear. The geese have traveled a long way, setting out as early as the end of September from their chill native tundra near the Arctic Circle, heading directly down the middle of North America, and touching down on the Louisiana coast about three or four weeks later.

The major influx over, the geese settle in, splashing about, honking and hunting for their preferred winter fare: three-cornered grass. Their powerful bills grub so voraciously at the fat roots of the plants that when they finish with an area there is no vegetation left at all.

By the first of March the blues and snows, rested, well fed and sleek, have started back north, mating en route, to lay their eggs and raise their young among rivulets of thawing ice in their Arctic barrens. In the Louisiana marshes, their strident cries are replaced by the delicate trills of the orchard oriole, common yellow-throat and other songbirds, which have come home for the summer after wintering in Central and South America. They join the year-round population of great egrets, bitterns and rails, and the cycle of teeming bird life begins anew.

A flock of blue and snow geese reconnoiter a marsh in the Sabine Wildlife Refuge near

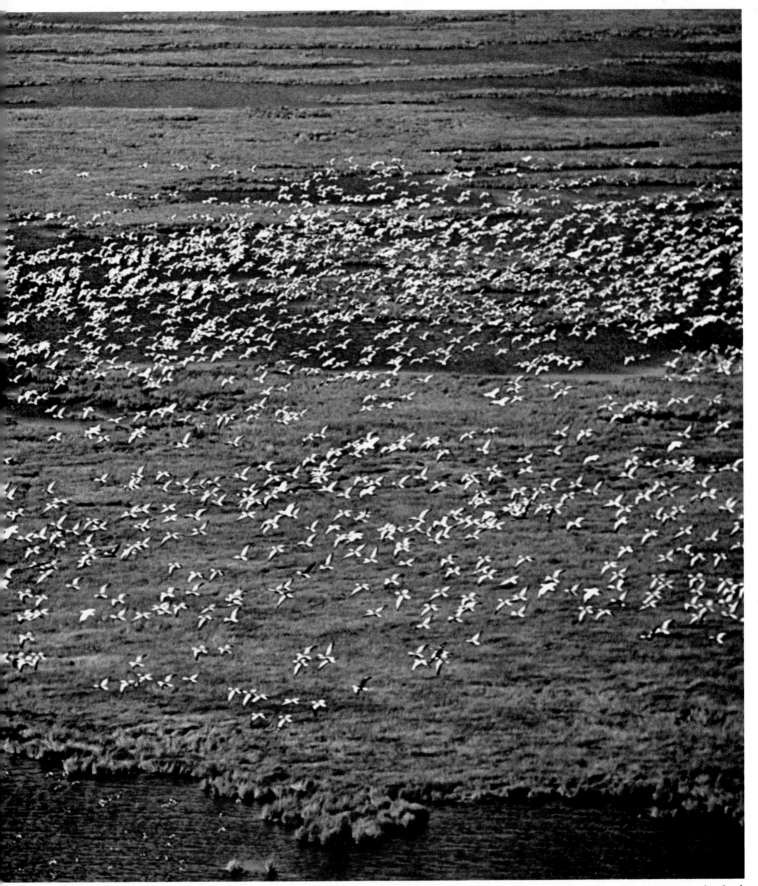

the Gulf Coast, ready to swoop at the sight of a tempting stand of grass. They may travel as much as 70 miles in pursuit of a feed.

Blue and snow geese gobble grit from the bottom of a sandy pond in the Sabine refuge. Like most wild fowl, geese need this substance for digestion. They are toothless, and the grit, lodged in their muscular gizzards, helps grind up the food they cannot chew.

Two Canada geese—a new strain that never goes to Canada but lives all year in Louisiana—survey a pond in the Rockefeller Wildlife Refuge. Some 150,000 of the original breed used to winter here before Midwestern grainfields lured many of them away.

At winter's end, a blue goose and a snow goose take off from the marsh to join the flocks headed north. Members of the same species

—differing only in color and markings—they travel about 4,500 air miles in the annual trek to and from their southern feeding grounds.

A protectively colored least bittern, a full-time marsh resident, forages in new coco grass.

Lured from hibernation by a warm sun and rising waters, a cottonmouth prowls for food.

A Gentle Change to Spring

Spring comes subtly in the marshland, without the dramatic rebirth that follows a stark northern winter. Because of the equable winter temperatures of the subtropical Gulf Coast and a growing season that extends from early February to mid-December, the onset of spring is hard to pinpoint. It brings changes though, and many new beginnings.

A fresh crop of wild millet awaits nesting songbirds; cattails and three-cornered grass that the wintering birds depleted are being replenished to nourish newborn muskrats and nutria. Marsh grasses also provide a nursery for fish, shrimp, oysters and crabs just in from their birth in the Gulf, and furnish a protective cover for the newly laid eggs of insects, birds and alligators.

With new food and new life, the marsh becomes a stalking ground for the predator. The cottonmouth snake seeks the eggs or nestlings of birds like the red-winged blackbird and the least bittern. The birds, in turn, are on the alert for some tasty insect —a mosquito or a larger mouthful in the form of a damsel fly.

On occasion the steady rhythms of springtime are jarred by cataclysm as the Mississippi goes on a rampage so mighty its floodwaters reach all the way to the marshes. Many creatures of the marsh drown or are forced to flee, and great swaths of vegetation are swept away. But the waters always recede and the marsh always recovers.

A male red-winged blackbird, perched amid blooming rushes, conspicuously flaunts his red epaulets during the spring breeding season.

Waiting to snap up a passing insect, this damsel fly clings motionless to a blade of marsh grass. A delicate kin of the dragonfly, it catches its prey on the move, scooping it up in midair with a quick, graceful dart.

Raised more than two feet above normal by rainfall and wind tides, the swollen water of a coastal marsh poses a threat to vegetation, which it may carry away, as well as to animals, which it may either drown or drive out. But the rich layer of new sediment deposited by the disturbed, muddy waters will benefit future generations of marsh plants and creatures.

5/ The Underwater Forest

. . . a properly protected marsh cannot be depleted.
It continually produces, like the legendary pitcher of wine
that is never emptied. WILLIAM A. NIERING/ *THE LIFE OF THE MARSH*

Where swamps and marshes meet in southern Louisiana, bayous become the trails of a vast underwater forest. Like a land forest, the aquatic kind is an environment all its own, with plants providing the basic foods as well as the protective cover for creatures large and small. As the waters run their southerly course, turning from fresh to brackish to salt as they mix with tides from the Gulf of Mexico, the denizens of this forest differ from zone to zone. But each area has its innumerable inhabitants, and just about anything that can crawl, hop, swim or plop is worth watching.

There is, for instance, the crawfish, also known as crayfish, crawdad, stone crab, mini-lobster or mud bug. Whatever it is called, the little armored beast abounds in Louisiana, and affords a fine excuse for spending some time in the wilder reaches of the southern bayou country. I remember one weekend long ago when my friend Jim and I went on a crawfish expedition in the lower Atchafalaya Basin. It was in March—the start of the four-month crawfish season—and what we had in mind was not studying the crawfish in its habitat, but catching and eating as many as we could.

Louisiana's brief winter had begun to turn into a wet spring, and as we drove southwest from New Orleans, on a dirt road pitted with clamshells and packed with dust, the daylight faded and trees alongside that had been bright and sparkling wet became ghostly and angular.

The road twisted and changed direction many times before we found a deserted spot beside a stream near the southernmost edge of the basin and pitched our tent. To the north of us, within the basin itself, the back waters of Belle River, Bayou Sorrel and Little Bayou Pigeon were and are famous for good crawfish catching, but it was a matter of pride for us to find our own secret place and make a big haul with enough left over to take home.

Jim and I considered ourselves experts on crawfish. The truth is that we knew only the more obvious facts—where to find them and how to cook and eat them. We did not know that there are at least 300 species in the world ranging from an inch to a foot long; or that there are more than 100 species in the United States; or that there are 29 in Louisiana, of which two—the red swamp crawfish and the white river crawfish —are the most common.

Like all animals, crawfish must consume oxygen and eliminate carbon dioxide to live. Like certain other crustaceans, crawfish can draw oxygen from the air, but derive their main supply from the oxygen molecules that are dissolved in the water and absorbed through their gills. The amount of dissolved oxygen in the underwater forest varies widely, depending on such matters as the flow rate of a stream (the faster it goes, the more oxygen it takes in); the temperature of the water (the cooler it is, the more oxygen it can hold); and the abundance of aquatic vegetation (the more plants, up to a certain point, the more oxygen they can contribute). The red swamp crawfish, which can get by on a low supply of dissolved oxygen, predominates in the southernmost bayous, while the white river crawfish, which needs more oxygen, is more prevalent in the northern part of the state, where streams are better aerated.

Cheerfully unaware of all this science, convinced simply by a feeling that we were going to find the best place for red crawfish, we slept soundly under the branches of a hackberry tree. I woke to the smell of catfish frying—the result of my tentmate's foray into the stream by which we had camped. The two he had caught were channel catfish, the kind most often caught in the swampland bayous; they survive even where the level of dissolved oxygen is too low for largemouth bass or bluegills. Their cat's whiskers, which somehow manage to look both fragile and lethal (and are neither), are odor receptors that can scent a meal of minnows or crawfish as far as 50 to 60 yards away. These receptors, properly called barbels, help to keep the species so well fed that channel catfish often reach a weight of 15 to 20 pounds. Jim's were smallish—only about two pounds apiece—but delicious;

there is no breakfast like a hot fried slice of fresh catfish between two pieces of French bread to fortify you for the exertion of slogging through swampland.

The watery webs of intermeshing bayous increase in complexity the farther south you go in this part of the state, so that choosing a place for crawfishing becomes pretty much a matter of whim. There are some criteria, however. You want water that is neither too deep nor too shallow; a depth of two to two and a half feet is just about perfect because it provides the right environment for the tender green plants, rich in carotene, that crawfish need to grow and to produce flavorful, bright yellow fat. It is not hard to find swampy areas of that description and, after surveying a few locations, we chose one near a narrow, overgrown road that looked as if it had not been used for at least a year.

Now we had to set our nets. Each of us had brought six, mine topped by strips of blue ribbon, Jim's by strips of red, to differentiate between them—in the bayou country every man tends to take pride in his own special knack for crawfishing. It took a while to carry the nets out into the water and submerge them, baited with fresh melts (Louisianans' term for pieces of raw beef spleen). Though we both wore boots, the going was tough because we kept stumbling over tangles of long alligator weeds intertwined with water primroses. Still, these obstacles meant that there probably were plenty of crawfish around.

Such plants provide a protective umbrella beneath which the crustaceans can hide from predators like grackles and herons, raccoons and minks. Foliage also camouflages the burrow that the female crawfish digs close to the stream after the mating season in May and June, when the male deposits his sperm in a pouch on her abdomen. However, the female does not lay her eggs—or release the sperm to fertilize them—until September.

All during the waiting period, and for several additional weeks before the eggs hatch, she lives in or beside her burrow. When the eggs open, the plant cover is still of some value as a shield from birds and animals, though it can't protect the infants—perfect miniatures of their parents—from catfish, sunfish, largemouth bass and bullfrogs, which hunt them. One small sunfish, for instance, can consume about 16 newborn crawfish in a period of 24 hours. Sheer numbers usually guarantee the survival of the crawfish, certainly of the red swamp species, since a female produces an average of 400 young each season.

Jim and I dropped our nets carefully, spacing them so that no one net lay within a 10-yard radius of another, and then squatted awhile on a

A four-inch red swamp crawfish emerges from its watery burrow in the muck. It digs its refuge anywhere from 24 to 40 inches deep, plugging the entrance with a cylindrical deposit of mud. When the crawfish surfaces, this "chimney" serves as an exit.

mud embankment. The day was warming, the air now bright and heavy with spring. Across the water where the land was drier, white-topped daisy fleabane and black-eyed Susans glowed like motes of sunlight. There was a gentle hum of life around us. For a while we watched a six-inch-long spotted salamander, its shiny black body highlighted with yellow-orange blotches, moving across the back of a turtle like a small costumed lizard on its way to a fancy-dress ball. The turtle itself was of the species known as the southern painted turtle. Compared to the map turtles I had seen at Bayou Dorcheat, it was gaudy, with a reddish-yellow network across its ebony-green back and a broad red stripe from head to tail. Its highly polished shell shone like wax.

When we went back and lifted the first of our nets, it held 15 to 20 crawfish—a large catch for one lifting. They were dark bronze in color and from three to seven inches long, and they surged together as the water drained away, snapping their claws together like diminutive lobsters. We emptied them into a gunny sack and set it in shallow water to keep the crawfish moist and alive. Then we dropped the net again and waded over to the next.

The rest of the day was a continuous round of lifting and dropping, wading and sweating. When the sun turned orange over the tops of the trees the crickets began to sing in the reeds, announcing the evening. Then a low buzz heralded the mosquitoes, zooming up from the surface of the underwater forest. Mosquitoes are mostly crepuscular—active in the twilight—and so we worked hurriedly, collecting the nets and carrying the gunny sacks back to the truck. One of Jim's cousins lived on Vermilion Bayou, about an hour's drive, Jim said, from where we were. He was wrong about the distance—it took almost two hours to get there—but he was right about the kind of welcome we could expect. A middle-aged man greeted us cheerfully at the door, and his wife did not seem fazed at the prospect of boiling what we estimated to be 50 pounds of crawfish—more than enough for the four of us to eat hot, with leftovers to take home the next day.

As we sat eating by the water's edge, the bayou air rose like heat waves in the dark. Jim threw one of the empty crawfish shells into the stream. There was a loud crack as a fish snapped at the shell: the underwater wilderness of the bayous is awake both night and day. What we were hearing was a sample of the workings of a nocturnal food chain; there are as many links in it as in its daylight counterpart. Catfish are night feeders, and so are salamanders, frogs and snakes. In one of the nocturnal food chains the big water snakes prey on small blue-gills, which feed on large May-fly nymphs, which eat tiny mosquito lar-vae, which eat the infinitesimal one-celled animals called protozoa, which in turn make a meal of aquatic plants.

Early the next morning, before Jim and I set out for home, I walked to the edge of the bayou. A thick mist hung like weightless gauze above the surface of the water. Pecan trees and water oaks glinted with dew. Near the stream a hackberry lay fallen, its taproot broken in the last hur-ricane, its trunk crumbling into the earth. The bayou was thick with mud. A fish swirled to the surface—a largemouth bass, its distinctive two-piece dorsal fin an inch or more high. Apparently there were no minnows near the surface for it to chase; with a switch of its powerful tail, it disappeared underwater. A light layer of green fungus covered the back of some of the trees along the bank; the morning sunlight turned it a pale emerald color. The crawfishing trip had been more than an adventure in good eating.

The following year I went back again to the underwater forests of south-ern Louisiana. This time I brought no nets; I simply wanted to observe more of the life that lay hidden beneath the surface of the water. All of the bayous, rivers, lakes, swamps, marshes, though interdependent, are small separate worlds teeming with life. For fishermen, of course, the at-tractions are many. The oak-shaded streams and the inland lakes, lined with cypress and clogged with hyacinths, hold channel catfish, bluegill and sac-a-lait ("bag of milk," the local term for white crappie, named for its fine-textured meat). Inshore coastal waters provide speckled trout, redfish, flounder, sheepshead and black drum. Pompano, red snap-per, Spanish mackerel and king mackerel in abundance lie not far out in the Gulf of Mexico.

But it was not only fish I expected to see. I wanted a glimpse of some of the other denizens of the underwater forest: crabs, oysters, shrimp —possibly alligators. I hoped also to spot some of the fur-bearing marsh animals that rely in part on underwater bounty. An hour or so from New Orleans I veered south and east until I came to one of the marsh lakes that stud the coastal parishes of the state. In such lakes the water is brackish—a mixture of fresh water coming down from the north and salt water from the Gulf brought in by the tides. By definition, water that contains less than .10 per cent salt—one part salt per thousand parts water—is fresh; brackish water may contain from one to 25 parts of salt; marine or sea water holds at least 25 parts salt, 35 parts at full strength. The farther south you go in the marshes, the more brackish the waters generally are, but rains and floods often reverse the trend momentarily so that a fisherman can catch fresh-water sunfish one day and on another day, in the same area, salt-water redfish.

Like dissolved oxygen, dissolved salt helps determine the types of plants and animals that can live in any given part of the bayou country. Water hyacinth and sac-a-lait must have fresh water; sargasso weed and red snapper must have salt water. When aquatic plants or animals adapted only to fresh-water habitats are inundated by salt water they lose liquid, dehydrate and die. Marine plants and animals, on the other hand, accumulate too much liquid if flooded by fresh water; eventually their cells burst like overinflated balloons. The populations of brackish water remain high because there are also plants and animals, such as cattails and catfish, that can exist in either fresh or faintly brackish environments, and there are others, such as oyster grass and oysters, that thrive in both highly brackish and marine environments.

In the swamp areas through which the first part of my drive took me, there were enough patches of dry land here and there for trees to get a foothold; but farther south the earth became unrelievedly flat. This was marshland that was only a few inches above sea level; it is inundated with water so much of the year that only aquatic grasses and reeds will grow. The Acadians in this part of the state—descendants of the exiled French-Canadians memorialized in Henry Wadsworth Longfellow's *Evangeline*—have their own name for this marshland. They call it *la prairie tremblante*—the trembling prairie.

The contrast between the tree-dotted swamps and the treeless marshes was vivid. The differences between the fresh, the brackish and the salt marshes were more subtle, especially in the species of plants that predominated. In the fresh-water marshes there were clumps of grasslike wild millet and tubular spike rushes that looked like clusters of green pencils two feet high. As the water became more brackish, spike rushes now mingled with cattails, which held their plump cylindrical "tails" high in the air, and with sawgrass, whose three- to four-foot blades are sharp as knives. In the saltiest marshland, the spike rushes and cattails were replaced by woody tangles of black mangrove, about four feet tall, and by oyster grass sporting seed heads that looked like lengths of braided rope.

The marsh lake where I decided to stop had a glassy surface that reflected a sky of silvery high-running clouds. The sunlight was strong and the air hot, but even so there was a gentleness, a kind of peace and privacy, that enveloped the whole broad marshland. I hitched a boat ride with some fishermen who were trawling the lake, using two long funnel-shaped nets. After an hour or so of slow cruising we pulled up one of the trawls and examined its contents. A few translucent gray shrimp wriggled around among flipping multicolored fish. The shrimp were too small—less than half an inch long—for me even to guess if they were the common brown or white species or the rarer pink shrimp. Actually, eggs are laid several miles offshore and the newly hatched shrimp are brought into the marshes by Gulf currents; after about three months inland, when they have grown to about four inches long, they swim back to the sea to spend the rest of their lives. But spending their infancy in brackish marsh ponds and lakes is crucial; while the salinity may be low, the water is shallow and brightly lighted enough to supply the algae, diatoms and bacteria on which the baby shrimp feed.

There was also a fair collection of the blue crabs in the catch and I reached down to pick one up for closer inspection. Suddenly something else rose against my hand, and a set of razor-sharp teeth grazed the tip of one finger, drawing blood. The long, bony alligator garfish that had cut me lay quietly beside the crab, its thin pointed jaws lined with teeth sharp enough to rip a large bass in two. The gar is a strange creature; it looks like the head of an alligator connected to the body of a fish, and grows to an average length of six feet, but with a width of only about 12 inches. It is uniquely adapted for survival. Not only are its eggs toxic and thus safe from predators, but the fish itself can tolerate high levels of brackishness along with low levels of aeration because it has evolved with a special sac for utilizing oxygen more economically than most fish do. My antagonist in the trawl was still young, about 18 inches long, but already aggressive.

Returning my attention to the blue crab I had tried to reach, I saw that it was being pinched by another crab that had already nipped off one claw. The first crab appeared to have no protection at all; it lay perfectly still, not even trying to fight back. It was a softshell. During the two or three years of its life, a crab sheds its hard casing 20 times or more in the process of growing to its full size of six to nine inches across; each time it sheds its shell it is temporarily soft. During its first months, a blue crab molts as often as once a week; when bigger, it sheds every month or two, the pace slowing as it matures. Before each molt, the crab forms a soft covering that envelops its entire body underneath its hard shell; when the time comes to shuck off its old armor

Deemed disloyal to the British Crown, Acadians

expelled from Canada in 1775—as seen in a romanticized drawing of a century later—found eventual haven in the bayou country.

the crab can split the seams down the sides and across the bottom rim of the shell and back out in a few minutes. Then it swells up to as much as twice its former size, and within 24 hours its wrinkled soft covering smooths and hardens. Only during these hours is it a softshell. If caught earlier, during the two-week premolting stage, the crab is a buster, so called locally to describe the bursting of the old shell after the new shell has hardened. Fishermen can find a market for the crabs in any stage, but the softshells are the rarest, since they live in that state for only 24 hours at a time, and also the most prized because nearly the entire crab is edible.

Later that afternoon, walking along the lake to a place where a series of floats bobbed on the surface of the water, I found bunches of reeds that had been torn up, tied together and dropped into the water not far from shore—left by some fisherman hoping to tempt busters to hide in them. Indeed, when I pulled up a bunch, I uncovered half a dozen of the molting crabs. The reed-lined edges of marsh lakes are favorite hiding places for the crabs while they change their outer frames. And a buster needs a hiding place, for it is immobile during the final molting stage and in the softshell stage is totally vulnerable to predators, including its own kind—as I had observed in the boat. Losing a claw does not present a serious problem to a softshell because it can regenerate its limbs; but the attacking hardshell crab is a cannibal that will kill as well as maim, and the buster's only safety is in seclusion. That in turn makes it susceptible to being caught by its human predators, who inspect their floated reed bunches regularly just as a trapper runs his trap lines.

Before evening one of the fishermen took me a few miles farther south in his boat. Nameless, countless bayous interlaced as the water increasingly began to take the place of the land. Before dark we reached another lake, salty enough to have the smell of the sea. Here the fisherman thrust a pair of long-handled tongs into the water and groped around the muddy bottom with them. A few minutes later, in the late light of sunset, we were feasting on oysters that were neither too salty in their taste nor too sweet but a mixture of the two—like the waters they had grown in.

The oyster is a mollusk of interesting ways and habits. It is at the same time both well protected from the vagaries of its environment and yet helpless. In the first stages of life it is soft bodied and free swimming. Then it grows a pair of tiny shells. At this stage each oyster spat, or spawn, must find something clean and hard to anchor onto; otherwise it will sink and be buried in mud. Once attached, it cannot detach itself; it no longer has any means of locomotion. This poses a seemingly insuperable problem in terms of reproduction and continuance of its kind. How, for instance, do a male and female oyster come together? The answer is that they don't. Each sends a milky-looking substance into the surrounding water, one containing eggs and the other sperm. The sperm swim to the eggs, and they join outside the parent bodies. It has been estimated that each female sends out 60 million eggs, each male a billion sperm—adequate insurance of survival in wind-churned, muddy water. Still the problem is not entirely solved, for oysters attach themselves at random. What happens if a random group in a given oyster bed is composed of only male members of the species? The oyster has adapted itself to that possibility too. Though most oysters begin life as males, some of these become female, usually just before or during the spawning season. How oysters change their sex is a matter that scientists are still trying to explain.

Not all the creatures of the underwater forest are so docile, as I discovered on a subsequent journey to marshes still farther south, almost to the southeasternmost tip of the state, where the Mississippi Delta meets the Gulf. One spring morning I got on a small freighter at New Orleans and stayed on it as far as it went down the Mississippi to a small settlement called Venice—an apt name, since the place lies six feet below sea level. As I stepped off onto the levee there, I faced a vast grassy plain, with bayous and small lakes glinting everywhere in the distance—a reminder that almost any place at the southern tip of the delta can be reached by water, if a man has just the right kind of boat and knows how to use it.

About half a mile west of the main levee there was another embankment—a back levee built for protection from the waters of the marsh and the Gulf beyond. Between the two slopes lay a scattering of houses, and here and there purple iris and thick leaves of banana plants gleamed in the sun.

By prearrangement, I spent that afternoon with an Acadian couple, Ulysses and Odette, in their simple and immaculately clean house overhanging the marsh on the far slope of the back levee. The house, built on pilings, effectively straddled the land and the water. On one side, a door led to the levee. On the other side, a door opened onto wooden steps leading down to a boat.

The Acadians—or Cajuns, as they are usually known in Louisiana

—are people well versed in the meaning of survival. They inherited the ability to keep going from their forefathers, who were driven out of Nova Scotia (then called Acadie) by the British in 1755. After much wandering, some of the exiles settled in Louisiana, and here their descendants have stayed, despite hurricanes, floods, plagues of yellow fever and other threats that would have buried a lesser people. They are as much a part of the bayou country now as any living thing to be found in it. The house looked as if it could blow away in the first heavy wind from the Gulf. But its two strong, smiling inhabitants seemed sure of themselves. The Acadians exude a sense of safety in an unsafe world. They know the wild realm of delta and marshland, inlet and bayou better than anyone around, and are better equipped to cope with its subtle moods and sometimes violent vagaries.

The next morning Ulysses took me to see the place where the river meets the sea. We went in a small motorboat, moving downstream into a breeze that carried with it the smell of salt. Gulls swarmed in the air ahead of us and dipped low over the grasses encroaching on either side of the river. The main trunk of the Mississippi had ended, and its many roots, or distributary streams, had begun. The water was thick and muddy. Then, almost without warning, we could see the open sea. Ahead of us the brown river current met the blue Gulf and the surface was churned into foam both by the confluence of the two and by the frenzied activity of the aquatic animals attracted to the agitated water. The surface was alive with shrimp and with the thrashing tails of long, thin eels that flicked like nerves torn loose. Overhead there were sea birds—ring-billed gulls, terns and black skimmers—in incredible numbers. I had heard about the birds that streaked, circled and plunged here to feed, but I had no idea there would be so many. Their cries mingled with the sound of the waves, drowning out everything else. Finally Ulysses shouted, "Now we go back, and my brother, he show you a place tonight; a different place."

On the way back we passed a huge, irregular mound of mud in the middle of the water. This was a mud lump, a curious kind of transitory island reportedly unique to the delta of the Mississippi. When the river deposits its burden of sediment in the Gulf, it drops the heavy sand particles first; the lightweight clay particles travel farther and are the last to fall. The sand creates natural levees that extend the delta seaward until at some later stage the sand deposits begin to pile on top of the clay deposits. The weight of the sand pushes the clay beneath it downward, forcing nearby areas of clay to bulge upward. These upwellings vary from tiny underwater domes to veritable islands, some of them 30 acres in area, that rise 10 to 12 feet above the water line. Mud lumps sometimes appear suddenly, and there are tales told about ships that have been stranded on such instant islands. The disappearance of the islands is a slower process, but inevitable as the waves of the Gulf gradually wear away at the mud.

That evening I went out in another boat with Ulysses' brother Octave, a trapper. For many years Acadians who dwell in the marshes have made a living by trapping muskrats and, in lesser numbers, wild minks. In the 1930s a few South American coypu, or nutria, were imported to Avery Island, a few miles inland from the Gulf, for breeding experiments. The experiments hadn't progressed very far when a hurricane blew the door of the cage open and the nutria escaped; within a few years they had bred so rapidly in the marshes that today Acadian trappers have more of these skins to trade than the muskrat skins that once provided their main livelihood.

The nutria and the muskrat, which are aquatic animals, share the marshes with the mink. Though the mink can live on dry land as well, it is an accomplished swimmer and diver. It is also, in the considered opinion of zoologists, one of the most vicious mammals extant—"murderous" and "bloodthirsty" being but two of the ways they characterize it. The description is somehow hard to reconcile with the creature's silky dark-brown fur and its small, slender body. The male, the larger of the sexes, seldom weighs more than four pounds. But there can be no doubt of the mink's savagery when it is on the hunt for food. It will sink its powerful canine teeth into just about anything that will satisfy its carnivorous appetite—birds, fish, frogs, mice. The muskrat, its cohabitor in the Louisiana marshes, is evidently a favored morsel. Endowed with a keen sense of smell, the mink will sniff a muskrat deep within the lodge it has built as a shelter, then will claw and dig with its sharp toes until it can work its body inside the lodge entrance and seize its prey.

Fortunately for the muskrats, and for the nutria as well, their tastes in food do not generally conflict with those of the mink, although the muskrat is known to eat its own kind at times. More often it feeds on favorite vegetables like bulrushes, cattails and pond lilies, supplementing them with mussels, salamanders and other aquatic creatures. The nutria is a total vegetarian, ravaging plants from leaves to roots.

The richness of the marsh larder was everywhere apparent as Octave and I traveled along in his pirogue. This is the true boat of the bayou, made from a hollowed-out cypress log. Local people claim that a pirogue can ride on a heavy dew. It was easy to believe, as we slid over marsh reeds that grew in water both shallow and deep. The strength and the grace of a pirogue, in the hands of a man who knows how to maneuver it, are something to marvel at. Waterways only two feet wide can be negotiated; almost as if the boat were weightless, it can be poled across mud flats from lake to lake. A pirogue is easily tipped over by inexperienced users, but with an Acadian in charge there is no problem.

For a while we rode beside a flat bank that looked solid. Octave stuck the pole into the wet crust of matted growth next to the boat. The pole came out dark and glistening. The top layer of the matting was solid with plants; below it was water, then below that the matting became solid again with dead plants that had sunk to the bottom and compacted as they decomposed to form peat.

Using a paddle again, Octave propelled us easily through the marsh. As the light began to fade, we rode up a small stream that narrowed ahead, with high reeds on either side. When the moon rose, the reeds took on a white-green aura. The moonlight reflected from the surface and lay all about like a cold green glow in the warm dampness of the reeds. It was as if we had entered a world that was the color of all plant life—the essence of green.

Then ahead of us, somewhere not too far off, a quick scream rang out. It sounded strangely human, and I stood up in alarm so fast that the pirogue almost overturned. Octave grinned and pushed me back down with one hand. "Mink," he said. "She screams. The muskrat, or the nutria, she makes a noise, but not like that." He pointed ahead of the boat. "There's a muskrat."

To our right, deep among the reeds, an animal was swimming. From what I could see of its sleek back, it seemed to be almost a foot and a half long and looked like an enormous field mouse. The word muskrat comes from the Algonquin Indian *musquash,* meaning "it is red"; but this animal's fur, wet and moonlit, seemed a gleaming black. The creature was carrying plants in its mouth, possibly intending them for home construction. In the marshes, muskrats build their lodges above the surface on rafts of water reeds or cattails or patches of peat, though the entrance is always underwater. They build by packing heaps of reeds and other vegetation together, plugging in the gaps with bits of moss,

As a female alligator warily surfaces in a fresh-water marsh, a weeks-old baby, atop her head, scouts for food amidst the water lettuce.

clay or peat. The lodges look like small-scale rounded wigwams, two to three feet high.

We rode on past the muskrat, with only the sound of water for company, a soft monotonous lapping. Octave picked up a handful of flat shells from the bottom of the boat and threw them hard into the water a few yards upstream. For a moment nothing happened; then, abruptly, harsh bellowing came out of the night. It sounded at first as if a small volcano had erupted around us. The noise was full and blunt—and suddenly over. The roar of a bull alligator at night has a singularly chilling effect, one that is hard to convey to people who have never heard it. Octave turned on a large flashlight and pointed it in the direction of the noise. About 30 yards upstream a pair of eyes glowed red and unblinking. The light limned the rest of the animal. It looked to be at least five or six feet long.

The alligator inhabits the swamps as well as the marshes, both fresh and salt water, and it has had a long history in Louisiana; it has been the subject of folk tale and fantasy ever since men settled the southern bayou country. It is one of those animals whose appearance is so impressive that it generates its own exaggerated image. The reality used to be equally impressive. John James Audubon, reporting on his own observations of alligators in Louisiana, wrote in 1826: "Before the Red River was opened to steam navigation they could be seen along shores by the hundreds, or on immense rafts of floating or stranded timber, the smaller on the backs of the larger, all groaning and bellowing like thousands of irritated bulls about to fight. All were so oblivious of man that unless shot at or otherwise disturbed they remained motionless. Boats or canoes could pass within yards of them unnoticed."

The reality today is considerably less spectacular. The popularity of alligator bags and shoes in Paris, London and New York earlier in this century resulted in the drastic depletion of the species in Louisiana. Since 1963 the hunting of alligators has been illegal in the state, and gradually the population has increased; it now numbers about 250,000, and a restricted hunting season has been reopened on an experimental basis. Alligators are to be seen now all along the coast, as well as scattered throughout the swamps. People who live near the marshes have complained at times of finding alligators in their garages at night. More than once an alligator has made its way into a church meeting in one of the small communities that border the wilder areas. The result of such a visit, to put it mildly, has been confusion.

Alligators are members of the underwater forest community because they need water to keep their hides wet. The dens they construct for their winter hibernation from November through February are always at the water's edge. The females go deep into the marsh for hibernation, but for the males a canal will do. In both sexes body functions are reduced during hibernation, and there is no feeding whatever. But sometimes, on a bright winter day warm enough to entice alligators outside their dens, several of these great creatures can be seen sunning together on a bank.

Their young have a harder time of it. The female leaves its eggs in an airtight heaped-up nest of grass and mud, and departs, coming back only in the eighth or ninth week. Her young are born with an egg tooth that enables them to break out of the shell. But they cannot escape the muddy vegetation heaped over them without the mother's help. Once outside, they are on their own—prey to herons, fish, turtles, raccoons and snakes. Only a small percentage reaches maturity. Yet once they make it that far, the alligators are among the sturdiest of survivors and a formidable threat to all other creatures of their environment.

A second bellow broke the silence, and Octave turned the pirogue around to go back. The roaring resounded for what seemed like minutes; then the only sound to be heard was the water's gentle lapping. As I watched Octave poling the boat with an unerring sense of direction, it occurred to me that the ability to navigate by instinct is a gift that the Acadians seem to share only with those other inhabitants of the coastal marshes, the birds. I was to learn about the comings and goings of the birds in another trip to the wilderness some years later.

Life among the Egrets

PHOTOGRAPHS BY VERNON MERRITT III

On spring evenings in the marshy southern fringes of Louisiana, the skies come alive with the measured beat of huge white wings as the great egrets come home to their nests and their hungry young. The marshes and beaches along the coast provide an ideal habitat for a great many aquatic birds, some transient, some that live there all year; but in spring the winter visitors return north, leaving the area to summer and permanent residents, notable among them the great egrets. These magnificent birds are the largest of the four species of egrets native to the United States, standing three feet tall, with a wingspan of five feet.

By mid-April the egrets have finished their courting and mating, have built their twiggy nests in bushes or on tree branches, and have laid and hatched their eggs. They then turn to the task of raising their young.

Egret pairs usually produce four chicks, and spend the next six weeks trying to satisfy the seemingly insatiable appetites of their offspring. The adults stalk the surrounding waters for small fish, frogs and crustaceans, which they store, partially digested, in their gullets and stomachs and take back to feed to the nestlings. By the end of May the parental ordeal is over and the chicks begin to fend for themselves.

Nesting time has its hazards for the egrets. Spring storms and floods can wreak havoc on a nesting colony. In addition, the egrets' natural enemies—hawks, raccoons, alligators and snapping turtles—are an ever-present danger. Alligators have been known to swat a tree or bush with their powerful tails to shake the young out of their nests.

The egrets had a worse enemy —man—during the days when the fashion in women's hats decreed that they be adorned with the luxuriant plumes, called aigrettes, that the birds sport during courtship and later lose. Plume hunters had almost wiped out the egrets in southern Louisiana by the turn of the century when a naturalist named Edward A. McIlhenny found eight of the birds in the swamp near his home on Avery Island and raised them to maturity. The next spring six of them returned to the island and established a colony, which now numbers some 20,000 egrets of various species. Here, and in other sanctuaries on the coast, the egrets survive and flourish, and each spring, as shown in the following pictures, they raise yet another generation to carry on.

Like a ballet dancer sur les pointes, an adult egret poises elegantly on the branch of a dead cypress tree. It stands on its toes, as all birds do (what appears to be the first joint of its leg is actually the heel of its foot). From this carefully balanced stance, the egret can launch instantly into flight.

Gracefully braking before landing, and crying its monotone "cuk-cuk," a great egret returns to its nest to provide its ravenous young with food it has caught and partially digested. Each egret parent makes about four trips a day between the nest and its food larder in nearby marshes and ponds.

As yet unable to fetch their own food, three egret chicks keep an alert watch for signs of a parent winging home with their next meal. At this age, about six weeks, they leave the nest only to hop about on nearby branches, but will soon be making solo flights.

The forthright technique employed by young egrets as mealtime nears is illustrated in this sequence of pictures. While its siblings sit by, the most aggressive chick—or perhaps the hungriest one—clamps a scissors hold on its parent's bill and agitates it vigorously to shake food into its own bill. Sometimes such aggressiveness defeats its purpose, as at far right, where the adult is so hard pressed it cannot disgorge any food. Occasionally the parent is pushed right off the nest.

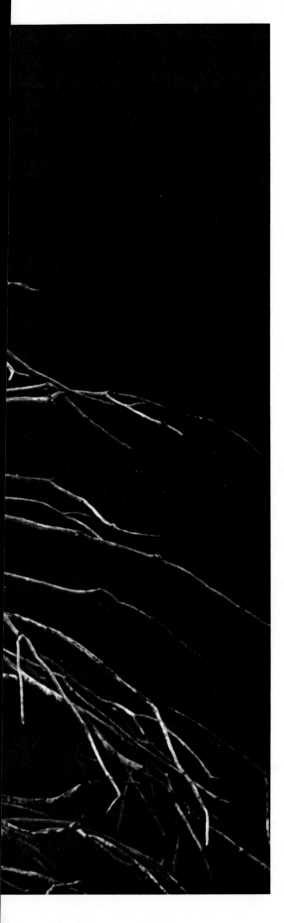

An adult egret (above) repairs the
flimsy, crudely made platform of twigs
that serves as its nest. Construction of
the nest is a shared project: the male
procures the materials, the female does
the building. Both take turns guarding
their home from twig-thieving birds.

One dead cypress tree provides sites
for two egret nests at different levels.
Some trees serve as multiple dwellings
with 10 or more nests, and suffer
the consequences: the birds' droppings,
which contain destructive uric acid,
often cause the death of a host tree.

In a no-holds-barred contest, one young egret nips another in the neck as a third chick watches. Often prompted by squabbles over food, such hostility is common during the nesting period, and no quarter is given—though deaths from these fierce encounters between young birds are rare.

Having lost their down, these two-week-old chicks look vulnerable and scrawny as they begin to acquire their first firm feathers. In a month they will have enough feathers to fly, but the spectacular aigrettes for which the species is famous—the so-called nuptial plumage—will not appear until the courtship period the next spring.

With half a dozen younger birds as an
interested audience, two egrets stage
a noisy flap over territorial rights.
Although egrets nest very close to one
another, they respect certain territorial
boundaries that are instinctively
recognized, and that cannot be crossed
except at the peril of the intruder.

6/ Sanctuary by the Sea

*Across the length of the United States . . . came the
pulsing beat of far-near wings — the sound of wild geese
in flight.*   McFADDEN DUFFY/ FROM BEYOND THE NORTH WIND

At its broadest point the state of Louisiana is no more than 270 miles
wide. But its shoreline, frayed at the edge like old tapestry and fringed
with thousands of islands, meanders for more than 8,000 miles. Here
along the Gulf of Mexico millions of acres of coastal marsh, and the bordering beach ridges, provide one of the world's largest natural aviaries
for waterfowl and wading birds, shore birds and songbirds. No fewer
than 411 varieties—more than half the species known to exist in North
America north of Mexico—have been sighted in Louisiana, the vast majority of them in this southern rim of the bayou country. At least 96 of
these species live in and around the marshes year round.

Among the tens of thousands of permanent residents are gulls, terns,
pelicans, skimmers, plovers, rails and wrens. Added to them are millions of other birds that populate the marshes part time: waterfowl
from the north that arrive in autumn and stay the winter, wading birds
returning from the south to spend the spring and summer breeding
here, and all sorts of transients that stop by for only a day or so on
their semiannual intercontinental travels.

March heralds the influx from points south, though a few species
may arrive in February or even in late January. With the first warm
breezes the migrating flocks begin pouring in over the Gulf. At the
height of the influx, which takes place over a period of about nine
weeks, more than five million of them cross the coastline every 24

hours. Many are big birds—herons and egrets and bitterns that fill the sky with flapping wings. But there are little birds too, warblers and vireos and hummingbirds. They have come from the peninsula of Yucatán across the Gulf, from the Central American isthmus or from South America. And the length of their various journeys requires a stamina that has nothing to do with the birds' size. A Louisiana heron may have flown 2,500 miles from southern Venezuela, a small purple martin 5,000 miles from southern Brazil.

Many of the incoming birds use the marshes and beach ridges merely as a stopover. The painted buntings and wood thrushes go on to other parts of Louisiana. The scarlet tanagers and rose-breasted grosbeaks travel as far as New England. About one of every 10 of the newcomers will be anhingas, ibises, their cousins the spoonbills, and members of the heron-egret-bittern family. And these will stay put along Louisiana's coastline until summer's end.

The influx from the south is spectacular enough, but it is only half of the drama. During the same months, several million birds that have wintered in the marshes—ducks, geese and coots—take wing to begin their way north along the Mississippi Flyway. This great migratory route, the most traveled of the four major American flyways, is shaped like an enormous funnel with its tip at the Louisiana coast. The neck of the funnel leads up the Mississippi River Valley, widens out at the Missouri and Ohio valleys, and continues to widen west and east until, at the funnel's mouth, the flyway almost spans the continent—from the northwestern tip of Alaska to the eastern shores of Hudson Bay.

Within this vast compass different birds take different directions. Mallards, pintails, ring-necked ducks and Canada geese use the so-called mallard route, generally northwest, to the Yukon Flats in Alaska, some 3,500 miles from bayou country. Blue geese turn northeast from the Mississippi to follow the Illinois River Valley as far as it goes. Then they continue across Canada to the Arctic tundras of Baffin Island—a 3,000-mile trip whose northern terminus is so remote even the Eskimos were unaware that Baffin was the blue goose's breeding ground until an intrepid wildlife scientist, J. Dewey Soper, tracked it down in 1929.

Although the massive seasonal movements of birds have been studied by man for centuries, the whole phenomenon of bird migrations, not only in Louisiana but worldwide, is only partially understood. Some theories about the migrations go back thousands of years. One suggested that birds flew to the moon for the off-season. Aristotle tried to account for the simultaneous arrival and exodus of species by conjecturing that one kind of bird was transmuted into another. The most popular ancient theory held that birds, like bears, hibernated, hiding in caves or tree hollows or even under the mud of swamps and marshes. Curiously, there has been recent proof that at least one species—the California poor-will—does indeed take shelter for the winter in a cavity in a canyon wall, entering a trancelike sleep and reducing its body temperature in order to survive the cold.

The poor-will is an exception, though, and a major source of puzzlement remains: why do some birds migrate while others, even members of the same species, do not? In the case of migrations southward food shortages seem to play a bigger motivating role than temperature changes. Many birds adjust to cold, even in the 40°-below of the sub-Arctic; the ruffed grouse of Labrador lives there year round. But many other species depart southward at a sign of threat to their food supply—when cold in the north, for example, begins to kill vegetation.

Just as the need for food appears to be the major southward lure in autumn, so the instinct to reproduce usually triggers the journey back in spring. The sexual glands of the birds enlarge, plumage brightens, restlessness increases and one evening the move northward gets under way. The destination of the migrant is always the same: the place where it was born, and where it will in turn produce its young.

Most migrations are leisurely affairs with daily breaks for feeding and sleeping. If the trip is to be a long one, a precautionary layer of fat will have formed under the bird's skin. In-flight speeds differ widely. Herons travel at about 20 mph, ducks and geese at 40 to 50 mph. Species with similar flying capabilities often travel together, though some flights are made up of a single species. The sexual composition of flights also varies. In the case of mallards and black ducks, the male and female fly together, courting and mating on the way north. Purple martins and red-winged blackbirds segregate the sexes in flight; the males go on ahead to establish a nesting territory before the females arrive.

Of the many questions raised by migration, the most baffling of all, perhaps, is how birds find their way across continents and seas to settle finally on the same bush or tree they occupied the previous year. Scientists have managed to pin down a few, but by no means all, parts of the puzzle. It is known, for instance, that the visual acuity of birds is two or three times that of humans, enabling them to see much more detail and to perceive tiny objects from great distances. Some day travelers seem to orient themselves by the sun; the night flyers appear to get their bearings from the constellations. But senses other than vision evidently come into play. No one has as yet satisfactorily explained, for example, the homing abilities of birds blown off course by winds, or the navigational skills invoked in cloudy weather.

Only a severe storm can force migrating birds down to the nearest available patch of ground; on the bayou coast in such circumstances, bushes may suddenly become so thick with birds that twigs and leaves seem to disappear. After one bad Gulf storm when I was a child, I remember walking along a beach on Grand Isle, a barrier island off southeastern Louisiana, and coming upon what I believed to be a bush made of birds. They were indigo buntings, hundreds of them, clustered so thickly they appeared to have grown and ripened there like berries. All along the beach other bushes were similarly laden. It was years before I learned why the birds were bunched in such incredible numbers.

Not long ago, more knowledgeable about birds and wanting to observe them in other than crisis conditions, I visited Avery Island, where large colonies of wading birds converge in spring and summer. Avery Island is a salt dome—one of 329 such curious formations along the Gulf. The domes are the product of salt beds, buried some 30,000 feet deep, formed more than 150 million years ago when ancient seas became landlocked and then evaporated. Because of the salt's light weight, it has gradually been squeezed upward by the pressure of the earth around it: most of the salt domes remain below ground level but some of them rise high enough to push the land above into a round shape. The most famous of the salt domes are the Five Islands, located inland near the shore of south-central Louisiana. Avery Island is the biggest of the five. It rises 152 feet at its highest point, and encompasses over 2,500 acres.

In 1892 the naturalist Edward Avery McIlhenny rescued eight snowy egrets from possible destruction by plume hunters and housed them in a flight-sized cage on Avery Island. From that nucleus has grown a present-day bird metropolis, a cageless sanctuary known as Bird City, complete with an artificial lake, where more than 100,000 wading birds gather during mating season. Though the site has been built up with artificial nesting platforms to supplement the trees and bushes, the birds remain as wild and free here as they are in the adjoining marshland.

The summer population begins to arrive very early in March, when budding green possesses the marshland and yellow jasmine is in bloom. As dusk descends, sharp croaking cries can be heard from afar—faint at first, then more piercing and plaintive. Flocks of snowy egrets move across the darkening sky like white arrows. They may have flown vast distances, yet when the birds first arrive at the island they show no sign of strain and they are at their most beautiful. The white of their feathers seems intensified, and indeed they are in full plumage now, for this is the start of their mating season.

There are other arrivals, too. The green heron, the yellow-crowned night heron, the least bittern and anhinga (known also as the snakebird for its habit of swimming with only its sinuous head and neck above water) cross the coastline in gleams and bursts of color, wheeling and shrieking as they descend. Little blue herons, slate colored with deep purple necks, fly in, and so do their larger cousins the Louisiana herons, their white bellies in sharp contrast to the bluish-gray feathers on their backs. From March through the middle of May the sky is filled with shafts of feathers and light, the air flooded with streams of birds, as if a rainbow had shattered and was falling in pieces into the marshes.

When they first arrive, the herons and egrets leave the sanctuary each morning for the surrounding marshes and lagoons, swamps and ponds to hunt for minnows, lizards and crawfish. But feeding is only one objective. There in the wilderness the male birds perform their courting ritual, spreading their plumes and strutting in front of the females, gurgling, taking to the air in short flights. Each male, having demonstrated both his beauty and his flying prowess, then descends to earth and to the particular female he has chosen to impress. Soon the pair seeks a branch of a tree or a bush or a platform in Bird City on which nesting will begin. Prudent instinct dictates the selection of a site; preferably it is surrounded by water on a branch at least six feet above the surface, relatively safe from tree-climbing predators like raccoons and snakes, and out of casual reach of alligators and garfish.

I watched a pair of snowy egrets that had picked the interlacing branches of a willow tree. Both male and female proceeded to flatten a place about 12 inches across, removing protuberant twigs with their bills and feet. The female then perched possessively on the site while the male went off in search of building materials. Returning with the first twig, he presented it to his mate in a great show of pomp; she raised her crest and fluffed her plumes in acknowledgment.

This is a standard ritual for the species: the male continues to procure twigs, the female to construct the nest for about three days, during which time the site is always guarded to prevent other birds from stealing the twigs for their own nests. Two or three days after the nest is completed, the bluish-green eggs begin to appear, one every other day

Blue geese and lesser snow geese, wintering in southwest Louisiana, fly into a marshy feeding ground at the Sabine National Wildlife Refuge.

until there are four or five in all. When brooding begins, the male and female again take turns and once the fledglings emerge both parents feed them. For the first feeding, one parent stands beside the nest and brings up some partially digested food from its gullet, nudging the newborn with its bill until they slowly respond. The young are fed several times a day, and soon they are anxiously grasping at the parent's bill the moment it returns to the nest. Between meals the young learn to walk, occasionally falling out of the tree into the water below. Sometimes they pull themselves back up, but often they are eaten by alligators.

The lessons of life in the marshland go on. One of the last—and most critical—occurs when a parent returns with a gullet full of food to a site that cannot be reached by the young unless they fly from the nest. One by one, the little birds flap over to reach the meal. After this they are ready to be guided to nearby ponds and taught to feed themselves.

With the first hint of cool weather in September and the appearance of the earliest birds from the north, the egrets, along with the other species that have spent the spring and summer on Avery Island, leave for the long flight south over the Gulf of Mexico to a warmer winter climate. Their departure is often at sunset: white wings and bodies, tinted with the deep orange of the sky, form a great long throat of light. The birds will not come back until the following spring, when they will again mate and produce another generation.

The migrations that sweep in from the north in the fall are equally memorable, especially when seen from the vantage point of one of the nine sanctuaries provided for birds and other wildlife along the coast itself. The Rockefeller Wildlife Refuge in southwestern Louisiana is one of the largest of them, 84,000 acres in extent, and last year I visited it to observe the great autumnal drama. I set out one October day just after dawn from the city of Lafayette, about 50 miles away. Cows roamed the fields along the road, followed closely by white-feathered cattle egrets looking for insects that had been stirred up in the grasses by the cattle. This species of egret is native to Africa and southern Asia, but has spread to every other continent and was first seen in Louisiana in 1955. Though generally the species is a migratory one that travels south in winter, many of the Louisiana cattle egrets inexplicably defy custom and live year round in the bayou country. Compared to other egrets, these are short-legged birds, with relatively short necks that they weave about, as geese do, when they search for food.

As I watched them, rain began to fall, heavy and violent—so thick it was hard to see ahead. I slowed the car almost to a stop and as I did so, two yellow-bellied water snakes glided across the road in front of me. In the swollen gray light, a crawfish picked its way across, claws held up. Through the rain it looked distorted, like a miniature prehistoric monster emerging from the reeds. There was another crawfish, and another—an army of them moving through the sheets of rain. A six-inch red-eared turtle was in their midst, as though being escorted to safety.

I had not traveled too far by the time the rain stopped. I was deep in marsh country. The stretches of wet green along the road were entirely flat; glints of autumn brown and yellow shimmered through the green. To the north, where the water was fresh, the trembling prairie was a sea of grass—wild millet and alligator weed. In the brackish waters toward the south the grasses were shorter but denser, their progress gulfward interrupted occasionally by low-growing black-green baccharis bushes and clumps of slender-bladed black rushes.

Water lay everywhere just below the surface, seeping through in places to form puddles and ponds. Where the water was fresh, its surface was masked by a green covering that looked like scum but was in fact made up of masses of duckweed. These minute floating plants, with leaves less than an eighth of an inch wide, reproduce so rapidly that they provide a continuous food source for waterfowl. In one pond a green-winged teal was paddling. The smallest of all duck species —about 14 inches long—it resembled a mechanical toy bobbing its head up and down as it fed on the duckweed. Then it upended itself so that all I could see was its tail as it probed underwater after some other plant. Moments later the teal was upright, eating duckweed again.

Scattered willows grew beside the road where the land had any height at all, and beyond them were russet cattails. As I neared the coast a few live oaks appeared, growing almost horizontal. The glare of the sky, a spectrum of grays, lent this seaside wilderness a look of limbo.

The Rockefeller refuge borders the Gulf for 26.5 miles. At the very southern tip of the Mississippi Flyway, it is one of the most strategically located wildlife areas in the United States and a winter home for hundreds of thousands of migratory waterfowl and marsh birds—geese, ducks, coots, gallinules and rails. The refuge has been state-owned since 1920. Under the supervision of the Louisiana Wild Life and Fisheries Commission this vast treeless expanse not only has been saved from encroaching civilization, but improved upon. To benefit the migratory waterfowl, natural ponds have been dammed to stabilize their water levels, and artificial ponds from 480 to 5,680 acres in size, called impoundments, have been constructed. Though migratory wading birds take advantage of the refuge in summer and there is a permanent population of water birds, the wintering migratory waterfowl are a particular pride of the refuge. The duck population alone, estimated at 75,000 in the 1950s, now reaches 400,000 in midwinter.

Along with the birds, thousands of alligators, otters, raccoons, muskrats, nutria and deer inhabit the refuge. The creatures are year-round residents—and so are a few research biologists. These dedicated men have a great deal to occupy them: banding birds, investigating migration patterns, pursuing the life history of the alligator and studying the entire ecology of the marsh.

As I drove in and parked near the research headquarters at the northwest corner of the refuge, a pair of Canada geese streaked overhead, their long necks stretched straight out as if reaching for some impossible destination. They were two of the 3,000 Canada geese that have been bred to be permanent residents in the refuge. I watched them circle and come down on one of the refuge impoundments. Their colors were harmonious: whitish jowls and black necks, white breasts, grayish-tan bodies and white tails. Beyond them was a flock of migrant blue geese, strutting together. In the distance, on a levee by a narrow bayou, stood a pale white-tailed deer, barely outlined against the grasses. Marsh animals tend to bleach out from constant exposure to sun and the normally rich brown coats of the deer are a reddish beige.

For a time outside the main building I talked with Ted Joanen, the chief of research. I was particularly curious to learn about the condition of the rare brown pelican. The official state bird—it appears on the state seal and hence on all state documents—the brown pelican was once a common sight on the inshore islands and the mud lumps at the mouth of the Mississippi River. In the early 1960s it disappeared from the bayou country. Scientists conjecture that pesticides contaminated the food the pelican ate and remained, harmlessly, in its fatty tissues until the pelican got into a stress situation. Then the poison surged through the bloodstream into the brain or the liver, with fatal result. Fledgling pelicans from Florida are being brought to the refuge and to a marine research laboratory at Grand Terre Island in small groups and are carefully protected. But the reestablishment of the species in Louisiana will be a slow process; the population is now estimated at only 400.

The brown pelican is immensely graceful when soaring, but an awkward waddler on the ground. It is easy to sight even from a distance,

Where southwestern Louisiana meets the Gulf of Mexico at the edge of bayou country, low tide bares a mud flat of silt, shells and clay.

because of its standing height—about two and a half feet—and its large scooplike bill. The bird is gentle if somewhat ponderous-looking, with a long neck the color of mahogany, the top of the head and sides of the neck whitish, the body grayish brown.

The pelican's quest for fish, the staple of its diet, is fun to watch. It wheels and turns in a half roll, then plunges into the sea and disappears beneath the surface. When the pelican reemerges, the pouch of its scoop bill contains several quarts of water full of fish. The bird thrusts its bill upward, contracting the pouch, and the water spills out through the corners of the mouth. Then, with an enormous gulp, the pelican swallows the fish, which it predigests and later regurgitates into the throats of its young. The babies are naked, sad and scruffy-looking. After the first soft natal down comes and goes, the birds are gray; not until the age of three do they grow mahogany-colored feathers.

While Ted Joanen and I stood talking, some of the young Canada geese in a flock nearby started a fight with another group that approached them. Within a few seconds, the gabble was such that it was almost impossible for us to hear each other. I yelled through the noise that I would like to see some of the other birds; we moved off and Joanen provided me with a guide and a station wagon. The station wagon, he explained, could go only a very short distance into the marshes of the refuge. After that, unless I wanted to use a boat, I would have to go on foot. I settled for the drive and the walk.

In this refuge, as in all wildlife refuges of the Gulf Coast and the coastal islands, the sky is never clear of birds. Somewhere overhead something is always on the wing. High above the rattling station wagon I saw a bald eagle. The great bird floated over the marsh haze, easily recognizable by its white head and white tail. Like the pelican, the eagle feeds largely on fish and is therefore rarely found far from water. And like the pelican, it faces the threat of extinction: pesticides in its diet make the bird infertile or cause its eggs to break before hatching.

Where the mud road met a stand of black rushes, my guide and I left the car and took a footpath deeper into the marsh. I stared unbelieving at the scene overhead. Green-winged teals, ring-necked ducks, mottled ducks, mallards, pintails and lesser scaup shattered the air repeatedly like fragments of an enormous explosion, as though some life force had burst apart. Though the flocks of ducks shared the sky, each kind kept to itself—a pattern they follow on land as well. Closer to the water a belted kingfisher, its crest bushy and its breast banded rust and white, hovered and waited for a minnow to come into view.

The scene on the ground was just as enthralling. Semipalmated plovers, like miniature gulls in clerical garb with single, wide gray or black breast rings under their white collars, stood curious and unafraid, watching us as we went by. A gray-brown clapper rail the size and shape of a young chicken ran across our path. Birds picked their way elegantly through the ponds, fishing as they went. The catch would be predictably good—croaker, redfish, flounder, sheepshead and other salt- and brackish-water fish inhabit the marsh waters.

Where the path ended, we came to a stop. Ahead lay reeds and grass and water: to travel farther on foot was impossible. Roseau cane and three-cornered grass rose tall around us. Then, from the northern horizon, we saw flights of migratory waterfowl heading for the marshes.

The first two flocks to pass by were American widgeons, the third shovelers. All flew in an unwavering direction, as if with the certainty of knowledge. I wondered about their numbers and whether they had been depleted along the way. Farther north along the flyway landowners have been known to flood their rice fields after harvest, forming ersatz marshes in order to entice the migrating waterfowl to descend. I am told that some of the birds are fooled and are shot by hunters. But most flocks are not deceived and continue down to the Gulf.

The flights I was watching dipped their wings over the marshes of the refuge and landed separately in different spots a mile or so from where we were standing. I could not make out the individual birds very clearly, but next day, as I was leaving the refuge, a flight of snow geese appeared on the horizon and landed in a rush only 200 yards from my car. I got out and looked at them—six adults, 12 young. The adults were a blinding white, with black wing tips; the young were a dusky gray. I looked especially at their eyes, set like those of all birds on opposite sides of the head. It occurred to me that though geese lack binocular vision, the arrangement of their eyes gives them horizon-wide vision on their journeys from Canada.

Now they began waddling about, ruffling their feathers after their flight, honking as if they recognized the place. Around them multicolored stretches of bayou country lay silent in the mist of early morning.

The Realm of the Cheniers

PHOTOGRAPHS BY DENNIS STOCK

Along the shore of southwestern Louisiana the chenier country extends for more than 100 miles, from Vermilion Bay in the center of Louisiana's coastline to Sabine Lake in the west at the Texas boundary—a testament to the ceaseless contest between earth and water in this part of the world. It is a low-lying area with vast salt marshes, but the ridge-like cheniers relieve the flatness, punctuating the wet marshlands like elongated islands. Each long ridge, varying from two to 10 feet above sea level, represents a former coastline where waves and currents of the Gulf piled up a mixture of river sediments and broken shells.

The coast has edged gradually farther out into the Gulf, leaving the cheniers to be surrounded by marsh. The oldest ridges, now some 10 miles inland from the Gulf, were formed almost 3,000 years ago; the youngest are barely 300 years old. The more substantial of them have provided high ground where vegetation has taken root; not the lush growth of the swampy inland bayous, but a more spare, frontier vegetation. The marshes lie right in the path of the storms and hurricanes that periodically sweep in off the Gulf, and only the hardy survive; but still the chenier plants and creatures endure, carrying on with sturdy persistence.

Much of the chenier country is not particularly wild; men have long farmed some of the larger ridges, which extend for miles. But on many cheniers man has left undisturbed the impressive clumps of live oaks that crown their low profiles, as well as the wild flowers and small birds that adorn their grassy places.

Roving the chenier country, photographer Dennis Stock found it "a subdued, gentle and aged country, where one should not search for melodramatic proportions. There are no grand vistas here; what is provided instead is a succession of subtle experiences of discovery."

As seen on the following pages, Stock's camera recorded both vivid and muted aspects of the cheniers: the quick movement of a grackle feeding among the reeds; the splashes of brightness supplied by a species of iris known as yellow flag, by a spiny thistle and by stark white egrets; the somber colors of the hardy, moss-covered live oaks. In these trees, the classic symbols of the cheniers, Stock sensed "a strength conferred both by age and by the simple fact of having endured for so long in such a vulnerable world."

A BOAT-TAILED GRACKLE IN MARSH REEDS

LIVE OAKS AND SPANISH MOSS

A WIND-DAMAGED LIVE OAK

A BUTTONBUSH BESIDE A POND

GREAT EGRETS AT THE GULF'S EDGE

A YELLOW FLAG

THE FLOWER HEAD OF A SPINY THISTLE, CLOSE UP

SUNSET ON GRAND CHENIER

Bibliography

*Also available in paperback.
†Available in paperback only.

Bent, Arthur Cleveland, *Life Histories of North American Marsh Birds.* Dover Publications, 1963.

Bent, Arthur Cleveland, *Life Histories of North American Wild Fowl,* 2 vols. Dover Publications, June 1962.

Brown, Clair A., *Louisiana Trees and Shrubs.* Claitor's Book Store, 1965.

Brown, Clair A., *Wildflowers of Louisiana and Adjoining States.* Louisiana State University Press, 1972.

Comeaux, Malcolm L., *Atchafalaya Swamp Life.* Louisiana State University, 1972.

Conant, Roger, *A Field Guide to the Reptiles and Amphibians of the United States and Canada East of the 100th Meridian.* Houghton Mifflin Company, 1958.

Davis, Edwin Adams, *Louisiana: The Pelican State.* Louisiana State University Press, 1959.

Drimmer, Frederick, ed., *The Animal Kingdom,* Vols. I and II. Doubleday and Company, 1954.

Dunn, Gordon E., and Banner I. Miller, *Atlantic Hurricanes,* rev. ed. Louisiana State University Press, 1964.

Hansen, Harry, ed., *Louisiana: A Guide to the State,* rev. ed. Hastings House, 1971.

*Harrar, Ellwood S. and J. George, *Guide to Southern Trees,* 2nd ed. Peter Smith, 1962.

Hochbaum, H. Albert, *The Travels and Traditions of Waterfowl.* Charles T. Branford Company, 1960.

Kane, Harnett T., *The Bayous of Louisiana.* William Morrow & Company, 1943.

Klots, Alexander B. and Elsie B., *Living Insects of the World.* Doubleday and Company, 1959.

Kniffen, Fred B., *Louisiana: Its Land and People.* Louisiana State University Press, 1968.

Kortright, Francis H., *The Ducks, Geese and Swans of North America.* Stackpole Company, 1953.

†Lincoln, Frederick C., *Migration of Birds.* United States Department of the Interior, 1950.

Linduska, Joseph P., ed., *Waterfowl Tomorrow.* United States Department of the Interior, 1964.

Lowery, George H., Jr., *Louisiana Birds.* Louisiana State University Press, 1960.

Oberholser, Harry C., *The Bird Life of Louisiana.* Louisiana Department of Conservation, 1938.

Palmer, Ralph S., ed., *Handbook of North American Birds,* Vol. 1. Yale University Press, 1962.

Peattie, Donald Culross, *A Natural History of Trees of Eastern and Central North America.* Houghton Mifflin Company, 1950.

Peterson, Roger Tory, *A Field Guide to the Birds of Texas and Adjacent States.* Houghton Mifflin Company, 1967.

Pough, Richard H., *Audubon Water Bird Guide—Water, Game and Large Land Birds.* Doubleday and Company, 1951.

Tannehill, Ivan Ray, *Hurricanes: Their Nature and History.* Princeton University Press, 1956.

Acknowledgments

The author and editors of this book are particularly indebted to Dolores S. Dundee, Professor of Biological Sciences, Louisiana State University, New Orleans, and Harold A. Dundee, Associate Professor of Zoology, Tulane University. They also wish to thank the following persons: John J. Lynch, Biologist, Lafayette. At Louisiana State University, Baton Rouge: Harry J. Bennett, Professor of Zoology; Clair A. Brown, Emeritus Professor of Botany; Dudley D. Culley Jr., Assistant Professor of Forestry and Wildlife Management; Leslie L. Glasgow, Professor and Assistant Director, School of Forestry and Wildlife Management; George H. Lowery Jr., Museum of Natural History; William G. McIntire, Director, Coastal Studies Institute; John Newsome, Bureau of Wildlife Research. At Louisiana Tourist Development Commission, Baton Rouge: Gus Cranow and Bryce Moreland. At Louisiana Wild Life and Fisheries Commission; in New Orleans: Hurley L. Campbell; Frank Davis; Robert N. Dennie; McFadden Duffy; Allan Ensminger; in Baton Rouge: Joe L. Herring and Robert E. Murry Sr.; in Opelousas: Kenneth E. Lantz; at Rockefeller Refuge, Grand Chenier: Ted Joanen. At Lacassine National Wildlife Refuge, Lake Arthur: James Roberts, Manager, and Gary N. Burke. And also, in New Orleans: Edward Berns, Marcelle Bienvenu, Angelo Chetta, Greg T. Faulkner; A. Bradley McPherson, Assistant Professor of Biology, Centenary College of Louisiana, Shreveport; Robert E. Potts, M.D., and Mrs. Potts, Convent; Edward McIlhenny Simmons, Avery Island; John Walther, Manager, Sabine National Wildlife Refuge, Sulpher; Joe D. White, Manager, Delta National Wildlife Refuge, Venice. In New York City: The National Audubon Society; Sidney S. Horenstein, Department of Invertebrate Paleontology, The American Museum of Natural History; Geraldine Krug; Larry G. Pardue, New York Botanical Garden; and at the New York Zoological Society: Donald Bruning, Associate Curator of Birds, and Joseph Davis, Scientific Assistant to the Director.

Picture Credits

Sources for pictures in this book are shown below. Credits for pictures from left to right are separated by semicolons; from top to bottom they are separated by dashes.

Cover—Evelyn Hofer. Front end papers 2, 3, 4, page 1—Evelyn Hofer. 2, 3—Thase Daniel. 4, 5—Vernon Merritt III. 6, 7—Evelyn Hofer. 8, 9—John Launois from Black Star. 10, 11—Vernon Merritt III. 12, 13—James H. Carmichael Jr. 18, 19—Maps produced by Hunting Surveys Limited. 25—Thase Daniel. 28—Drawings by Stephen Negrycz. 33 through 39—Russell Munson. 40—Dan Guravich. 41—Russell Munson. 42, 43—Dan Guravich. 46—Thase Daniel. 49—Russell Munson. 53—Thase Daniel; Beecher Berry except bottom Dan McCoy. 58 through 67—Robert Walch. 70—Thase Daniel. 72-73—Evelyn Hofer. 78—Russell Munson. 85—Thase Daniel. 86, 87—Dan McCoy. 88—Evelyn Hofer. 89—Dan McCoy except bottom left Evelyn Hofer. 90 through 93—Dan McCoy. 94, 95—Left Dr. Robert H. Potts Jr.; Thase Daniel—Thase Daniel; Dan McCoy; right Dan McCoy. 96—Dan McCoy. 97—Ann Moreton—Evelyn Hofer. 98, 99—Dan McCoy. 100, 101—James H. Carmichael Jr. 104—Stephanie Dinkins (© 1971). 107—Jan Bolte. 110—Thase Daniel. 112, 113—James H. Carmichael Jr. 117—Dan McCoy. 118 through 123—Vernon Merritt III. 124 through 127—Dan McCoy. 130—Thase Daniel. 134, 135—The Bettmann Archive. 140, 141—Dr. E. R. Degginger. 145 through 161—Vernon Merritt III. 164, 165—Dan McCoy. 169 through 179—Dennis Stock from Magnum.

Index

Numerals in italics indicate a photograph or drawing of the subject mentioned.